STOPPING THE VOICES IN MY HEAD

ALSO, BY

MIKE WILLIAMSON

WORKING IN THE REALMS OF SPIRIT

SCHIZOPHRENIA OR SPIRIT POSSESSION

WHAT ARE GHOSTS & HOW TO EXORCISE THEM

STOPPING THE VOICES IN MY HEAD

BY

MIKE WILLIAMSON

Email author.mikewilliamson@yahoo.com

British Library Cataloguing in Publication Data
A catalogue record for this book is available from the British Library

ISBN
9780993021848

PART ONE

PART TWO

I have written this book for those interested in the general subject, those experiencing similar problems, mental health professionals, and spirit release therapists, to show how the spirit world can interact with the physical world. In part one I have given an introduction into how the world of spirit works and why they can sometimes affect our physical world. How negative spirits prey on the vulnerable for their entertainment. I have started with the normal course of life and I've explained the different ways we can work with our guides and who they are.

I've shown for different reasons how things can go wrong and how they can affect our mental and physical well-being. There are two case studies of haunted houses and how they were resolved.

In part two there is an in-depth study of a lady who was hearing voices, and had been diagnosed as schizophrenic and put on medication. How the medication was given to combat the symptoms but had no effect on the cause. She had a five-year history and her case was resolved over a period of ten months.

With approval from Harriet, this is a full case history, taken from recordings and e-mails of the events and struggles that took place. The case shows how education, understanding and self-discipline and sheer determination were required to overcome the spiritual invasion that she experienced.

The successes brought laughter and encouragement, and misunderstanding and failures brought tears of frustration, yet determination to win.

PART ONE

THE JOURNEY OF THE SOUL

The soul/spirit exists at the source, which is pure and untainted, from where it will enter the spirit realms and begin its journey. As a young soul, it will be like a baby treading the path to enlightenment, being guided and helped by those more advanced souls until it is ready to walk the path alone. As soon as the soul begins its journey of enlightenment, it becomes tainted with the negativity caused by recently arrived souls who are still reconciling their last life in the physical world. It will spend many eons learning to understand these emotions, and how it can move forward on its journey of enlightenment in the spirit realms before it even considers the next step, which is to incarnate into the physical realms. While in the spirit realms, it will work with other souls and learn to help humankind understand and achieve perfection. This can take many years, but as the soul is eternal, time is not a problem. There will come a time when the only way to progress further will be to experience adversities first-hand, instead of observing them through the experiences of souls already on the earth plane. This is when the soul will incarnate into a physical body. There is a lot of preparation involved when embarking on the journey through the physical world.

To start, the soul will have specific goals it wishes to achieve, to experience different situations for its progression. Once these have been decided, a plan will be drawn up, and other souls will be asked to assist. Some will be asked to oversee the plan and make sure the incarnating soul stays roughly on course to achieve its goals. These souls will act as guides to help and communicate with the spirit to continually assess and adjust, so the experiences are fulfilled. It doesn't matter if all the goals are not accomplished, as there will be many incarnations before the soul can return to the source. So, having established a plan and chosen the souls who will look after the incarnating soul, it is then time to select the environment, culture and time for the journey to start. This will be in the future as the soul cannot incarnate in the past. Once this has been established, it's time to make requests to other souls intending to embark on their journey through the physical world. The first consideration is parents, and the soul needs to find other souls who are planning to have children on the earth plane and ask if they can be one of them. The soul will consult with many spirits until they find at least three couples who are happy to help. The reason for choosing a few couples is some may not survive childbirth or disease, and others may not meet on the earth plane. Life on the earth plane is difficult, and it is a hostile and toxic environment to survive in. There are so many ways for physical life to end – stillbirth, disease, war, accident, starvation, to name but a few. Every soul who makes the journey intends to stay as long as possible, and only if they are unlucky enough to die through unforeseen circumstances (such as the few I have listed above) will their life be cut short. Those in the spirit realms do not terminate a life but will take advantage of the opportunity to learn when a life is beset by disease or cut short, whatever the reason. Before incarnating, the soul will bank their memories and experiences until they return from the physical because they are irrelevant to the new incarnation. Any guidance will be supplied by the guides.

In most cases, the incarnating spirit will initially be aware of spirit, but gradually, as they grow, they will lose that awareness as they learn to use their physical senses more and more. Their focus will be on the physical world, which is all around them, rather than the spirit realms, which will not be so obvious any longer. Some may, if their journey requires it, become aware at a later stage of their life and others not at all, as that knowledge is not needed in this incarnation.

It is now that the trials and tests begin, with sorrows, problems, difficulties, and for a time all will seem confused. Although the soul is striving to do the right thing, it feels as though it is in a fog. The soul finds itself up against people, with human problems, and then spiritual difficulties come crowding in until the soul doesn't know which way to turn or what to do. It is then that the temptation comes to throw everything over. The thought then comes, 'I was better off sticking to the physical, I'm sick and tired of struggling to understand.' This is the moment of choice when the soul must resolve to carry on and trust the guides. Everyone will have to go through this stage, so it's better to stick to the path and get it over with. Otherwise they will never know how close to achieving their goals they are.

Having completed an average life span, the spirit will, in an ideal world, gradually become more aware again of the spirit realms. Loved ones will draw close in preparation for their transition back to the spirit realms. Once the transition has been made, then it is time to overcome any lingering ailments and emotions of the body and assess the life just completed. The memories of previous incarnations can now be accessed and experiences can be put into perspective. When this is done and loved ones who have been part of the journey have arrived back to the spirit realms, it is then time to move forward on a new pathway, either in the spirit realms for a while or another incarnation on the earth plane.

This process will be repeated over many lifetimes, and the soul will spend thousands of years in the spirit realms and on the earth plane until the soul has overcome all negativity and emotions. It is only then that it can return to the source.

THE SOUL IS PERFECT AND WILL NOT DIVIDE

There are many thoughts as to what the soul is, dating back to the ancient Greeks. In many religious, mythological and philosophical traditions, the soul is the incorporeal essence of a living being. The soul or psyche meaning ('to breathe') are the mental abilities of a living being, with reason, character, feeling, consciousness, memory, perception, thinking, etc.

In Judeo-Christianity, only humans have an immortal soul (although immortality is disputed within Judaism). For example, the Catholic theologian Thomas Aquinas said all organisms had a soul, but only human souls are immortal.

Other religions, notably Jainism and Hinduism, believe all living things from the largest mammals to the smallest bacterium are the souls themselves and have a physical representative (the body) in the physical world. The soul is the self, and the body is only the mechanism to experience the karma of life. Some teach that non-biological entities, such as rivers and mountains, possess souls. This belief is called animism and is widespread in the East and becoming more accepted in the western world. The current consensus of modern science is that there is no evidence to support the existence of the soul when traditionally defined as the spiritual breath of the body. In metaphysics, the concept of the soul may be equated with the mind to refer to the consciousness and intellect of the individual.The soul is perfect but can be covered by emotions and negativity, just as a football can get covered in mud. Gradually, as the subconscious deals with the feelings and negative energy, the soul once again shines through. This is the journey of the soul, to continually overcome the negative energy that surrounds us at all times, until finally nothing affects the fine vibrations that the soul has achieved because the soul can shrug off the negative energies that permeate the physical and spiritual realms. Example: imagine the soul as the football with a dense exterior, picking up the mud and dirt of the field. You can cleanse it, but it is going to get muddy again because you are exposing it to the same or similar conditions as before. Once you realise it doesn't get so muddy in dry conditions or sandy situations, then you will have dealt with the denser vibrations that cover the soul. As the soul progresses, the finer energies and emotions, such as happiness, caring, love, etc., are processed, so eventually, the soul can move forward without any encumbrance, such as emotions or outside influence. The soul only has one emotion that is now able to shine, which was lost in the bombardment of energies from other souls – and that is unconditional love.

SPIRITUAL

Many psychiatrists believe the soul can be fragmented, and these fragments can be infiltrated by negative spirits. That is not true; according to the spirit world, the soul is and will always remain perfect. The soul has always been; it cannot cease to exist; it is eternal. It is the fear that this can happen that causes the disharmony and, therefore, the problems that manifest. The thoughts of man can affect the mind of the individual, and depending on their understanding causes dense energy around them. It's when one conquers fear and thinks positive thoughts that they can overcome the difficulties they are experiencing.

Both animals and humans have souls, although they are not the same. Souls that inhabit animals are a different type of soul. They are still of the spirit world and, as with humans, when the body dies the soul will return to the spirit realms. Animal souls come in seven different types and will only inhabit certain groups of animals. These are:

(1) all types of cats,

(2) all types of dogs including wolves and hyena,

(3) horses, cattle, zebra, etc.,

(4) birds,

(5) fish,

(6) rodents,

(7) insects.

They will always stay in the same group. Human souls inhabit only humans and no other group. There are beliefs in certain religions that depending on how we conduct ourselves depends on whether we progress as humans or revert to, for example, insects. There are no lower species, we are all here to balance life and experiences with respect for all species.

The spirit is the spark of the creator that we all carry within our soul. It is the driving force that pushes us to co-create our reality with guidance from the spirit realms. This is where our thoughts are manifested; once created they continue to exist in the ether where they can cause either good or bad reactions depending on the progress of the spirit creating them or receiving them. Over the many incarnations the individual will go through, the thoughts become more refined as the spirit learns the effects of their thoughts. There are more light beings working, sending healing to the planet and humanity, than ever before, which is why humanity is slowly becoming more aware of how fragile our planet is. It is also why more people are aware of the spirit world and how important it is to live in harmony.

GUIDES

Guides are old souls who have spent many years in the spirit realms and on the earth plane, working with humanity and giving help and understanding to their mediums. We are all mediums at different stages of enlightenment, and we are guided by our friends in spirit towards the objectives we set ourselves, while still in the spirit realms. Guides work only with one medium. We do not share them with others, although on rare occasions a guide may come through another person for a specific reason. We choose from amongst our friends before we were born, to assist us on our journey through life. As we chose them many years before we were born, they cannot be family or friends from the earth plane. If you think about it, once you pass over you would want to be there when your children and grandchildren pass before you move on. That can take 200 years or so, and then you will want to put your last life in order before you even think about another life on the earth plane. It is a privilege to be selected to look after the well-being of someone who is entering the physical world. Sometimes we hear mediums say their mother/father is one of their guides. That is not so, but the link between parent and child can be strong enough that the parent may wish to try and help, which they can sometimes do, but they are not guides. Guides come from all times and places where humanity has existed. It's not unusual for a guide having had their last life on the earth plane hundreds or even thousands of years ago. Fame on the earth plane is not fame in spirit; it would be rare if you had a guide who was a famous figure in history, as the perception of who they were would detract from what they are doing and can take away their credibility as the spirit.

There are many different vibrations, and while we generally accept the physical and spiritual, it doesn't mean there aren't other vibrations that some can attune to, where there may be angels and nature spirits, etc.

Devils and demons are manifestations of the religious communities to encourage the masses to follow the particular god of choice, through fear of an eternity in hell punished for mistakes made during life on the earth plane. The term 'angel' comes from the Greek *angelos,* which means messenger. Sometimes guides are referred to as guardian angels, and angel is just another name for a guide. They give us guidance in our daily lives so that we can achieve the goals we set for ourselves in this life. They will help us strengthen our willpower, lighten our mind and mood, assist us with self-healing, and help us become more compassionate with those around us.

They help us connect with the right resources to reach our goals. They also offer wisdom and comfort when we feel lost. They guide and protect us in our decisions, helping us to make the right choices at the right time. It is far better to be guided on our journey than wander aimlessly. That is what our guides are there for, to keep us on the right path, to achieve the goals we set ourselves when we chose to incarnate. Because we have free will, we will sometimes go in the wrong direction, and this is when our guides gently steer us back on track, protecting us from bad decisions. Suppose you are on a steep path of learning; when you falter your guides help you to overcome the difficult parts of your pathway. There is a poem called 'Footprints in the Sand' (author disputed) A poem about how guides carry the load when we're under stress or overburdened with life, which perfectly demonstrates the assistance our guides give us. We rarely recognise this help as we are too busy trying to overcome those rocky parts of our lives.

Some people are naturally aware of their guides and can communicate with them regularly. You can contact them by merely speaking to them out loud, or by using your inner voice. Guides are very much aware of the problems that we face every day. They have their specific areas of expertise, commonly associated with their personal experiences. They have also spent eons learning how to heal and communicate with us, and they will sometimes specialise in certain types of healing or areas of the mind and body.

The purpose of guides is to provide help and guidance to humans. As spirits, they have higher vibrational frequencies than humans do, so we usually cannot see them or hear them, but we can sometimes feel their presence. Guides have had many lives as ordinary humans until such a point in time when they have mastered all their earthly lessons, not needing to incarnate in a physical body again. They work closely with humans to comfort, guide, teach and enlighten us in achieving our soul's purpose. Because guides work within a higher energy vibration – much higher than ours – we need to raise our vibrations to connect with them. When we ask questions or pray, our guides do answer. The response may come in the form of a sign, gut feeling, coincidence, an idea, or thought that manifests in the following days or weeks. You may not even realise you have received a response, as often people have mistaken the guide's help as their own ideas or solutions to problems.

There are sites on the internet who will sell you a spirit for companionship. These 'spirits' are supposed to help you with your development and you become their keeper. You can also purchase spells for whatever you desire. Spirits are individual souls and cannot be bought it's like buying energy and you don't know whether they will help or hinder your progress. We all have spirits who are guides to help us as explained, they are friends you knew when you were in spirit, who are trying to guide us through a life on the physical plane. We all choose our guides and don't swap them for others during our life time.

YOU CANNOT BE REGRESSED INTO A PREVIOUS LIFE

Many people experience unjustifiable fears or memories of things they believe have happened to them. The fact that they can't remember the experience with any clarity does nothing to change the fact that they still believe something happened to them. For instance, a fear of being burnt or drowned, killed, blinded, etc., these are a few of the likely memories people have at some time in their life. There are also less stressful memories, such as remembering a time or place that is familiar to them, yet they have never been there. They believe it is an experience from a previous life, yet there is no evidence to persuade them this is so. They are happy to accept the concept as there are mediums who will tell them it is a memory from a past life. That may well be true, but it is not 'their' previous life but that of a spirit who may have attached themselves to them.

It is a common belief that we can tap into the memories of a previous life. That is because when people are in a relaxed meditation, they can talk about a life that they think was theirs. Deep relaxing meditation is very close to a trance state, which is the same state a light trance medium achieves when they allow their guides to come through. The life spoken about is not the patients. It is of a spirit who is also present who speaks through the regressed person. It is not possible to regress to a previous life because all memory of any prior existence is locked away like a form of amnesia. Those people who are aware of the spirit realms will know about the spirit world in a general sense but nothing specific to an earlier life. The reason for this is so past experiences don't interfere with our current life decisions. We all arrive on the earth plane with a clean slate and chart our journey through this life based on current experience and understanding. Yes, our guides do guide us, but they don't know about our past lives either. To them, we are the spirit they have been working with in the spirit realms, who have asked for their assistance during our current life.

There have been instances where a child has been able to give details and intimate knowledge of another existence. They are picking up the thoughts and feelings of a spirit and believe they are their thoughts and memories. It is common knowledge that young children are more in the spirit world than the physical up until the age when they start to mix with other children. It is quite common for them to be aware of spirit, like imaginary friends. During my travels helping lost souls, it is not unusual for a child to complain of seeing a spirit in their room. Because they don't understand how the 'person' got there or who they are, they become frightened, especially if the spirit is lost or confused, this will make them unsettling to a child.

People don't have to be a medium or in a trance to pick up spirit thoughts. We can pick them up at any time as we are all spirit; We may not recognise the thought as coming from another mind, i.e. spirit, as our thoughts are focused on our own mind. The difference between a medium and a person who is not aware is that the medium can recognise extraneous thoughts and keep the focus to get more information in a controlled way instead of parts of the thoughts. It is only with practice that mediums can recognise the thoughts or feelings being given by spirit and can listen without breaking the flow. The reason people can be interfered with by spirit is that the interference is more obvious and can't be denied, whereas guides are less intrusive.

YOUR MIND IS YOUR SOUL, NOT YOUR BRAIN

There is a significant difference between the mind and the brain: the brain is organic, and the mind is the soul/spirit. The brain is responsible for the smooth running of the physical body. If anything goes wrong in the brain, then problems arise in the body in a physical sense. If the brain becomes damaged or medication affects the balance of the chemicals in the brain, it can cause an imbalance which can cause all sorts of problems – multiple sclerosis, Parkinson's disease and Alzheimer's, to name a few which are all physical illnesses with pathology. A damaged brain can also cause mental aberrations, which may be caused by the side effects of drugs.

The mind, however, is the connection between the physical body and the spirit. The link to the mind can be influenced by spirits who are around the individual or attached to the aura. The spirits can affect people's emotions, which can present as mental illness. These include schizophrenia, anxiety, multiple personality disorder, paranoia or depression, some of the more common mental illnesses which are not organic (and have no pathology) but spiritual, and are often misdiagnosed by doctors and psychiatrists as problems in the brain.

The mind is the part of us that has emotions, memories, feelings, consciousness, character, perception, thinking, etc. It is how we communicate with spirit and how they communicate with us. They can affect our emotions, feelings, smell and sight, and they can also give us dreams and nightmares. Not all communication is negative; in fact, most is helpful and encouraging, as in clairvoyant readings. We must be aware, even if we don't develop our psychic abilities, that we can still be influenced by thoughts and emotions that we pick up from spirits around us. This is especially true if we are going through trauma when our senses are heightened. The higher self is used a great deal in development and psychiatry as though it is separate from us. It's the soul or spiritual side of ourselves. It is said to be the connection between us and the divine or higher spiritual consciousness, and by connecting with this higher self, we can find enlightenment. We connect with our soul all the time, even if we are not aware of it; when we ask questions, we are communicating through our minds with our guides.

SENSES

We are in a physical body and need to use that body to communicate with each other. We have five ways of communicating, and each sense is enhanced by one of our other senses. We talk, see, hear, smell and feel, and all this is done automatically without thinking how we do it. These are all physical senses that we use every day of our lives. If we lose one of these communication skills, another will be enhanced simply by focusing on it. For instance, loss of sight enhances the hearing, touch and smell, and these enhancements are automatic. We all have a sixth sense, although many do not recognise when they are using it. This is the sense that is intangible but nevertheless in use daily by most people, the sense that we use to connect to our guides in the spirit world.

The spirit world communicates with each other by thought, and those thoughts are as clear to them as verbal communication is to us, and every spirit is adding their knowledge to a pool. Each will, therefore, be able to understand the requirements of other spirits so they can work together for the common good. This level of awareness requires complete harmony, which can't be achieved while in a physical body. There are too many distractions from aches and pains, emotions and outside stimuli that the body is subject to, that we can't ignore. It is impossible to reach this state of awareness for most people, until we have returned to the spirit world and reconciled our earthly journey and re-assimilated back into our natural being as spirit. It is only then when we have no pressure from life's worries that we can again have complete harmony with other souls in the spirit world. This state of consciousness is not immediate; it takes the soul time to settle down after a life in the physical world.

When I speak about the above, I am not talking about souls who have newly arrived from an incarnation. They will stay around the physical world and in the spirit realms until their loved ones have also returned to the spirit realms before moving on.

GHOSTS

Apparitions, poltergeist, visions, spectres, spirits, ghouls, guides, manifestations, phantoms, shades, wraiths, shadows, banshees, ghosts and souls are all different names for the same thing.

Ghosts are not figments of our imagination or hallucinations; they are real, they are the soul or spirit of a dead person or animal that can appear to the living. They interact because they wish to communicate for a myriad of reasons, from messages of comfort and love to interfering with our thoughts, misleading us and causing pain and distress. Most spirits are helpful and loving, but there will always be those who are confused and will lash out at anyone they can. They often do this to attract attention to their plight, but some intentionally want to cause distress. These are the spirits who have not yet reconciled themselves with their circumstances, i.e. that they have died.

In pre-literate cultures dating back to animism or ancestor worship, the belief in the existence of an afterlife as well as manifestations of the spirits of the dead were widespread. Some religious practices, funeral rites, exorcisms and some practices of spiritualism and ritual magic are explicitly designed to help the spirits of the dead rest. Ghosts of humans and animals are usually described as solitary, although it is not uncommon for there to be more than one, and there have been stories of ghostly armies as well. It was thought they haunted specific locations, objects or people they were associated with in life. Although this is a myth as spirits can attach themselves to anyone, place or object, it's accepted that eighteen per cent of people have seen a ghost, although I suspect that figure to be much higher. The opinion of science is that ghosts do not exist and their existence is impossible to verify. Despite centuries of investigation, there is no scientific evidence that any location is inhabited by spirits. They say ghost sightings may be related to degenerative brain diseases such as Alzheimer's disease. We know that as people get closer to passing on, they start seeing loved ones gathering to receive them back to their natural habitat, the spirit realms. They are not hallucinating – what they are seeing and hearing is real.

TRANCE

Trance is a state of controlled consciousness that allows the mind to raise its awareness to the vibrations of spirit. This was done by meditation, or hypnosis in the early days. The mediums had the help of a mesmeriser or a hypnotist (so named after the Austrian physician F. A. Mesmer) to help them achieve this subconscious state. This allowed the medium's subconscious to connect with spirit. While they were in this condition, they were not aware of what was going on during the time they were in a trance. It would take a while to go in and out of a deep trance and when they regained their consciousness, they would be disorientated for a while until they were settled. This was how they communicated with spirit guides and others, as the medium had no awareness of who was coming through or what they said. Although they were able to bring spirit through, they didn't always know if the spirit was a guide. They just had to trust that the communicator was there with the best intentions; this was not always so. Nowadays, deep trance is not used as often, as many more mediums can convey communication either in a light trance or by being inspired or overshadowed by their guides. This is safer for the medium because, in a deep trance, the body is on a higher vibration than normal and can be harmed if touched or disturbed without prior warning.

Light trance is where the medium will meditate until they are in a receptive state of consciousness, yet still aware of their surroundings, and allow their guide to come forward and take over the body. The medium is aware at all times of what is happening. Through practice, they learn to recognise when they have a guide or an imposter with them. If need be, they can regain control of their body just by opening their eyes. This type of trance is useful for teaching and learning about the spirit world and guides and to get philosophical teachings from spirit guides. It is also useful when removing unwanted spirits and lost souls from people and houses. That is because the lost soul can be brought through the medium and talk about their dilemma and understand what has happened to them. Once they know, they are escorted to the spirit realms.

With overshadowing, the guides come close but do not control the body; they just inspire the medium in what to say when doing an address or answering questions.

Both types of trance can be dangerous if the medium doesn't know what they are doing. That's why it should be developed slowly and with another medium working in partnership with the trance medium. The partner will sit with the trance medium and develop with them and get to know the trance medium's guides almost as well as their own. They can then monitor and protect the trance medium by controlling the proceedings. Some hazards are not knowing who is coming through, unable to control the trance by stopping when required, or getting imposters coming in. By this, I mean the spirit is not a guide, and sometimes they don't want to leave. That is one of the reasons for light trance as the medium can remove the spirit much easier as they are aware of what is going on. While in a deep trance, the medium is not in control and can't come back at will. They have to wait for the spirit to finish what they are saying, and may need help when coming back to a normal conscious state by their partner.

It is essential to develop contact with guides and get to know what they feel like and establish a relationship so that the medium knows who is coming through when going into a trance. There will always be those who wish to communicate with the physical world and will impose their will on the medium if the medium is not vigilant. Although the spirit can be removed, it can be traumatic for the medium if the spirit is not removed correctly, as they can cause discomfort for the medium in terms of emotions and feelings. These emotions can linger for days and resurface when least expected in the form of anxiety, depression, pain or just feeling out of sorts. Some developing mediums think if they ask the spirit if they are sovereign three times, they cannot lie. But if they are going to pretend to be a guide, then they can also tell lies. Why would they force themselves on a medium? To gain access to the physical world through the medium because they did not want to leave. These spirits aren't trained to look after the medium while they are in a trance.

When preparing to go into a trance, the medium should first be aware of a guide with them and monitor them as they come through to make sure they are getting one of their own guides. By monitoring who is coming, they can stop imposters who are pretending to be guides. The importance of getting the right spirit is there will be trust between the medium and guide, and the medium will know they will be protected and that everything that is said is in the best interest of the sitters.

The above applies to both deep trance and light trance, although when doing spirit release, the medium will allow the lost soul to come through them under strict control. This control is administered by the medium's guides, the medium and the medium's partner.

SOUL RESCUE

Soul rescue is when a spirit is confused or lost after passing to spirit and mediums and spirit release therapists can assist them in finding their way home.

While this is not something most mediums get involved in, there is a need, and some mediums develop specially to do this work. Make no mistake, this work can be dangerous if not done correctly, the medium can be attacked mentally by the spirit, particularly if the spirit doesn't want to leave. They will try to unbalance the medium by giving pain and discomfort to make it difficult for them to concentrate. It is up to the medium to make sure they are adequately protected. This is done by sitting in a rescue circle and practising working with one's guides and forming a tight bond with them and their partner.

There are several ways of rescuing lost souls, and it depends on the circumstances as to which is the best way of working. It can be done with an experienced medium working clairvoyantly, or if the medium has clear communication with their guides, then the guides will direct proceedings which the medium will carry out. Neither of these methods requires light trance, but if you want the client to get first-hand knowledge of who and why they are being haunted, then the trance method is best as they can hear what is being said by the spirit.

An experienced medium will be directed by their partner, who is clairvoyant and aware of lost souls in the house or the circle, to focus on a particular spirit and bring them through. Once the spirit is through, then the partner can discuss their predicament and resolve the problems that restrict the spirit from going to the light.

When the spirit is no longer confused and fully aware of their situation, they can then be taken to the light, where they will meet their loved ones who are waiting for them. The trance medium will then open their eyes and break contact with the spirit. Sometimes more than one spirit can be helped if their situation is similar, as they can also hear what is said to the spirit that comes through. We should always be aware that all sorts of people from all walks of life and all ages can get lost. It is not a permanent situation as eventually all spirits will be reconciled with their loved ones.

The use of sage, salt, holy water, prayer, religious items like the cross, and passages from the Bible or other religious works is a myth. These items will have no direct effect on the spirits as they are physical, and the spirit is not. However, sometimes one or the other will work temporally because the spirit has the belief gained during their life that they can be affected by them. If we look at this logically, a spirit whose life was lived within the Islamic faith will not be affected by the cross or passages from the Bible, as they didn't and still don't have that belief. The same as Christians won't be affected by sage or other herbs, which are burnt to try and drive them out.

Simply put, if the spirit believes, then it will have a short-term effect, but in the long term, it's a waste of time. This is why it's essential to deal with each situation individually. Some spirits will refuse to move on, and under these circumstances the free will of the client takes precedence; the spirit will be removed and put in the care of their guides, who the medium will introduce them to.

ENERGIES

All physical matter is composed of atoms, and each atom is a form of characterised energy. Each element is made in an identical way. When you blend one form of energy with another it produces a third substance, and so on. In this way chemical changes are brought about. Take the power stations that produce our electricity. To bring about a change in the existing state of specified matter, additional energies must be applied, for example we apply heat energy to boil water. In the same way our guides are able to apply the appropriate energies to produce the required result whether it is healing or protection.

We are all made up of energy as is the whole universe. These energies can be used for good or bad, they are just energy; it depends on the application and intent. The nuclear power used for producing electricity can also be used to destroy things. Energy can be used to enhance our lives or cause damage to us. Discarnate spirits don't have bodies, they are pure energy; some are dark and heavy and some are light and bright. We have a physical body which is affected by our spiritual energy or aura which intermingles with the physical world. Spirit is naturally on a higher vibration than us which is why mediums have to raise their energy to interact with the spirit world. Thoughts are energy and we can send uplifting or depressing thoughts to others. Example: If someone around you is happy it can lift you out of a low mood just as easily as a low mood can bring you down. Spirit can use energy to shield or block or heal by blending the correct energy for a specific purpose. As thoughts are energy it pays to be mindful of your thoughts and how you project them. When we put protection around a person or place, it will only remain by their agreement. Everyone has free will and can neutralise the protection just by thinking. If someone has experienced interference from the spirit realms it can be difficult to accept that it's gone. They have become so used to the presence of spirit they expect them to come back and cause interference and no amount of invisible protection will convince them otherwise. This is why they need to hear what the spirit has to say and see them removed.

HEALING

Everybody is a healer to some degree, as it is the most natural thing. Take a mother who comforts a child that is hurt – that's healing. When a medium develops their mediumship, healing is a part of that whether they do healing, or not. Most mediums ask for healing in their prayers but don't actively place their hands on a patient. It doesn't mean they can't heal, just that their priorities are in developing their communication skills. Those who dedicate their development to healing are learning to work with their guides and allowing them to pass the healing energies through the medium without restriction. The more experienced the healer, the less they interfere with the healing rays. The intention is for the healer to be a clear channel, to allow the healing rays to come through for the greatest benefit of the patient. The novice must be careful not to give of themselves as this will take away their own energies (magnetic healing). During development, they will learn that the clearer the channel, the more beneficial the healing is for the patient. When a healer puts their hands close to the patient if, after a few minutes, they move their hands gently from side to side they will feel resistance almost like magnetism, this tells them that they are in the right place and that their guides are working. The healer doesn't have to touch the patient. Some people don't like to be touched. There are places that your hands shouldn't go when a man is giving healing to a woman and the same for a man. Depending on how the healer is trained will dictate how they work.

Some say put your hands over the different areas of the body that need healing. Others say all healing can be done by placing your hands over the shoulders.
By placing your hands over different parts of the body, you can give the patient confidence that you know where the problem is and work directly on the injured part. Massage and manipulation have no place in healing unless you're qualified in that discipline.
The guides will work on balancing the physical with the emotional, spiritual and etheric bodies, and may use many different healing energies in one session. Some guides will specialise in specific ailments, and it's not up to the healer which healing energies are used, or how much benefit the patient receives. Sometimes the healing will only ease the patient, and it depends on the circumstances. If the patient requires surgery, then healing is not the answer. For instance, if you break a leg, you would go to a hospital, or if the patient has cut themselves badly, then it's the hospital. That's not to say healing won't benefit the patient, it will, but it won't replace stitches or plaster. If you have a disease, then medication will help. What I'm saying is healing is not a replacement for a doctor, but the two can work alongside each other, and the patient will benefit.

When working with soul rescue, the medium is responsible for detecting and helping lost souls. Therefore, the medium must develop their senses and mediumship to a high degree to understand the problem and find a resolution for lost souls. The medium deals with the contact and dialogue with the lost soul, and the guides help bring the lost souls to the medium. With the assistance of their guides, the medium will help the lost soul to reconnect with their loved ones in the spirit world.

The view of the medium is, interference is coming from earthbound spirits who are confused or lost or don't want to leave the physical world. By staying around the earth plane, they can influence people with their thoughts and emotions, to the degree that those affected believe the thoughts, emotions, moods, and pain are their own. It is very easy to be influenced in this way, and it can lead to all sorts of mental diagnoses by the medical profession. The doctors are looking at the patient and see the symptoms as they present themselves, rather than looking for the cause. The cause may be a problem with the chemistry of the brain, damage to the brain or side effects from medication and must be ruled out. Any 'disease' of the brain that has no pathology must be investigated to see if it is spirit interference, which comes through the mind. The mind is not organic and will not be affected by medication, that will only mask the problem; it doesn't deal with it. Helping lost souls reunite with their loved one is a form of healing, and helping them overcome their physical discomforts is healing the spirit.

It's not always possible to be in the same place as the patient; this is when we use remote healing. We ask our guides to send healing to the patient, and as thoughts are tangible, they receive the healing they need. All healing works on all living things, including plants and places where there has been negativity. How many times have you felt bad vibes when entering a room? You are feeling the negative energy of what has transpired, and by asking for healing, our guides can transmute the negativity. Other times it is just bad energy that can be received from someone in the room. Sometimes it is a spirit that is causing the negativity, and this is when soul rescue is needed.

WHY DO SPIRITS HAUNT HOUSES?

It is a fact that when our bodies die, our life force continues in another way. We come from the spirit world, and return after life in the physical world has ended. We don't necessarily change for the good when we die. Some are unhappy with their life, or consider it unfinished and wish to continue interacting with those left behind. That can lead to all sorts of problems for those of us who are trying to live our lives the best way we can. Life can be a difficult journey at the best of times, but with interference from beyond the grave, it can make it much more difficult.

One of the reasons spirits want to make contact is to let those left behind know they're still around. There are ways to do this without frightening people, such as mediums, but many of those who have passed don't know how to make contact. Then some are confused and suffering and are asking for help. They don't know how to get help, so they try to make their presence known by moving things or making noises in people's houses. Sometimes they stand close to people, and their pain can be felt, or they have a particular smell about them like perfume or tobacco, which people can smell.

Some are angry or just nasty, and find they can affect people in all sorts of ways, mainly with emotions and pains, without being found out. They know what they're doing and purposely set about disturbing people for their amusement.

Let's take the first group. They've been removed from their loved ones, either suddenly or through illness, and just want to reassure them that they are safe and well. Although they don't intend to frighten, the results of them making their presence known can. The people of this world are becoming more accepting of the spirit world due to the vast amount of media coverage. Unfortunately, anyone can have spirits in their house. Most don't know about it because they are not sensitive enough. Increasingly, people are becoming more aware of this phenomenon because the subject is talked about more openly. That's not to say it hasn't been going on all along, just that people are more open these days. With the current mindset, those who pass over are also aware of the possibility they can make contact, so they will try in whatever way they can. Wouldn't you if you thought it would ease a loved one's pain at losing a husband, wife or family member? Although they're only trying to show their love, sometimes it can scare people.

Some get lost or are confused, for instance, if they are on drugs, perhaps to ease the pain. When they pass, their mind is sometimes still in that state because they don't realise the drugs only affect the brain. Once they have passed, the drugs no longer affect them, so is it any wonder they're confused about what's happened to them? Then some don't believe there is anything else when they die; imagine their surprise when they find there's more! They desperately want to get in touch, so they can tell everyone there is more to life than the physical. They may move things or make noises to try and attract attention. That is another type of haunting – not nasty or out to cause fear, but it can frighten. Sometimes they're asking for help because they don't understand what's happened to them.

Then some want revenge for the wrongs that have been done to them. They'll take it out on anyone they can; their view is, it was done to me, so I'm going to get my own back, it doesn't matter who. They'll take it out on anyone they can, it won't make them feel better, but the lost souls will carry on doing it until they see sense. Some can be very stubborn. They know what they're doing, and all the while there are no repercussions. They will continue until they are stopped or made to see sense.

Some are downright nasty and enjoy causing upset and frightening people. They do it for fun, to watch people suffer. They especially like it when people don't know they're attacking them because they know they won't get caught. They'll attack anyone they can, and once a suitable subject is found, they will stay with them for years. There is no time in spirit, so it doesn't matter to them how long it takes. These tend to be the spirits who look upon what they do as a skill, and they will study different ways to upset or annoy people. They will play with your emotions, your moods, the pains in your body (making them worse or more frequent), your perception of others, and how they treat you. They will also give you feelings of depression or paranoia and can make people think they are mentally unstable. They will make your feelings go up and down like a yo-yo, but won't usually cause physical harm as they will have to start all over again with someone else if they get caught.

In some cases, they completely control the mind (possession) to the degree that the person being attacked is unaware of their surroundings for up to an hour at a time, and in some cases longer. People have been sectioned or diagnosed as mentally ill, when all that is happening is that they are being spoken continuously to or are having their emotions interfered with by these nasty spirits. In some cases, it will make people go mad with a constant stream of chatter going on at all times of the day and night.

I must point out I am not talking about heaven or whatever you want to call it. I am talking about the spirit realms that are around the physical world. Most people pass to heaven without any problems, regardless of how they die. It's only a small percentage that get lost. If you consider how many people die each day, if one per cent gets lost and you multiply that by one year, then that's a lot of people. If you then consider the nasty spirits who know what they're doing, they will have been dead for quite a while, to have learned how to do the things they do. So, if you think of the number of people who have died over the past two or three hundred years, and longer, there are a lot of lost or nasty spirits out there. Is it any wonder some houses are haunted? And it's not necessarily old houses, many old houses have been cleared away to build new ones. It is the location and the prospect of interacting that draws the spirit.

We are a dedicated team of three mediums of varying abilities. While some of us are clairvoyant (clear seeing), the rest of us are clairsentient (clear sensing). We meet once a week to communicate with the spirit realms and help lost souls find their way to the light. We've found over the years there are many reasons why souls are lost. One of the main reasons is they don't realise they've died. We also go to people's homes and help the lost souls who may inadvertently be frightening them. Some realise what has happened to them and sometimes play games with the people in the houses. Most of them, once we have talked to them and helped them to understand, are happy to be taken on to meet their loved ones in the light. But there are a few that enjoy frightening people. These we have to remove so the people in the houses can get some peace. We usually escort them off the premises and put them in the hands of their guides who will take them and talk to them. While with their guides, they can't interfere with the physical world. On some occasions we manage to escort them to the light, where once they feel the warmth and see their loved ones, they usually have a change of heart and stay there.

Many people think children don't get lost because they're innocent and go straight to the light, but we must remember children get confused as well. There are those in the spirit realms who, although they are lost, will collect children and try to keep them safe until help comes, from either heaven or a soul rescue circle who will help them and take them to the light, where they can be with their family. Please don't think all children get lost; they don't. If you think of the areas around the world where children live in poverty or are exploited in whatever way, then you will understand some of them will stray from the light through mistrust or ignorance. They are as likely as a confused adult to require help. Most of the time, family are there to meet them, but if you don't know your family because maybe you're an orphan, then it's hard to trust a stranger if you have been abused or misled during your life. So, you see, children can also have problems getting back home to the light.

Apart from houses and places being haunted, people can also have spirit attach themselves to them. This is, if you like, a personal haunting and nobody else in the house is affected, except by the reaction of the individual who has the attachment and the feelings and discomfort that are given by the spirit who has invaded their aura. We have to recognise what type of problem we are dealing with, otherwise we would be unsuccessful in helping the situation.

Spirits can attach themselves because they may feel an affinity with the individual and are usually confused as to what's happened to them. When this happens – if the spirit died of, say a heart attack – then the pain may be felt by the individual as if it's their own. The spirit doesn't usually intend to cause pain or interfere with the individual's emotions. It's just how they feel, and these feelings are felt by the person who has the attachment. Some know exactly what they are doing and take pleasure in causing discomfort. In both cases, it is essential to recognise what we are dealing with and approach the solution in the right way. We usually find those who are confused and lost, once they understand their situation, are glad of our help in taking them to the light. It's those who know what they are doing that can be more difficult, although they can be removed. In one of the following cases, we came across some nasty individuals who were making a lady's life a misery. Fortunately, they had a religious belief which we were able to use to our advantage. We must remember there are millions of people in this world who have different religious beliefs or none at all. These spirits have to be persuaded that it's in their best interest to leave or be removed. I must point out that we work with our guides who deal with the spiritual side of life, and without their input, it is less likely that we could deal with these spirits. We work as a team, our guides on one side of life, and us on the other. Most of the time, we are successful, but when a person doesn't want us to help, then we don't have the authority, and there is nothing we can do. Everyone has a choice, even if they make it without the necessary understanding

I have written about some of the situations we've come across while attending some recent houses, where people had spiritual disturbances. It is as we found them and what we did to improve their situation. What we do can be dangerous to our peace of mind, so if you wish to get involved in this sort of work, then please first develop your gifts under tuition from an experienced medium who specialises in soul rescue. It's a long and challenging journey, but the satisfaction you get from helping not only the people who live in the houses but also those in spirit is worth the hard work you will have to undertake. More mediums are working in this way these days, but you must be discerning about who you work with. It's not for money or ego; it's for the benefit of all those who need help in this world and the next.

HAUNTING IN HAMPSHIRE

It was towards the end of October 2019 that our team received a call from a lady called Tina. Tina asked if we could help, as she had paranormal activity in her house. She said it started just after Christmas 2018 when her daughter Alice and her granddaughter Joyce were staying with them. Joyce had received a toy cooker for Christmas, which played a tune when the timer ran down. Late one evening, just after everyone had gone to bed, the music started to play and then stopped. No one took any notice because they thought it was just the spring winding down. But it played again in the middle of the night, so Tina's husband, Harry, went downstairs and took the batteries out. It was then he realised the tune was played by battery, not springs. He returned upstairs, but no sooner had he got into bed than the tune played again. He awakened Tina and told her what had happened, but she just thought he was dreaming. While they were talking, much to Tina's surprise the tune played again. Tina and Harry went downstairs and when Harry showed Tina the space where the batteries went, Tina went a little pale. They couldn't understand how it had played, so they decided to deal with it in the morning. They returned to bed to get a good night's sleep. After they had been in bed for about ten minutes, the tune played again. After about an hour of repeated playing, it suddenly stopped, and they dozed off. The following morning, they decided to take the toy back and get a replacement.

Over the next few nights, Alice complained that it was freezing in the room where she was sleeping. Harry checked the radiator and said it was working fine, but he couldn't explain why it was so cold in there. That night Joyce woke up crying and would not stay in the room where she was sleeping. Joyce said there were strange people in the room. When Alice took her back to her room, she told Tina there was an eerie feeling in the room her daughter was sleeping in, and she felt it would be better for all of them if she had her daughter in with her. The next day, after Alice and Joyce had gone home, Tina and Harry were left to wonder what was going on. Over the next few months, they heard strange noises and bangs but tried to ignore them. Each time Joyce came to stay, the bedroom she was sleeping in got very cold and she seemed to get very agitated. Alice complained she was like it every time she came home after staying with her grandparents, and it took a few days for her to calm down again. One day Tina went into the downstairs toilet only to find she was standing in a pool of water. She thought there was a leak, and after mopping it up asked Harry to check and see if he could find the problem. Upon investigation by her husband and a plumber friend, no water leaks were found and no explanation could be given for how the water got there. There was only Tina and Harry in the house at the time. Tina also said on another occasion about a month later; she was cooking Sunday lunch. When she opened a kitchen cupboard, the salt and pepper pots were thrown at her, narrowly missing her head. When she shouted in surprise, Harry came to see what the commotion was about, but there was nothing to be seen except the salt and pepper pots on the floor. When I asked how Tina had found us, she said a friend at the local spiritualist church had told her about us. She asked if there was anything we could do. I replied, yes, we would come around and deal with it for her. I told her there would be three of our team coming if that was OK. Tina said that would be fine.

Upon arrival a few days later, the first thing we noticed was a dark foreboding atmosphere pervading the whole house. We sat down and discussed the problems that Tina and Harry were experiencing. It so happened that Joyce was staying with them when we visited. Because Joyce was so young, Harry said he would take her out and would Tina call him when we'd finished.

I explained that an energy field, a sort of protection, had been created around their house, so the spirits couldn't leave until we had talked to them. Once we had ascertained whether they wanted to go to heaven or not, we could help where needed. When we had finished, there would be no spirits left inside the protection. Although, after some time, their loved ones could come and visit, they would not let their presence be known. I explained to Tina that one of us would go into a light trance and bring the spirits through to talk so that she could hear what they had to say.

I asked if there were any questions before we started, and Tina asked how many we had found around her house. I explained there was more than one, and they were scattered around the house. There were two upstairs in the back bedroom and quite a few in the small bedroom at the front of the house. She said the small bedroom was always cold, and when Joyce came she was afraid to sleep in that room. I told her there were no nasty spirits in the main bedroom, but there were a number on the stairs watching us. There was a little boy in the downstairs toilet with polio and several what could only be described as urchins in the lounge with a stern-looking woman. In the dining room was a nasty looking man dressed as a vicar, with a cane in his hand, and there were several children in the kitchen.

After everyone had settled down, I asked Jane to bring through a nasty looking man who was standing by the stairs. The conversation went like this:

"Good afternoon," I said.

"What do you want here?" the man said.

"I want to know why you're here and what you're doing here," I replied.

He said, "That's none of your business, I don't want to talk to you, and you should leave before you get yourselves in trouble."

"We're not leaving; we're here to sort out the problems that you and your friends are causing to the people that live in the house."

"What happens in this house is no business of yours, it's our house, and we'll do what we like."

"It is our business. Tina and Harry asked us to sort it out, which gives us the authority to question and remove those of you that are causing trouble."

"Well, there's nothing you can do, so get out, I no longer want to talk to you, and if you know what's good for you, you'll leave."

I said, "We can't leave because we haven't cleared the house yet, but if you would like to go to heaven, we would be happy to help you. The alternative is for us to escort you off the premises and introduce you to your guides who will look after you."
"Well, I don't want to go to heaven, and my friends and I are staying here."
"I'm sorry, but there are only two choices, and staying here is not one of them. If you don't leave, we'll have to remove you," I said.
He refused to leave, so we had to pass him and his friends over to their guides. Once we had watched them go, Jane opened her eyes as she came out of trance.
Tina asked, "What if they come back?"
I explained about the energy field that was put around the house. This would make it difficult for them to return, and their guides wouldn't allow them to interfere with anyone else.
She asked, "Why couldn't you stop them permanently?"
"They have free will, and we are not able, nor would we wish to take that away from anyone. They'll come to an understanding eventually, but obviously, that time is not now."
I asked Danny to get the vicar who was in the dining room, and we would see what he had to say. When the vicar came through, it got icy, but we ignored that and just carried on.
I said, "Good afternoon vicar, how can we help you?"

"You can stop meddling in things you don't know anything about and leave while you're still sane," he replied.
"May I ask why you're here?" I said.
"I'm here to make sure the children behave and learn the word of God."
"How do you make them behave?"
"Children have to learn when to speak and when to be silent."
"Is that why you have the cane to show them who is boss?"
"I do God's work, and if it means I have to beat the devil out of them, then they should thank me for putting them on the road to salvation."
"Is that why the children are here?"
"They're wayward, and they're here so we can straighten them out, they will then grow up as god-fearing adults.
"So, this is a home, and you're in charge of their education, is that right?"
"Enough of this, be on your way and don't interfere."
"I'm sorry, but you don't seem to realise you have passed over, and so have the children, you should be with your god now, and so should they. You should all be at peace; the children are no longer your responsibility."
"Don't be ridiculous, whether I'm alive or not doesn't matter. Don't you realise it's their last chance before the devil gets them? I cannot let him win, and these children must learn to respect their elders and behave."

"I'm afraid we're going to have to take them to heaven, we'll take you too if you want to go."

"How dare you, who do you think you are? Meddling in things beyond your comprehension will get you into a lot of trouble, my boy."

"Am I to take it that you don't want us to take you to heaven?"

"I no longer want to talk to you, you're in the devil's hands, and if you don't stop what you're doing, you will never be saved."

"OK then as you don't want our help, we'll have to ask your guides to look after you. If at any time you come to your senses, then just ask out loud for help, and someone will be there for you. Now I'm afraid you will have to leave, goodbye."

"I will return and make you learn the lessons of the Bible you'll see," he said as he left.

We thought it would be best to sort the children out, so I explained to Tina it was better if I could get them to realise, they were dead rather than tell them, as it sometimes comes as quite a shock for them.

I asked Danny to bring through one of the children who was in the kitchen. The little girl he brought through was about ten years old and looked as though she hadn't eaten in weeks. She was dirty and her clothes were not much better than rags. I asked her what her name was.

"My name is Grace, sir," she said.

"Hello Grace, I'm Mike, are you alright?" I asked.

"Yes, I suppose so, but that man was horrible, he was always hitting us for no reason."

"Well, he's gone now. Can you tell me what you think happened to you? What's the last thing you remember?"
"Well we were all in the big room asleep, and it got very dark and smelled horrible, my eyes started hurting and I couldn't breathe."
"Why do you think that was?"
"I don't know, it got hot then I went to sleep again."
"What happened next?"
"I was standing up; it was very dark. But I could see a little girl on the floor. I don't know who she was, but she looked very sad, even though she was asleep."
"Was that little girl about your age and looked a bit like you?"
"Yes, she did. Was it me?"
"If it was you, what do you think must have happened to you?"
"Well if I was looking down at me, I can't be standing up and lying down, does that mean I died?"
"Yes, it does. Where do people go when they die?"
"If you're good, you go to God, and if you're bad, you go to the devil. The vicar said we were all bad and we would go to hell. Is that where we are?"
"No, you're lost, and we've come to take you to heaven. Would you and your friends like to go there?"
"Will we be allowed? The vicar said we would never go to heaven because we were bad."
"You're not bad, and yes you can go to heaven. Would you all like to go?"
"Yes, please, can we all go together, please?" Grace was quite excited.

"Yes, of course, then you'll have your friends with you in heaven, won't you? Was it one of the children who threw the salt and pepper pots at the lady?"
"Yes, only we were throwing them at the matron because she was pulling my friend's hair. I'm sorry if it frightened her, we didn't mean to."
"That's alright, at least you got yourselves noticed, that's one of the reasons we're here now. It was one of your friends making the music play as well, wasn't it?"
"Yes, she liked to listen to it; it made her happy."
"OK that's alright. Now can you open your eyes big and wide and tell me what you can see?"
The reason we ask the spirits to open their eyes is that we want them to open their senses to see, which is how the spirit world sees things. That's one of the reasons people get lost, and they are only aware of the earth plane.
"I can see a long tunnel with a light at the end."
"OK, that's the light from heaven you can see. When you're ready we're going to take you there. Are you or your friends in any pain?"
"Yes, and one of the boys has got a bad leg, so don't go too fast, because he won't be able to keep up and he might get lost," she said with concern.
Because they are spirit and not physical, their physical ailments no longer exist in the spirit world, but because they have been aware in life of their ailments, they don't even consider their spirit cannot be less than whole. Therefore, when we remove their ailments, what we're doing is asking our guides to help the spirits

realise they no longer need to carry their illness or disfigurements.
"Well let's make everyone better first. We're going to take the pain away and make your friend's leg better. Everyone alright now?"
"Oh, thank you, he can walk now, and he's jumping up and down."
"OK, now we can go to heaven."
When we arrived in heaven, the children knew no one; they had been abandoned as babies, so we asked our guides to find someone to look after them. They brought forward some kindly ladies who took the children away to safety.
We then spoke with the matron, and after we explained what had happened to her, she asked us if she could go to heaven. We said we would take her to meet her husband. She told us the children were in a home for wayward children, there had been a fire, and all had perished.
We then brought the little boy with polio through.
"Hello, what's your name?"
"My name's Colin. Who are you?"
"We've come to help you; do you know what's happened to you?"
"I was in the hospital and I was very ill. It went dark, then I was here. Do you know where my mummy is? I can't find her, she was with me in hospital, but now she's gone."
"What happens to people when they're very ill?"
"Sometimes, they die, and sometimes they get better."
"Do you think you got better?"

"No, I'd still be with mummy if I was, so I must have died then."
"Yes, I afraid so, but that was a long time ago, you've been lost for a while, and then you were brought here."
"I'm sorry about the water I tried to wash my hands and couldn't turn the water off."
"That's OK, no harm done."
"Why can't I be with mummy?"
"You can, now that you understand what's happened to you; first, we're going to make you better, then we're going to take you to your mummy. How do you feel now?"
"I feel much better, and my arms and hands are alright now. Where's my mummy, I want to show her?" he said excitedly.
"Open your eyes and tell me what you can see."
"I can see a big light just over there."
"OK, we're going into that light; it's the entrance to heaven."
"Will mummy be there? She wasn't old, you know."
"I know, but that was a long time ago, she grew old and died, and she's waiting for you. Can you see her over there?"
"Oh yes, can I go to her, please?"
"Yes, off you go."
"Thank you."
"You're welcome," I said as he went running over to his mother and the rest of his family.
We spoke to the rest of the lost souls who were in the house and resolved their problems; once it was clear, the atmosphere was much lighter.

Tina telephoned us a week later as we had asked her to. She said things were peaceful, and there were no more strange things happening. She said Joyce was fine now and she was quite happy to sleep in the front bedroom again. When she went home, she was her usual self, so her mother was less concerned about her staying with her grandparents.

We have to remember the pains and ailments of the body only belong to the physical and the spiritual body is always whole. The reason the spirits suffer is that they don't realise they no longer have a physical body to feel pain. That's why we can make them feel better.

The names have been changed to provide anonymity as this visit only took place on 28 October 2019.

HAUNTING IN BRIGHTON

I went to a house near Brighton because the lady was having spiritual problems. I asked her what problems she was getting, and she said.

"There are spirits in my house doing all sorts of things which are frightening me."

I asked, "What sort of things?"

She then told me, "Most nights, my bed is being shaken; sometimes somebody gets into bed with me. One night as I got out of bed, someone grabbed my ankle, and I had to kick to get them off. When I turned the light on, there was no one there. I hear loud bangs coming from the bedroom at the front of the house day and night. Lights turn on and off by themselves. I live alone and I'm terrified. Can you do anything to stop it?"

I said, "I'll bring one of my colleagues and we'll remove the spirits that are causing you so many problems."

When we arrived, I felt an evil presence, and as I walked around the house, I was aware of quite a few spirits, good and bad. We sat down and I explained how we were going to remove the spirits and asked if she had any questions before we started.

She asked, "How many are there?"

I told her, "There are quite a few, but we'll deal with them."

I explained Danny would go into a light trance and bring the spirits through so all could hear what is said. She asked, "What is light trance?"

"It's when a medium allows a spirit to overshadow them and use their voice to speak with us. The medium will control them in so far as they can only stay as long as the medium allows them to. Because Danny will only be in a light trance, he will be aware of what is going on at all times and can come out of trance just by opening his eyes. There's nothing to be afraid of; it's just as though Danny has closed his eyes."

She seemed satisfied for the moment, and we decided to proceed with the removal of the spirits.

We started with the man who was messing around in the bedroom, and I asked Danny to bring him through. I asked him his name, which he refused to give, saying it was none of my business. So, I asked him what he thought he was doing frightening the lady by shaking her bed and grabbing her leg.

He said, "I'm looking after her."

I replied, "How are you doing that?"

"By letting her know she isn't alone and there's someone around."

"There are nicer ways of doing that. She doesn't want your help and she wants' you to leave."

"I'm quite comfortable in the house and wasn't planning on leaving for some time."

"Do you know where you are apart from being in the house?"

"I'm just in this house, and it's better than the dark and cold where I have been."

"Do you know what's happened to you?"

"The last thing I remember is falling down the stairs. I was unconscious and they took me to the hospital."

"How do you know you were taken to the hospital if you were unconscious?"

He thought for a moment.
"Because I saw them take me."
Then he said, "I could see myself lying at the bottom of the stairs and thought how is this happening? Then I was somewhere else and it was cold and dark. I saw this house with a light above it and came in; I don't want to go out there again, so I'm going to stay here."
I asked him. "How could you be in two places at once, looking at yourself at the bottom of the stairs and lying on the floor?"
That made him think; then, he realised he couldn't, and that's when realised, he was dead.
"I must be dead then."
"Yes, you are, and it's not nice to frighten people. Where do you think people go when they die?"
"They either go to heaven or hell, depending on how good they've been."
"Would you like to go to heaven?"
"I don't think they would let me go there because I haven't been very nice to the lady that lives here."
"You can go to heaven; I'm sure the lady wouldn't object. What's your name?"
" Albert" he replied.
"So, Mary, is your wife then?" I said.
That took him a little by surprise, and he asked, "How do you know?"
"As I tune in to you, I'm able to pick up on your wife who's in heaven. Would you like to see her again?"
"If I'm allowed, yes, I would."
"We'll take you to her."

We took him to the light, where she was waiting. As they hugged, they both said. "Thank you."

I asked him one last question before we said goodbye, which was, "What year did you fall down the stairs?"

"1907."

When Danny opened his eyes, the lady was in tears as she had felt the emotions of their reunion. When she settled down, I said, "We have a few more to talk to, is that OK?"

"Yes, I hope they're not all so lost."

I asked Danny to bring through the woman who was standing in the corner, watching us. When she came through, I asked, "How can we help you?"

"I have a lot of lost children here that I've been looking after, can you take us to heaven please?"

"Of course, we will, are they all aware of what's happened to them?"

"I've told them they've died, and that I'm trying to find a way of taking them to see their loved ones. That's why they stayed with me."

We gathered the children together and took them and the lady to heaven where they were reunited with their families.

I thought it was time to deal with the man I had picked up in the spare bedroom, where we'd heard noises ever since we arrived.

I said, "There's a man of average build with not much hair. He isn't a happy man and he is throwing his weight around, and that's why we hear noises."

Danny closed his eyes and tuned in to the man.

He said, “What do you think you’re doing? I’ve just sorted out who I want in my house, and you come along and start taking them away.”
I pointed out that it wasn’t his house, and those we had spoken to had gone to a better place where their loved ones were. He was outraged
He said, “How dare you interfere with my plans, this is my house; I claimed it, and I will do what I like in my own home.”
I asked him if he knew what had happened to him, and he said, “Yes, of course.”
I asked him to tell me, and he replied, “I died in a fire, and I’ve been wandering all over till I found this house.”
“You can’t stay here; this house belongs to the lady, and she just wants to be left in peace.”
“There’s plenty of room, why does she have to be so greedy. Once I’ve rearranged a few things I’m sure we can get along?”
I told him he didn’t belong, and the lady wanted him out
I asked him, “Where should people go when they die?”
“Wherever they can find some peace.”
“There are other places where you can go, where you wouldn’t upset the living.”
To which he replied, “Do you mean heaven?”
“Yes, if you want to.”
“It’s not real, I haven’t seen it, and I’ve looked.”
“It is real, but you aren’t looking in the right way.”
“What do you mean in the right way? I can see you.”

"But you don't live in this world anymore, and you can't see everything in your world. Let me show you what you're missing."
"OK, how are you going to do that?"
"Simple. Open your eyes and you'll see a lot of people you've been missing."
"Where did they come from?"
"You're looking with your senses now instead of your eyes, and you're now looking in your world."
"But I still can't see heaven," he said.
"That's because you don't know where to look. What else can you see apart from those strange looking people?"
"I can see a tunnel with a light at the end."
"Yes, that's the entrance to heaven. Would you like me to take you to see your family?"
"They won't be there yet, I'm only 35, they were all too young to die when I did."
"What year did you die?" I asked.
"1933," he said.
When I told him, it was 2018 he was surprised as he hadn't been aware of the amount of time that had passed
"Would you like me to take you to see them?" I asked.
"Well, if they'll have me in heaven, I haven't been all that nice, you know."
"Yes, I know, but you can go to heaven anyway. There are people there who have done far worse than you."
"OK, let's go and see."
So, I took him to meet his family and to his surprise, they were all there waiting for him. He said thanks and

asked if he could stay. I said, of course, go in peace and he left. When Danny opened his eyes, he said, "There were loads of people waiting for him, and he got all choked up."

The lady asked, "Are there any more?"

I said, "Yes, we've got a young boy standing over there who looks like he could do with some help. He's about 12 years old with dark hair and nothing on his feet. He's dressed in dirty grey trousers, which come down to his knees and has a grey top on."

"Yes," said Danny. "I can sense him. Do you want me to bring him through?"

"Yes, please," I said.

When the boy was through, I asked his name.

"Tom," he said.

"Do you know where you are?" I asked.

"No, I've been wandering in the dark, and it was cold until I saw this house and came in. It's warm here, but there were some nasty people here, so I had to hide."

"What's the last thing you remember before you were in the dark?"

"I was working up a chimney, and I got stuck; they couldn't get me out."

"I see, then what happened?"

"I was there for a long time, and my nose was blocked with soot, I tried to open my mouth to breathe, but it got filled with soot, my chest hurt and that's all I can remember."

"So, what do you think happens when you can't breathe?"

"You die. Is that what happened to me?"

"Yes, I'm afraid it is."
"But if I'm dead, how can I talk to you?"
"Well, your body is dead, but you are still alive in another way."
"Do you mean I'm a ghost?"
"That's sometimes what they call you, but I prefer to call you a spirit. Are you in any pain?"
"Well, my chest is hurting and my sides are sore."
"OK we'll take that away so you'll feel better. There, how's that?"
With a smile, Tom said, "Yes, and I can breathe again. What do I do now?"
"Would you like to go to heaven?"
"Is that where dead people go?"
"Yes, it's where you came from before you were born. Where your mum and dad and all your family are."
"But they can't be, they were all right when I went to work."
"What year was it when you died?"
"I don't know, 1800 and something, I think."
"Well, it's 2018 now, that's more than two hundred years ago, you've been dead a long time. Would you like us to take you to heaven so you can see them again?"
"Yes, please, I don't want to stay here."
"OK, open your eyes and tell me what you can see."
"I can see light at the end of what looks like a tunnel."
"Yes, that's the entrance to heaven, we're going to go into that tunnel to heaven, but before we go can you see the other children in this house?" I asked.
"Yes, there are quite a few, can they come with us?"

"Yes, our guides are just getting them lined up. Right, now we're ready to go, it won't take long."
"What're guides?" Tom asked.
"They're friends of ours who help us to help people like you when you're lost. They work with us from your side of life. Here we are, what can you see now?"
"I can see lots of people, and there are my mum and dad. Can I go now?"
"Yes, you're safe now. Goodbye."
"Goodbye and thanks, mister."
All the children went to their loved ones, and Danny opened his eyes.
The lady said, "There were a lot of people here, is that all of them?"
"Yes, now you can have a bit of peace."
"Will they come back again?" she asked.
"No, they won't, we've put protection around your house, so you won't get others coming to disturb you. What you need to do now is get on with your life. Don't think about whether there's anyone here. That would be an invitation for others to come through the protection."
She asked, "What's protection, and how does it work?"
"It's an energy field that our guides put up before we come, so the nasty ones can't run away and come back after we've been. Then when we've finished, they show your guides how to keep it there so that you won't be bothered again."
We chatted a bit then said our goodbyes knowing she wouldn't have any more problems.

I telephoned a few weeks later just to make sure she was alright. She said since we went to her house, she's had no more problems, she doesn't ache or get pains like before, and she's sleeping much better.

PART TWO

VOICES IN MY HEAD

The previous cases were all about discarnate spirits affecting more than one person, be it a cry for help or just interference. There is another type of interference that is more accurately described as hearing voices, whether externally or internally. There can be more than one voice and male or female. When it's internal sometimes it's a thought rather than a voice. Before we can help the individual, we must discern how the voices are heard, and they may be from spirit or sometimes mistaken for your inner voice, the voice you 'hear' when you count to ten in your head or read to yourself. Once we know if the voice is spirit and how the voice is received, we can then work towards a solution, although it will rarely be a quick fix. The reason for this is the patient may have had the symptoms for a long time and may also be on medication. If, for instance, the problem has been going on for several years, then it will not always be resolved in one sitting. The patient will need to understand how they are receiving the voices, where they're coming from and why. It may take a while to re-educate the patient regarding the cause before attempting removal. Although we can often remove the offending spirit in one sitting, the fact they've been hearing the voices for a long time creates an expectation in the patient. The fact that they expect to hear the voices turns in to a habit which they often find hard to break.

To them, hearing the voices is normal, however abusive or controlling they are. Most people will feel a loss when the voices are removed, so we have to remove them slowly. Most of the time, the voices come back because the patient is unable to close down to spirit. Even if they can protect themselves, they need to learn not to think about or listen to see if they are still there as that just invites others. Everyone has a little voice talking inside their head, it's called inner speech, and you can hear it when you're thinking or silently reading. Some hear voices the same way as when someone is talking to them (which they are) but inside their heads. There can be more than one voice, and rarely is it anyone known to the patient. The voices can be abusive and suggestive and also horrible; they are also constant. The patient may also be experiencing mood changes or being touched and feeling pain, which is not theirs. They may also be seeing spirits or frightening faces.

They usually start after a traumatic experience or when the patient has been taking recreational drugs. They can also be the side effects of medication or brought on by stress. We must rule out any underlying brain problem that may also cause people to hear voices. I have found that most people who are hearing voices isolate themselves from friends and family. They are also put on strong medication to numb the brain; this does nothing to alleviate the voices as they are coming through the mind. So, the first thing is to help the patient get back control of their mind.

The cause has been blamed on all sorts of factors, from environmental to genetic, to drugs and brain damage.

HEARING VOICES IN KENT

I received an email asking for help from a lady in Kent called Harriet. She was hearing voices and being disturbed by spirit. She had severe mood swings and she got very angry for no apparent reason. The voices were telling her she was ugly and nobody liked her, and she should throw herself in front of a car. She felt someone touching her when she went to bed and consequently had disturbed nights. Harriet had been diagnosed with schizophrenia and bipolar disorder and had been prescribed 60mg of Duloxetine, which is an antidepressant medicine. It's for depression and anxiety and also for nerve pain, such as fibromyalgia. Harriet is 29 and lives about two-and-a-half hours away, and it was going to be challenging to give her the help she needed, so I found a medium in her area who might be able to help. I got an angry email back saying she was prepared to travel and didn't care what it cost. I advised her to try the local medium, and if it didn't help, then I would look at the situation again.

About two months later she emailed me saying she had read one of my books and the lady she was seeing was of no help, would I think again. I told her we could try working together over the internet, but if we start, we must see it through to the end because if we didn't, things would get worse. Harriet agreed to this, so I set up a meeting place halfway between us where we could introduce ourselves, and I could see what problems she was having.

I met Harriet and her parents, and she told me her story.

HARRIET

Harriet was born in Lewisham hospital in London on 23/05/1990, and raised in London. One of three sisters of which she was second born. Her father immigrated from Jamaica when he was young, her mother was from Granada. Her father had drinking/anger/cheating issues, it wasn't a happy marriage at all, fights were frequent. Harriet didn't get along well with her older sister, but got along extremely well with Charlotte her younger sister. Her older sister Tamara didn't like her and picked on her often. She would keep her younger sister away and kept them apart most days, so Harriet often played games by herself. Harriet was seriously shy which didn't help matters much. Her mother told her that Harriet used to see what spirits in the house were doing, she would go to her saying she saw her bedroom door swing open and shut and fridge magnets move. Her mother's side were quite spiritual, people in her family often saw, heard and felt spirit. Two were mediums and her auntie can feel, and used to see them when she was younger. Her grandmother is very open too. Harriet knew spirits existed but hated seeing ANY form of it, because she was terrified of them, being young and not fully understanding it. So, she was aware of them all through her childhood, but nothing dramatic happened until she moved to Australia.

Her parents divorced and they moved from house to house. Harriet was diagnosed with cancer at 13, a rare skin cancer called Mycosis fungoides. Her mother met and remarried and moved into the house in Belvedere London where Harriet had experiences with a ghost in her bedroom. She was extremely uncomfortable living there, as it always made her feel scared, and just plain creepy. Her older sister Tamara no longer lived in the family home. So, it was just her parents and sister Charlotte from then on. Harriet loved to draw so wanted a career as an artist. She focused on that most of her life. They moved to Kent by the sea, where she went to college and university to study fine art, worked in a retail store, met her boyfriend, got engaged, moved to Australia got a job as a tattooist, and then the spiritual interference started. Things went from bad to worse and when her relationship broke up her mother told her to come home and we'll sort it out.

When Harriet got home, she spoke to countless mediums and went on line seeking help. She was told she had demons and an incubus, thought forms she'd created, and it was loved ones talking to her.

Her mind wasn't hers it was like someone had hacked in and taken control, she didn't know what was happening or how to handle it and got very confused. She got super angry and moody and wanted to be alone all the time. She would get horrible images and then nice ones in her head and dreams which became nightmares. Harriet heard about spirit keeping and she thought she would get some good spirits to clear out the bad ones, that's what they told her and she bought some angels, fairies, dragons and fantasy creatures but it just made it worse. The voices became constant and loud she couldn't get any peace. It was like having someone constantly saying horrible things in her ear, and couldn't get rid of them!

I said, "So what's happening now?"

Harriet said, "I'm fighting an invisible spirit, and it's scary sometimes, to the point I want to jump in bed and never leave again. When I go to bed, I can feel someone touching me, mainly on my side and back. I have been sexually assaulted several times, which is hard to talk about. I can't even drink because they easily influence me to do sexual things, and when I sleep, horrible thoughts roll in again and again. I feel like I have nothing to keep me sane; I'm fighting all the time. It's so hard, but not many understand, the voices tell me nobody likes me and I'm not worth bothering about. I also get depressed and anxious, which is why the doctor gave me the pills, but they don't do anything to stop the anxiety and depression; just make me feel tired. They're supposed to give me more energy, remove depression and sort out my anxiety and stop my mood swings. They diagnosed me with bipolar disorder and borderline schizophrenia. It's hard to tell which is spirit and which is me.

"A long time ago, I used to spirit keep, and I'm still doing it now, where I bought good white guides to help with earthbound protection, I thought they would help! But nothing, I'm still doing it now and have a keep of pure angels around me (what I was told). I bought them from a spirit-keeping site where they also sell spells and arch angels, but still have the same problems with earthbound beings, I had them all this time. Waste of money! But I still have them with me, I think.

"I get outraged all of a sudden and go into a rage, and my mum helps me to calm down by talking and hugging me, which helps.

"Several spirits are talking in my head, and there's only so many times I can hear 'self-harm' or 'kill yourself' without it affecting me. Once in half awake half asleep, I was sexually assaulted, and it felt real. It made me scared and nervous; I also felt as though I was being strangled, twice, so I get scared when I go to bed. The touches are nonstop, and it feels never-ending. Sometimes, it gets so bad I have to sleep with mum, it's scary and makes me super depressed. I try to be happy all the time, but sometimes I cry because it's so hard to be happy when this happens to you, generally upsets me, and that's not me at all, am I being influenced by spirit? So, when 'I'm' crying, it's serious. Right now, the tiredness is a big problem, all I want to do is sleep and be 'intimate' which I don't because it's super creepy when I do, this thing seems to be male. I don't know if you've spoken to people who were sexually assaulted, but I have been a few times.

"But the toll of all of this has, well, I believe, affected my brain a bit, and I find myself depressed and having anxiety too."

While Harriet was talking, I was aware of two spirits with her, so I had a talk with them and resolved their confusion and took them to the light. One of them said Harriet had a lot of spirits hanging around her, shouting abuse, and generally trying to upset her. He said they had been there for a long time and would be difficult to remove.

I explained to Harriet and her parents that I had removed two spirits that were interfering with her moods and making her angry and depressed and causing anxiety. I also told them that she was open to the spirit world, and anyone who wanted could come in and talk to her; that we would work on her controlling her mind so she could block the voices, and teach her how to protect herself.

I asked her how she heard the voices, and Harriet said, "I can hear male and female voices audibly, and they come and go as they feel like it. When I'm being touched or poked, I'm aware of a male with me, and I get verbal abuse at the same time. This interference only happens at night, and there are times when I can't move, as if I'm paralysed. This usually happens as I'm waking up. I pray each night and ask Archangel Michael to protect me, and I am still spirit keeping, but it doesn't seem to work."

I told Harriet that it would not be an easy fix as there were a lot of different issues to deal with, and the first was to learn how to close down. I explained that prayers were not a good idea at the moment as when she prayed, she opened up to spirit and remained open all night. Harriet has already said she didn't think the spirit keeping was working, and I said to stop trying to bring in spirits she didn't know as that only added to the confusion. I also told her that we would start by helping her control her mind and thoughts so that she could block out the voices; that it would depend on her determination as to how long it would take to regain control of her mind, and it would take time, but as she

got stronger, the voices would gradually fade.
I explained that her mind and her brain were separate but intertwined, and the medication would only affect the brain as it was organic, as were the drugs. The mind is the spiritual part she had to regain control of. She asked how we could do that, so I told her we would start with a simple exercise, which she would do twice a day. She was to sit comfortably and close her eyes and picture in her mind's eye a candle, and every time it disappeared, she was to picture it again until she could picture it at will without losing the candle. Then every time she started to hear voices, she should think of the candle to the exclusion of everything else, and as her mind was full of the candle, it would automatically block out the voices. I asked what help had she had so far, and this is what she told me.

"I'll start from when I was committed to the mental institute. I think I was sent to the hospital in Feb 2019 for three weeks. They put me on quite a bit of medication. I didn't realise how much until I started thinking about it. So scary knowing that they thought I needed all that crap! My care wasn't the best; in fact, I was terrified, humiliated. It was just plain wrong. I always felt I didn't belong there and started to think maybe I was right. But I couldn't do anything about it! I had no choice but to take the meds they gave to me. They never made me feel any better at all; I felt worse; the voices were the same if not more noticeable! I wasn't in the right frame of mind and didn't know who to listen too, the voices or the medical team. Little did I know that both were wrong! I couldn't listen to the voices, being negative, shouting lies and hate all the time and the medical team thinking I was insane. They thought I had some kind of split personality. No one believed that I had spiritual interference, and I had little to no clue about it either; it was a living hell.

"Care was no better; it felt strict and uncaring; they didn't care one bit that I was suffering and thought meds were the only thing to sort it out. I kept complaining that I can still hear the voices, but they did little to nothing, Then I started getting angry, upset and scared and I started acting out horribly, by attempting to self-harm and shout and scream, because no one cared or listened. It's like they thought I was making this all up, and they thought they were better than me or something. I didn't like anyone there, and I wasn't the type to be rude about anyone, but even I thought they were all mean. The only thing they did was separate me from the others and increased my meds. I felt numb, sleepy and dead like a zombie but was still stuck with the voices. Imagine being completely paralysed, not being able to move at all, and just stuck in one horrible place where you think everyone hates you and wants the absolute worst thing to happen to you. And you only have your thoughts, your brain and your mind. But they're corrupted as hell. You can't think what you want because the spirits change them into your worst fears, so you can't imagine anything! You can't have a quiet moment. Because the voices are shouting, screaming at you all the time, trying to get your attention. The only things they say are hurtful, disgusting, hateful, downright vile. All the time, no rest or breaks 24/7 every-day of your life! With no escape. You can't dream because your dreams aren't your own, or they're manipulated. You can't sleep to escape, not being awake. And I had to deal with that for not only those three weeks in the ward but years as well; it just seemed worse in the ward. I couldn't escape the ward and was constantly reminded of the pain and suffering the other people were going through. I honestly just wanted to die; nothing was worse than dealing with this all on my own. No one, no people, just me, I had to do this by myself. I had to be strong and just ignore the voices as much as I could; they were trying to make me like them. Horrible, and the voices wanted me to change into a bitter, hateful, disgusting, vile piece of crap like them. But deep down, I knew it wasn't me, and just tried to stay positive.

"I honestly thought the more meds I had in me, the better to deal with this, but nothing was working, and I didn't know why. I was in a living hell. They gave me pills daily, those were antipsychotics – Olanzapine – to help with 'voices', quite a high dose, because I remembered that I kept asking about the voices, and them putting the dose up. Antidepressant – Prozac/Fluoxetine to help with depression and anxiety. Benzodiazepines – Diazepam to help with calming me down, and not getting angry or agitated, it's a sedative too. It was given to me nearly every-day. But it was when needed because it's highly addictive. Beta-blocker – Propranolol to reduce anxiety symptoms. That's all I remember to be honest about meds. Once I was out, though, I changed a few meds for others because I was still (of course) hearing voices, so I tried a few things.

“General care was fine. I guess nothing to write home about; I went to a few speaking classes where you just sit down and talk about your feelings. I don't know, I thought they were a waste of time, and not once made me feel better. It was good to socialise, but other than that nothing. No one was going through what I was going through; I felt they just talked about how other people, famous people, also had mental disorders. And it’s common, normal, I just had to manage it in these groups. You know the funny thing is I pretty much knew it wasn't me this whole time and knew it was spiritual. So, it didn't count for me all this. Yes, some days, I thought it was me, but honestly, I knew it wasn’t completely me if that makes sense and that it was spiritual. I knew there was something negative and horrible pushing me, but I could not find anyone in the same boat there. I desperately kept talking to other people there, asking if they were experiencing the same thing, but no one! Not a celeb, not another person, I felt so alone! The classes meant nothing to me. All they ever really focused on was socialising, that's it. Nothing else really mattered than them forcing me and others to socialise. Never mind me hearing voices or my anger issues, no I had to socialise. I get why they had to, and I get that of course socialising is a good thing and I did need it. But at the time, I thought I was going to see a professional, to talk about my emotions and feelings, and see more doctors, but that never really happened. I saw the doctor a few times, but only for meds and blood tests, blood pressure checks, medical check-ups, etc. Never really talking things through. I had to ask for that, and just got someone, probably not even a mental health person at all, just one of the staff members, I think. And the talks were nothing special, just keep going, you're doing great and stay strong, the normal stupid kind of ramblings you get when your kind to someone.

"I tell you now I wasn't impressed at all, it just seemed so unprofessional and rushed. It was just obvious they wanted space for new mentally ill people and wanted the old ones out. Never felt safe, relaxed or comfortable there, I heard screams, crying and angry people during the day and night every-day. It was just plain to see all they wanted was to kick you out. But they needed to socialise you first, so you don't relapse and come back, so you're stable to join society again. Which I get, but what I didn't seem to get was how strongly they just focused on that. Scary even, some people didn't seem ready to go back into society. Yet they pushed them out regardless; it wasn't a club to socialise.

"I did see the main doctor there but only twice. He was the guy who diagnosed me with 'borderline personality disorder'. So uncaring and mean. Pretty much laughed in my face about my hearing voices from the dead. But I was strict, I kept saying that was the case, and the name I got was Fred. But he was saying it wasn't spirit pretty much and that I had some sort of split personality. I wasn't going to convince him anytime soon, that was for sure. There were other people in there too, like the crisis team and other professional faces, which I didn't see anywhere else other than the two meetings I had. Including the doctor, so only twice my whole time I had been there. They were there to offer support; they were the same too. nice though, nicer than the doctor! I was so angry he wasn't taking me seriously, even though I knew hearing spirits would sound and be like a big stretch for most people, but still, I thought he would be nicer about it, even if he didn't believe. I just felt like a joke. The others were nicer, but I still felt they felt I had what the doctor said. I can't blame them! If the doctor said I had that, then, of course they're going to agree, he's the professional guy after all. I had no choice but to take that label and go with it because I was alone with my true feelings. I felt if I didn't accept it, then they would just keep me locked up there if I kept on complaining about it. So, I had to accept I had what they said and agreed to treatment. I hated it admitting it was me when it clearly wasn't. It felt weak.

"After that, I was pretty much allowed to go home, promised I'd keep taking my meds, and just left without really saying goodbye. I know it's not their fault, just doing their job and don't know anything about spirits, but still. I never want to go back or end up there again. After that, I was visited every day by the crisis team to check I was taking my meds, and that's it. And to check that I'm OK. I used to take: antipsychotics – Olanzapine, Aripiprazole and Asenapine. Antidepressants – Cymbalta/Duloxetine, Prozac/Fluoxetine. Beta blocker (reduce anxiety, symptoms) – Propranolol. Mood stabilisers – Lamotrigine Benzodiazepines (it's a calming/sedative pill) – Diazepam."

I gave Harriet some healing because she was getting agitated and also removed a lady who was playing with her emotions. Once she had calmed down, I explained to her what I had done and told her to try and stay calm. I then told her again I wanted her to practise meditating and to imagine a candle and picture it in her mind. To focus on the candle and exclude anything else so there was nothing in her mind but the candle. She was to hold that image and everytime it went away to bring it back this would help her to block the spirits and get control of her mind.

It was then time to leave, and we decided on a weekly talk on Skype to monitor progress and deal with situations as they arose.

I said, "Hello, how're you getting on with the candle?"
Harriet said, "I'm finding it difficult to focus, and it keeps disappearing after a few seconds."
I said, "It's not going to be easy, but with practice, you should be able to hold it a little longer each time. It's important that you practise twice a day, and every time it goes, bring it back into your mind. By focusing, you make it harder for any other thoughts to come into your mind. Initially, you will get a lot of interference while meditating, but gradually, you will get less as you learn to focus."
While we were talking, I removed another man from Harriet who had got in because she was wide open. So, I decided to introduce her to one of her guides as a focal point when she was asking spirit for help.
I said, "One of your guides has stepped forward, his name is Kaz and he's Egyptian, about 5" 6" and he is wearing an off-white robe. He's quite stocky and has a beard, has dark hair down to his shoulders, and he has something in his hand. Can you see what he's holding?"
Harriet said, "I can't see."
I said, "Let me know when you can."
The reason for this verification is so I know she is tuning in to the same spirit as me.
I asked Kaz to help Harriet to protect herself, and he said, "I will help, but she has to make an effort because I need to know by her actions that she doesn't want the interference to continue."

The next week

I said, "Hi, how are things?"
Harriet said, "Things are the same, but I'm managing better with everything happening. I've been dragged into half-awake half-asleep, which was scary. I'm angrier and having strong impulses, but manage them with distractions, like music, TV and changing thought patterns. It's super hard, and I do struggle, I call my guide 'Kaz' but it seems it's not working as well as I hoped. I hoped the 'male' earthbound would have gone by now, but seems to have gotten worst. I believe 'Kaz' is helping, but feel he struggles with this male earthbound. I get sexual touches and hear voices still. I call 'Kaz' which makes me feel calmer, but the presence is powerful and it won't stop. I'm staying as calm as I can, but it's getting a bit much, I haven't slept well in three days and it's draining, I'm being shaken awake, and keep waking up. But the male earthbound is loud and stubborn. I believe he's the main one who's influencing me to do these things, manipulating me. But he seems to be the one who's cuddling me at night. I try and try to get him to leave, but nothing's working."
I said, "Keep doing what you're doing. Kaz is helping, but he has to allow you to build up your strength. It may seem difficult at the moment, but it will get easier. Have you considered you're getting rid of the male earthbound, but as soon as you do, another takes his place pretending to be him, so you'll think it's not working? We need to build up your confidence in your guides, so to start, I want you to place yourself in a

pyramid with Kaz with a purple light around you for protection. Once you've visualised that thank Kaz for his help and know that you're protected. I've cleared you to give you some space."

Harriet said, "I'll keep practising; it's funny ever since I started doing the practices, I feel stronger! My confidence is getting better, and concentrating on my distractions and Kaz seem to be working. I'm now managing better with the earth bounds and ignoring them better. It does seem like a long path, but I believe in Kaz! It's hard when he gets rid of one, and another possibly comes in, so frustrating. I do believe it was the same guy, but to know it would be someone else taking his place, it's hurtful. I'll try my best and keep asking for them to be sent to the light. So, thank you and thank you for removing the man, it's creepy knowing what this earthbound was doing with me. Kaz knows I try, but it gets on top of me sometimes, and I don't know what to do! But I'll keep at it. I still get the presence around me, seems like a male again. But I don't want to keep asking you for help, and I'll try and see if Kaz and I can do this for a few weeks and see how it goes.

SEPTEMBER 2019

I said, "How are you getting on?"
Harriet said, "I feel a lot calmer, my dreams seem to be getting better, not so many nightmares, still feel a presence around me, but feel so much better knowing Kaz is around. I said the phrase you gave me last night before bed and I felt protected. I still feel someone in bed with me, but I'm much better at managing it than before. The anger impulses are still there, though, which is quite strong still. But last night was pretty much the same for me; I just feel I can handle it better. It's weird though I feel calmer, I still get the earthbound spirits around me, not sure what to make of it. But thank you so much for getting rid of that man! I still feel a heavy presence of a male figure around me, and the touches are still there, but again I'm managing it better and having Kaz on my side helps."

OCTOBER 2019

Harriet wrote, "I spoke to the doctor about my feelings, not about the spirits, had to lie a lot, and he said try this low dose of a mood stabiliser. I wasn't sure if I should try it, but he gave it to me just in case I changed my mind. I haven't taken it yet, still debating, but tempted, if it means it will sort out my brain side of things. Because I'm very depressed and have anxiety, which makes me feel weak fighting against these spirits day in day out, and they know it. I had a hard time even going to the appointment when they make me tired and fill my head with doubt. But if it helps one per cent, it's better than nothing. I know it would do zip for the mind, but if my brain's weak, then I'm an easier target! Which gives them more opportunities to attack me harder, which they are doing right now. I need my brain to be strong so that I can fight the mind. I believe I think that's what I'm trying to say, it's only temporary until I can get back on my feet with my life. Right now, I have no friends, no partner, no career, no life! Just at home with no purpose, and it makes my situation/depression worse. It's like having someone continually chatting horrible things in your ear, and you can't get rid of them! I'm fighting an invisible spirit, and it's scary sometimes, to the point I want to jump in bed and never leave again. I need to stand on my own two feet, which I've been doing a little more with your help. Going on the treadmill and working out, volunteering, all good stuff! I have to start from scratch, but I will hang in there! And talking helps, so thank you for reading this; it's hard to talk about. I can't even drink because they easily influence me to do sexual things and sleep, and horrible thoughts roll in again and again. So, I feel like I've nothing to keep me sane! I'm fighting so hard all the time! Not many people think so, besides you, of course! Sorry, I didn't tell you sooner about the attacks, was again hard to explain. With the doctor's pills, I'm going to leave them until Saturday and see how I feel. They're meant to give me more energy, remove depression and sort out my anxiety, and stop my mood swings, not the spirits, but my own. Hopefully, that'll help me recognise which is mine and which is spirit! Which is still kind of hard, I might hold off until I speak to you next actually that might be easier. Just don't want you to get cross or angry going behind your back taking pills. They gave me a month's supply on a low dose; if I don't like it, I can ween myself off very easily. I expressed I didn't want anything too harsh, so they gave me one with fewer side effects, and reviews are right! Sorry for chatting your ear off! But I wanted to say this for the reason why I thought it might be wise to take something. Or not. I haven't taken anything yet."

I said, "Hi Harriet, thank you for the update it's constructive. How are you getting on?"

Harriet said, "When I try to meditate with the candle, I'm getting a lot of interference. I'm also getting interference most of the day with the voices constantly talking, making it hard to concentrate on anything. Sometimes chatty but mostly undermining my confidence. Can you remove the negative spirits?"

I said, "I could if they got too much, and I've been

removing them when we talk. But you're so used to them; you unconsciously invite them back. The only way is for you to learn to protect yourself by blocking them, and that's what the exercise with the candle is for, to gain control of your mind. How long are you able to hold the picture in your mind?"

Harriet said, "About a second before lots of thoughts come into my mind."

I said, "It will be hard working with the candle, but it will get easier the more you practise. The idea is to clear the mind and only allow your thoughts. What are your hobbies? What do you like doing?"

Harriet said, "I like to go to my room and draw. But it's getting difficult to concentrate."

I said, "Can you draw downstairs where there's someone else in the room with you?"

Harriet said, "I like music and watching television, but again I find it hard to focus, and that makes me angry, and I go into a sudden surge of rage. That's when I have trouble staying in the same room as other people, they seem to irritate me just by being there, and I go to my room to be by myself."

I said, "Count to ten when you feel angry and try to slow down your breathing. If you concentrate on your breathing, it'll help you control your moods. Do you think you could stay downstairs for one hour to start with for a week? Then gradually extend the time by ten minutes each day until you can stay there for two hours a day while focusing on your drawing, or the television or just chatting. Then if you want to go to your room, you make a conscious decision to do so?"

It was obvious the spirits were increasing the pressure on Harriet to try to keep her under their control; every time she made a decision, she was taking control away from them.

Harriet said, "I also get very anxious if I have to go out."

I said, "OK, how about if you take a walk each morning for ten minutes and increase the time as you feel more able and providing the weather is OK?"

Because of her anxiety when going out, Harriet has no social life and can't work, as she finds it hard to concentrate.

I said, "We're going to take back control of your life and eventually block out the voices so you can be normal again. How long have you heard voices?"

Harriet said, "For about five years and they've gradually got worse. At first, I tried talking to them, but they just ignored me and kept saying things like, you're not good enough for him, or he doesn't like you and why don't you cut your arm, or kill yourself. I'm still getting touched when I go to bed, which makes it difficult to sleep."

I said, "When you feel as though you're being touched, put your hand on the spot as though brushing off a fly, that'll stop it."

When we next spoke Harriet said, "I've asked Kaz for help, and things got a little easier for a while, but then went back to normal. Has my guide stopped helping me?"

I said, "The idea's not for you to hand over the burden, you need to continue to try and help yourself and Kaz will assist."

Harriet said, "I am having trouble with the candle meditation, and when I'm going to meditate, I get thoughts saying why bother it's not going to work."
I said, "Those thoughts are interference to stop you from getting control; if you decide to do something, then you must do it. The spirits will try and put thoughts in your mind as to why you shouldn't meditate. All the while, they can distract you, you won't move forward."
Harriet said, "It's been a struggle, but I managed to increase the time I spend with the rest of the family by 30 minutes, it's very hard, but the deep breathing helps. I've been doing a bit of drawing, but I find it hard to focus and get impatient, and I managed to take a walk on two occasions. I'm still getting touched when I'm in bed."
I said, "I suggest you put a pillow behind you because the pressure of the pillow on your back will neutralise the feeling of being touched. Stay with it, as it'll take a bit of time, but gradually you should see some improvement as you continue to work on the different areas of your life."
Harriet said, "I can't talk for long. I've been throwing up all night. I've been sick, but I'm sure it won't last long. As for interference, things have been easier, still getting emotions but nothing I can't handle. Also, I got a voluntary job at an animal shelter, which I'll be going to twice a week starting next week. I'm meeting a male friend tomorrow, nothing serious, but ever since I made the time to go and see him, I've been feeling sick. I don't think it's related to spirit, but it's been annoying. If you give spirit an inch, they will make the most of the

opportunity. I know they're making me feel worse, I'm going anyway, but it feels a bit creepy when the subject is brought up about him. My illness has been my main problem this week, and I've been stressed out, and spirit's playing on it. Just feel a constantly sick feeling to the stomach and barely able to do what I wanted this week but managed anyway, but it hasn't been easy. A constant fight. I'm going back to bed as I'm tired. I managed an hour's walk this morning and felt like throwing up the whole time, and now I feel worse. I think I should have stayed in bed."

I said, "It sounds like you have caught something, and you're right; they will take advantage of your illness, to push you further down with your emotions. From what you say, you seem to have it figured out. I hope you feel better when you meet your friend tomorrow."

From what Harriet says she is getting attacked, but she's got enough to deal with at the moment, we'll sort it out when she's ready. It's hard to concentrate when someone's feeling sick, but it's one of the first things spirit will do to stop you from concentrating. If you can work through it, it'll go.

NOVEMBER 2019

I spoke to Harriet on the phone as her laptop isn't working at the moment.

Harriet said, "I'm having a rough time right now, I'm getting headaches which won't go away, I'm taking my tablets, but they don't seem to be working. I'm not sure whether I'm coming down with something or it's spiritual. I've asked Kaz for help, and I'm getting some powerful, disturbing thoughts that are getting me depressed. I know spirit is interfering with my emotions also, and it's hard to handle, and my dreams aren't any better either. I ask for help, but nothing is working; I need your help because things are getting worse. The voices are bringing me down a lot, and there's a lot of talk about attempting suicide, which is scary. They give me a strong will to act on certain actions. I know not to do it, but it's still worrying, I'm trying to stay strong though. I haven't been meditating; there's been too much going on, and I can't concentrate."

I said, "You need to start working on the candle regardless, even if it's not for long. We need to get a routine going so that you can block out some of the interference. You're getting attacked from all sides. You can do this, just a little bit at a time. Have you put the pillow behind you when you're in bed? Do some drawing and listen to some music to redirect your mind and thoughts."

DECEMBER 2019

Harriet's laptop was still playing up but had a brief conversation on the phone.
I said, "How are things?"
Harriet said, "I'm getting on well with my walking, I've been out every day this week. I still get nasty voices telling me none of the people I see likes me."
I said, "They don't know you; they're strangers, so it's of no concern."
Harriet said, "I've started to use the pillow, and I'm getting less disturbance with touching, but I still get voices. I don't hear the voices when you're talking to me; it's like they're listening to what we're saying. I've also started to work with the candle, and I can hold the picture a bit longer now, I'm doing it twice a day. Things are better as sometimes I can focus on what I'm doing, and the voices fade a bit. Would it be OK to go to a meditation group?"
I said, "It's better if you don't, as we don't know the medium and whether she can protect you if you have difficulties and also, she may not believe in negative spirits. Keep working on the candle as that's the key to your success."
Harriet said, "I'm starting to hold the candle for about a minute before I lose it and have to get it back, and I'm finding the candle comes to mind if I get an attack, so at last, it's becoming automatic. The animal shelter where I'm volunteering is helping as I don't get hardly any interference because I'm focused on the animals. I'm getting less interference at night and feel more rested

when I wake up in the morning, and the paralysis has stopped. I was getting voices the other day, and a thought came in to do some drawing, which I did, and the voices went away for a while."

I said, "That's good news; you're starting to receive encouragement from your guides. Don't look for them, but if you get a thought, follow it, as it's your guides communicating with you. Your guides won't talk to you but only give you thoughts, but the negative spirits will talk, touch or play with your emotions. Don't take any notice or look for thoughts from your guides, as it may not be them. If you feel the need to do something, examine where it's coming from. If you're comfortable go ahead, with practice it'll become obvious where the feeling's coming from. Try to put spirit out of your mind. I know it's hard at this time, but the sooner you can, the easier it'll be."

Harriet said, "When I meditate on the candle, I'm getting three candles, which is confusing."

I said, "That's interference, blow the other two out and focus on the one you put there."

Harriet said her laptop is working, so I will record what's said, for the record.

I said, "Hi, Harriet, how are things?"

Harriet said, "I'm meditating on the candle, which is really good now."

I said, "You've just got one candle now?"

Harriet said, "I blew out the other two candles, the one that's coming on the right side and the one behind my head, just got one candle now straight ahead on which I'm focusing. I've been doing that, and it looks like it's getting better. I was getting so confused about which one to focus on."

I said, "So when you focus on the candle, you don't hear voices?"

Harriet said, "No, not as much no, I don't think so. I do get distracted by my thoughts and probably interference from negative spirits, normally I've just concentrated my thoughts on the candle. I have my headphones on, and I don't even notice the music, I just focus on the candle and everything just zones out."

I said, "OK, so when you meditate, you listen to music?"

Harriet said, "Yes."

I said, "When you don't listen to music, do you hear the voices?"

Harriet said, "When I listen to music, I still get the voices, but because I'm focused on something else like the candle, they're more in the background. But I don't know, it depends."

I said, "It depends on how you're feeling as well?"

Harriet said, "Yes, if I'm in a better mood, it's not too bad, it was hard at first because I felt I had to quieten my mind to focus on the candle and I had the music in my ear. I was thinking how will I concentrate, I just tried to accept it was there, and I just focused on the candle and tried to drown it out. So, I did that, but I still get voices during the meditation. It's very faint or hardly there at all, and it's mainly the visions like they're trying to distract my mind from the candle more than its voices. They give me images and bring up stuff to try and stop me from focusing."

I said, "They'll try to stop you any way they can. During

the normal course of the day, do you hear voices all the time?"

Harriet said, "Yes, pretty much."

I said, "Do you automatically bring the candle up?"

Harriet said, "I try to yes, and sometimes it's there already, as I said before. Like I'm just thinking, and it's there, I don't have to concentrate on It, it's just there straight away. All I can think about now is the candle, just focusing on the candle when I'm out, or inside the house. I'm focusing on the candle all the time, and it's drummed in there now."

I said, "So do the voices disturb you as much as they used to?"

Harriet said, "No, I feel like they're trying to, they're pushing me, but I know it's just using the candle and stuff. Because I know the reason behind it, but honestly no, I don't think so. I think it's more the candle now because I keep focusing on it and just forget about the voices."

I said, "Good, so that's working OK; we'll keep that going for a while longer. Then we'll change your meditation so you don't have to think of the candle anymore because you'll automatically block the interference, but not yet."

Harriet said, "So you're saying this could be another kind of meditation?"

I said, "No, don't worry about it at the moment as you're not quite ready, but you're progressing nicely."

Harriet said, "OK, meditation's good, it's working for me, and I haven't missed a single day of doing it, so I'm proud of myself."

I said, "Since you've been doing it every day, things have got better haven't they?"
Harriet said, "They have, yes. I'm getting less anger as well, and I'm dealing with it a lot better. I feel like they're not attacking me while I'm awake now, it's more like when I'm asleep I think, or more like when I'm half-awake because my dreams have become more intense. Other than that, no, it's been pretty good during the day. It's just that now I'm afraid to go to sleep because I know I'm going to get hell when I'm asleep."
I said, "Are you saying prayers before you go to sleep?"
Harriet said, "No, you told me not to."
I said, "Good."
Harriet said, "Didn't you say that when I'm meditating as well, it's like opening up?"
I said, "Meditating is opening up, you're opening up under your control and meditating for a specific thing. Sometimes when people meditate, they haven't got anything in their mind, and that's when it's easier for a spirit to influence the meditation and take you to horrible places or scenarios."
Harriet said, "Oh, OK, I see."
I said, "When you meditate with something in mind like the candle, your mind is focused, and it's more difficult for spirit to control what you see or feel. How're you getting on with the medication?"
Harriet said, "I'm probably ill today, I think I've got flu. I don't know whether that's due to the pills or not because I've got symptoms of it, it's just me; I know it's not spirit. I don't know whether that's just me coming off them, I'm gradually weaning myself off taking 16mg

and 30mg alternately as the doctor said. So, I'm just trying to deal with it and get on with it, nothing different spiritually wise, that's good."

I said, "So now that you're reducing your medication, are you feeling any adverse effects other than the flu-like feeling?"

Harriet said, "No, not at all, no."

I said, "So that would indicate the pills aren't doing anything as far as spirit is concerned. If, while reducing your pills, you started getting problems that would indicate the pills were helping, but you haven't been feeling any worse. If we stick to what the doctor said, you will soon be on the minimum dose."

Harriet said, "Yes."

I said, "OK, that's good; is there anything else?"

Harriet said, "No, that's it for now."

I said, "OK, see you next week."

I said, "Hi, how are things?"

Harriet said, "OK, meditation is going great! I'm focusing way more on the candle, which is good, I think. Also, is Kaz holding an apple, I could be wrong, but I felt it was an apple he wanted to show me that he was holding like to say perhaps he's a teacher for me or some sort."

I said, "Well done, so we know you're in touch with one of your guides."

Harriet said, "I was glad when I tuned in to Kaz and saw the apple in his hand, so happy I got it right, scared too but happy."

I said, "I don't want you trying to tune in to Kaz."
Harriet said, "No, I haven't. He just showed himself. If anything, I've been asking him not to intervene as much. I wanted to see if I could do it on my own, if I could keep them at bay myself. I know they help me when I'm meditating, which is great, but it gets confusing too because I think, is it them, or negative spirits that are messing with me, doing all that stuff and telling me to do certain things? It was hard trying to determine what was them and what wasn't, so I just went with my gut feeling and just thought the bright room and the protection has to be them. I was just trying to figure it out, it still got confusing, but I just imagine having a white room with the candle on the ground, with me meditating and having a box around me. Like an invisible kind of box but solid, and that's keeping them at bay while I'm meditating. It's hard trying to focus on all that while I'm concentrating on the flame as well. I know my focus was just supposed to concentrate on the flame, so I try not to visualise a white room too much and just visualise the candle on the floor, and yeah, it seems to work."
I said, "When you're visualising the candle, and you've got the white room there, do you feel the walls of the white room are your protection?"
Harriet said, "Yes, it is yeah, that's how it feels."
I said, "So you know the walls are there whether you see them or not. You know your protection is there, so you don't have to visualise them anymore. If you think about it, your meditation is compromised; remember I said keep it simple. Otherwise, you'll be led astray. Well,

you have the white room, and the walls were put there by negative spirit so they could draw you into a controlled meditation, not yours but theirs. Your meditation should only have the candle, nothing else."
Harriet said, "Yes. That's sneaky. OK, I'll be more careful. I could get annoyed, but I'm not giving them the satisfaction. You know I said about an invisible wall, is that them as well? It's not a bubble anymore; it's like a box, and I'm inside an invisible box. That seems to be protecting me, even when I'm out, it just comes in my head just like the candle. It makes me feel safer as well, and protected."
I said, "Did you change it or did someone else?"
Harriet said, "Oh, you think it's been changed?"
I said, "Yes, it makes you feel secure, but it's a ploy."
Harriet said, "The candle has been perfect like I say, I'm seeing it everywhere now. But then it started getting confusing with the other candles like I said when I saw two more candles. I started getting suspicious because I was only visualising one candle in front of me. You confirmed that I was right, and I blew the others out, and they disappeared. I know they can see and hear everything too, I keep forgetting that they're always there, the negative spirits, so they know what I'm doing all the time."
I said, "Get rid of the box and focus on your bubble of protection."
Harriet said, "It's another trick. How will I know when it's them?"
I said, "With practise, don't accept anything unless we set it up or you think of it yourself. When you hear a

voice, and you've got to decide whether it's a voice or thought, instinctively you can feel which it is, can't you? Trust your feelings, and your feelings will be right."

Harriet said, "I can determine now way better, way better than before if it's voice or thought. The thing is with voice and thought they're kind of similar to me, so it depends on what they say, and I'm trying to determine whether it's a thought. It's tough to tell the difference."

I said, "OK, so you're having difficulty in telling the voice from the thought?"

Harriet said, "Yes, I am."

I said, "How do you hear the thought?"

Harriet said, "When I hear the thought, it's usually when I'm distracted, and they come when I'm doing something. The voices come when I'm not focused on anything, and they normally slip in then. I feel like it's my guides because I'm not thinking about the voices, I'm completely involved with what I'm doing."

I said, "OK, so when you're focused and doing something, the voices are quiet; when your mind is drifting, you hear the voices, is that right?"

Harriet said, "That's right."

I said, "Then you need to focus on what you're doing when you hear the voices to keep your mind under your control."

Harriet said, "Oh, OK gotcha, I was thinking they speak to me then when my mind's quieter, that's what it's like."

I said, "Meditation is used in development to quieten the mind and allow spirit to come in, and what you're doing is quietening the mind and starting to drift and you get a thought, not a voice, come in redirecting you back to where you were."

Harriet said, "Yeah, that's what it feels like."

I said, "That's a thought from one of your guides. When you get the voice, they're not directing you back to where you were. They're trying to take you somewhere else."

Harriet said, "Yes."

I said, "That's one way to tell the difference; the voice is audible as well, isn't it, and the thought isn't."

Harriet said, "Yes, that's right. I keep thinking thought is like speaking as well, that's why I keep getting mixed up, it's more like what you think inside your head."

I said, "Yes, that's another thing about development, you have to learn to tell the difference between what are your thoughts and what isn't. That's what you're doing at the moment."

Harriet said, "It's so hard, so the voice is more audible, but the thoughts are like they could be coming from you, but maybe not."

I said, "Thoughts are silent, aren't they?"

Harriet said, "Yes, that's it; got it."

I said, "When you go to bed at night, what do you do mentally?"

Harriet said, "Oh, funnily enough, I think of the candle, every time I go to bed now, I think of the candle and meditate on it even while I'm trying to sleep. It just comes up. It does seem to calm me down a lot, and it feels terrific."

I said, "Most people have trouble going to sleep

because their mind is too active, and what you're doing is calming your mind down, clearing your mind. When there is nothing to focus on, you'll just drop off because there's nothing to keep your mind occupied. Do you still get touched? (Harriet paused for a moment in thought) If you have got to think about it, the answer is no."

Harriet said, "That's a good point. No, that's great. I still kind of think there is somebody behind me, but it's probably just the stuffed cat. I don't know whether there's someone there or not."

I said, "If you think there's someone behind, you just put a block up."

Harriet said, "Yes, great, it's funny as well because I get a thought, and the candle appears."

I said, "What happens is, you don't think about it, but a thought comes into your mind. That's your guides directing you. It's the most vulnerable time of the day when you're between sleep and awake, so what they're doing is getting you protected while you're going to sleep. Be careful if there's something else apart from the candle. It could be a negative spirit getting in first. You may still be getting dreams, but don't worry about that at the moment, we're working towards that."

Harriet said, "OK, that's good, I thought like you said they're just dreams, and you're right when I wake up in the morning, I remember what you said it's just dreams, let it go. Because it seems so much is aimed at me, I feel like it's not normal, like it's an attack. I don't know whether I'm paranoid about it, but it feels like it is. To a point where it's annoying me so much, I'm bringing the candle up all the time when before I wasn't. Now the fact that I have these dreams that are very abnormal to me, they're happening every night, there seems to be no break, it's every night, constant, same things, random, hurtful, the past and stuff trying to scare me and annoy me."

I said, "How're you getting on with your job?"

Harriet said, "OK, it's pretty good at the moment."

I said, "When you're getting out of the house, do you feel more comfortable?"

Harriet said, "I feel more comfortable going out now than I did, even though the voices try and tell me stupid things. As I said, the candle just comes up again, and I have my protection as well, which is good. I don't know; I like that when it comes around me, it's like I don't have to think about it. I used to be not scared about going out, but just being anxious about it. But now when I'm going out, I feel like I'm more protected. I feel like more things are happening, and seeing with my own eyes, the result of the work I've been doing is helping. It's giving me courage with the candle that something is happening because I've been wondering. I do this candle and what am I going to see afterward, is it going to help me, is it going to be obvious, is it going to be subtle? I just try to have something to hold on to, telling myself this is worth it, just keep doing it. Even when I was ill or wanted a drink, I told myself no, I have to do this even when I was tired, I knew I had to get up and meditate, keep doing it, and it's worked."

I said, "So if you look back now to last August, which is when we started talking, it's been four months, look how far you've come. And you need to remember

you've done this with all your hard work, you've had a lot of courage to overcome the interference, it's not over, but you can see the difference."
Harriet said, "I was so worried about letting you and mum down."
I said, "The only person you would let down is yourself. You won't let me down and you won't let your mum down because you're trying, you're working at it. You're succeeding, and it's getting easier, and there's no reason why you shouldn't continue to succeed. Now you might be thinking to yourself you're feeling settled enough to go and look for a full-time job, but it's too soon, so be patient. Until we get the pills sorted out, you don't want to be taking such a big step."
Harriet said, "No, that's what I'm worried about the most. I'm scared that the pains will come back in my arm, and I'm scared how I'm going to be when I'm off them."
I said, "You'll be in full control when you come off them because so far, you've felt no difference, and we'll only reduce them when you're ready."
Harriet said, "I want to come off them as soon as I can so I can see what difference it makes. I was thinking of being on the lower dose in about a week."
I said, "That's too soon. Keep alternating the dose until you run out of 60mg, then give it a week and see how you feel. We have to be cautious, and then we can see what the doctor thinks. It's good that you have your mum monitoring you because she'll notice any change long before we do. Call it a backup. One difficulty with what I do is I'm continually fighting against the

medication and its side effects. So, the less medication you take, the more control you have. That's not to say everyone should stop taking medication as it has its place for those who may have a chemical imbalance or brain malfunction."

Harriet said, "Even if they aren't doing anything for me now, there's still the side effects, which is why I need to get off them."

I said, "Yes, it's been proven in clinical trials that antipsychotics and antidepressants can damage the brain."

Harriet said, "Even though I'm not noticing the side effects, there must be something mum sees that I'm not."

I said, "You have to remember it takes a while for them to get into the system, and by that time, although you will be getting side effects, you're only concentrating on any benefits you may be getting. When you come off the pills, you'll get withdrawal symptoms, which you'll need to work through until the medication is out of your system."

Harriet said, "Since I went on the medication, I'm not sure what it's doing; it doesn't seem to be doing anything positive for me."

I said, "That's because the medication is trying to alleviate the symptoms and not the cause."

Harriet said, "What about my depression?"

I said, "Do you think you have depression?"

Harriet said, "No, they told me I did and gave me antidepressants, but nothing changed, I was still getting anxious hearing the voices."

I said, "Yes, but you now accept that we all have moods which can bring us down but also lift us. The problem for you is you don't know if it's you or interference. Now you know where the voices are coming from, and you can block them sometimes, you don't get so anxious, do you?"
Harriet said, "No, I know I'll be able to control them once I've got the meditation worked out."
I said, "You know there'll be backward steps initially until you have mastered the meditation, but you'll overcome those as you progress. It's a natural cycle of life, we all get bad moods at times."
Harriet said, "The spirit guides won't force you to do anything uncomfortable, would they?"
I said, "Like what?"
Harriet said, "Well, basically I don't like the light on when I meditate, I like to have it off. But I think they want me to have it on."
I said, "It's your meditation, turn the light off if you want. After all, you've got your eyes closed anyway."
Harriet said, "How do I know when my spirit guides want me to do something?"
I said, "They'll tell you."
Harriet said, "But what if they ask me to do something that makes me feel uncomfortable to do. Do I still do it?"
I said, "They won't ask you to do something that makes you uncomfortable because that's detrimental to what they're trying to do."
Harriet said, "Oh, OK."
I said, "What they're doing is helping you to help

yourself. We're getting you to a stage where you don't have to think about the candle. You just get on with life and forget about spirit. That's what we're working for. The idea is to get you to a place where you have the voices under control, and if you hear a voice, you can just block it out. When you get to that stage, you can then focus on life."

Harriet said, "That could take another year, though, couldn't it?"

I said, "It could, but the speed you're going it will probably be less; after all, you've had this problem for five years; it's going to take time. It's only been four months since we started talking."

Harriet said, "I thought it would take about a week, but I can see why it'll take longer, it's hard work. But it's getting easier. When I get this under control, will my guides talk to me?"

I said, "No, they 're not going to start talking to you because then you'll start thinking you've got interference again. If they do communicate, it'll be by thought. You'll recognise it when it comes, but don't look for it, just forget about spirit. There's a difference between communicating with spirit and what you're doing. The difference is the voices coming in are put into your head by spirits that're around you. You see, when I go to a house where they're experiencing interference, it usually affects more than one person, like moving things, making everyone feel cold or hearing or seeing spirit. They're earthbound spirits that I can talk to, and I can help on their way back to the spirit world. The spirits you've got with you are focusing on you; they're not affecting the rest of the household. That's because their focus is purely on you, they're trying to control you. I can still talk to them, but it's not time yet. At the moment, we just need to remove them when they get too intense. Have you ever had episodes where you say, sit down at one o clock, and next thing you know, it's three o clock?"

Harriet said, "No, I don't think so."

I said, "Well, if that happens, that's when spirit possesses you, you're not aware of time passing because your conscious mind is blocked. It's all about education. You know a lot more about how and why now so you can deal with it better without being afraid."

Harriet said, "When I was meditating one time someone sat down in front of me and held their hands out to me. I couldn't see their face, and I thought this isn't right, was that a guide?"

I said, "No, it was interference. They're trying to control your meditation. If you're aware of anything other than the candle and you feel uncomfortable then it's not right. You must either get rid of them or open your eyes, that'll clear it and then go back to focus on the candle. Your guides won't force themselves on you. If you have another guide come forward, Kaz will introduce the new guide. If it's not logical, reject it."

Harriet said, "Ok that's it, see you next week?"

I said, "Ok."

JANUARY 2020

Harriet wrote, "OK, so last night I had horrible dreams, knew straight away I'm being attacked, so I just ignored it and went back to sleep. Before that, though, I tried to quiet my mind so I could sleep better, but I was struggling hard. I couldn't picture the candle and was finding it harder to keep it there, after trying for 15 mins I fell asleep and forgot about it, then had the dreams. I woke up and decided to meditate but wasn't focusing on the candle. It seemed useless. I still had a faint vision of it, so I tried focusing on it but got distracted from images, thoughts and visions, horrible visions. I knew it was the negative spirits, but never had I had it so bad that it took nearly complete control. It was so frustrating. I kept opening my eyes to double-check the candle in front of me, so I had some kind of reference just to start to imagine it easier in my head again. But with little to no luck. It was so hard to focus on it. I did the 30 mins but felt that I hardly did anything. I couldn't hold the candle for long at all. But I stayed in control and kept still and tried as much as possible to keep the candle in mind. It wasn't a great session, but thanks to you I know now it's just another attack, and I need to focus more on it, and not to give up, I will let you know how it goes."

I said, "How are you doing? You had a bit of a setback."

Harriet said, "Yes, I did. A horrible one. I still do, to be honest. But it's getting better because every time I focus on the candle, it's staying in my mind longer each time I do it. I'm attacked viciously, but I'm managing through it if that makes sense."

I said, "So, by focusing on the candle, you're blocking them out?"

Harriet said, "Yes, it's like I'm working twice as hard this time doing the meditation on the candle than I used to before."

I said, "Now you can see how easy it is for them to undermine your meditation. Because your meditation was becoming easier, you weren't as diligent and never noticed spirit creeping in."

Harriet said, "So because I was finding it easy, they were able to get in? So was my meditation OK before that?"

I said, "Your meditation was fine. When you meditate, anything that's not the candle must be ignored; your concentration is only on the candle. That way, you will stop any interference from creeping in."

Harriet said, "Oh, OK, that's funny because I'm thinking more of the candle right in front of me and picturing it in my mind. I have the candle right in front of me, and do I have to have a white background?"

I said, "What do you put in the background?"

Harriet said, "I get a white A3 piece of paper, and I put the candle on it so I can imagine it with a white background easier."

I said, "Why do you want a white background?"

Harriet said, "I don't know, maybe because I was thinking it was like picturing it in there made it easier."

I said, "Take the piece of paper away; the only thing you're focusing on is the candle, nothing else."

Harriet said, "OK, that's so much easier, so it doesn't matter what kind of background it is as long as it's the

candle?"
I said, "Well, no, because we're not interested in the background, just the candle."
Harriet said, "I'm so confused, I can't tell which are my thoughts or the spirits around me; it's so confusing."
I said, "That's why we focus on the candle; the only thing you've got in your mind is the candle."
Harriet said, "OK, right, OK."
I said, "Any other thoughts that come in, you've got to push them out."
Harriet said, "Oh, OK, right. So just focus on the candle and nothing else. The candle is right in front of me; I close my eyes and imagine the same candle in my head, is that OK?"
I said, "That's exactly what you're supposed to be doing; it gives you a focal point."
Harriet said, "I forget what the candle looks like when they manipulate it all the time, so I have to remind myself. I have to open my eyes quickly and close my eyes quickly just to get it refocused, then imagine it again."
I said, "That's fine."
Harriet said, "That's cool because it does help."
I said, "Are you managing to block the voices out more now?"
Harriet said, "No, not really."
I said, "Is that because you haven't got the focus back properly.?"
Harriet said, "Maybe, I don't know, I still have horrible dreams too, maybe it's because I'm not getting the focus back properly. It's getting better each time I do

the meditation."
I said, "Well, you have to make up some ground, haven't you?"
Harriet said, "I do, that's what I said to myself. I need a few more weeks of doing this because I'm not happy with myself. I don't have it in my head as much as I used to, and it's annoying me. So, I want to focus until I get it permanently in my head more."
I said, "OK, so when you were doing it before, and things were going well, it automatically came up, didn't it?"
Harriet said, "It did, and it blocked out the voices, but now it's not doing that. I even do it at night just before I go to sleep because it helps me to sleep. It's hell trying to keep my focus; there's so much distraction, and so many thoughts going into my head. I just forget about it, and I have to remind myself to bring it back, and they're trying to have conversations. They keep talking to me all the time during my meditation, and I say no and try to focus. They try to mimic me to make me think of things I shouldn't be or answering their questions when I'm not, all these tricks I'm now noticing that they're doing."
I said, "That's because you recognise the interference."
Harriet said, "That's awesome, and I was thinking I wasn't making so much progress because of what happened with the attack. I know I'm still getting attacked now, I can feel when I'm getting attacks more than I used too. When I meditate on the candle, the difference is so crazy. I can't focus as much on the candle as I did before. I just notice it a lot more, and it's

just sad."
I said, "That's why I told you at first, it was going to get easier, then it was going to get hard."
Harriet said, "Yes, definitely, I'll never give up, but I was thinking this is such a struggle, what am I doing wrong? Before, I got it so easy in my head but now it's so hard to keep it there, I'm so struggling. I feel like I'm not getting the help from my spirit guides to try to motivate me to do it. I feel like they want me to do it on my own, so I learn. I think it's paying off I'm focusing more on the candle even with the attacks and as bad as they are, but I need to learn how to deal with it. I thought I would accept it, that I'm being attacked, and just overcome it. Focus more on the candle and just take it day by day and see what happens. The candle does calm me down; it's just annoying during the week; it wasn't as good as the previous week, so I was just getting annoyed with myself, but it's getting better bit by bit."
I said, "How is everything else?"
Harriet said, "I also noticed when I'm working at the Red Cross even though the interference is bad at the moment, I'm managing it better. When I'm on the till and there's an attack happening, I can't close my eyes, but if I think of the candle and try to relax and ignore it, it fades away. I just completely forget about it. Whereas before, I kept thinking about it and thinking why am I being attacked and what's happening. Now I just think, let it go, think of the candle and everything calms down. I get confused as to whether it's my guides coming through to help sometimes. Can you ask my guides to step back so I can tell who's there? If I know it's not my

guides I won't get sucked in so easily."

I said, "Your guides are standing by but not interfering, to give you a chance to grow stronger, controlling your thoughts."

Harriet said, "Good, it makes it so much easier if I know it's not them. The spirits pretend they're my guides saying Kaz said to do this and do that, he's happy, he's sad. I know that isn't the case because he's not judgemental. It's so easy to tell who's talking if I know my guides are standing back. I've stopped asking my guides, I want to do it myself, I know they help sometimes, but it's best when I do it on my own."

I said, "Take a break for a day and then start again. Don't worry about whether you block the wrong spirits, better to block them all than none. The fact that you know how much control they've had doesn't change anything. Don't doubt yourself and stop thinking; just go with your gut feeling. The voices are louder because they want to keep you off balance. You remember when you first started meditating with music, you thought it would distract you? Then once you got into it, the music faded into the background? Well so will the voices once you believe in yourself and concentrate on the candle. That's a step forward now that you can tell from where the thoughts are coming. Remember, when we first started, it was difficult but got easier. It will get easier. How are you getting on with the pills?"

Harriet said, "I haven't noticed anything; to be honest, I feel the same."

I said, "You're still alternating, are you?"

Harriet said, "Yes, I asked my mum to see how many of

the stronger dose we had left, she said there were five until I go on to the lower dose. So, it's not going to be long now until I'm on the weakest dose possible. I'm feeling better now I'm not ill or anything. I'm still a bit worried about my arm, but nothing's happened; yet, I thought the spirits would play on it, but they haven't yet."

I said, "What's wrong with your arm?"

Harriet said, "Do you remember when I said about the pain in my arm? That's why I went on the tablets; I just thought I might get a sensation back again."

I said, "Why would you?"

Harriet said, "Because I'm coming off the tablets, they're a painkiller as well."

I said, "OK, so if you get sudden pains, it's not you, they're put on you. Just tell yourself it's not yours and mean it, you'd be surprised at how easily we accept the pain that's coming from others. You have to say and mean it; it's the intent that makes it work."

Harriet said, "Yes, it's the intent I struggle with sometimes. Not with the candle but the pains, I just think it's earthly. I don't picture the spirits, to be honest, and sort it out that way. It's still quite crazy how they can do it. Maybe I'm in denial; I just don't fully believe how they can give you pain. But I know they can, so I need to consider that too."

I said, "What you have to remember is that if you get a pain, and there's no reason for you to have that pain, – like for instance, if you knock your arm, it's going to hurt – if it hurts and you haven't banged it, then it's not your pain."

Harriet said, "OK. I was wondering when I said they've been attacking me. I mean, they've been attacking me. It reminds me of how it was before I first spoke to you; it was that bad. I thought, wow, because I know everything I know now, it just doesn't bother me as much as it did then."
I said, "Education is a wonderful thing."
Harriet said, "I'm learning from that too. I didn't realise how persuasive and how strong they could be too. I had no hope before if I didn't know what's happening, and even now, it's difficult to take in. It would've been just so bad these few weeks, is this all because of the candle?"
I said, "That's right, yes."
Harriet said, "So they're threatened by me meditating on the candle?"
I said, "Of course, they're threatened, you're learning to block them and stop them interfering with your mind."
Harriet said, "But it feels like I'm not."
I said, "But you were, seeing it now the way they're attacking you is no stronger than the way they were attacking you before. But it's not having the same impact because you understand better."
Harriet said, "Yes, definitely, a hundred per cent."
I said, "So you're more in control of things, you see one of the things that helps them is you being fearful. If you're afraid, then you back off, and they come in stronger and overwhelm you, but you're not doing that, now are you?"
Harriet said, "No, not at all."
I said, "You're standing up to them."

Harriet said, "Yes, that's right, so they're bullies."
I said, "Yes, that's what they are, bullies."
Harriet said, "So I am standing up to them; I know it's a setback with them attacking me."
I said, "It's not a setback it's part of the course, no one's going to get it perfect first time, you're going to move forward, and then you're going to slip back a step then move forward and slip back a step, but you'll keep moving forward if you continue to fight."
Harriet said, "So there's nothing to be ashamed of?"
I said, "Not at all, you should be proud of yourself."
Harriet said, surprised, "Oh, really?"
I said, "Yes, look how much more you understand about what they're doing, and what they're trying to do, and how you're combatting them."
Harriet said, "I know, but it feels like it's not working because they're still attacking me. That's the mentality I have in my head because they're still doing it, it's not working."
I said, "Well, we knew it wasn't going to be a quick fix, didn't we? You just have to be patient and keep working at it."
Harriet said, "With the candle, eventually, it will be like they're not there, and I can't hear them?"
I said, "Yes."
Harriet said, "I see, so would it be like the image of a candle blocking what's happening, or would it be like just not there. How does it work?"
I said, "You focus on the candle, and you exclude everything else like you've got blinkers on, and with you concentrating on the candle, nothing else will be able

to get into your mind. Gradually, once you have control of the candle and you stop the voices, we'll then change the candle to something else. Something more agreeable to you and your day-to-day living."

Harriet said, "Would that still be meditation?"

I said, "Initially, yes, but you'll stop meditating at some stage because you'll no longer need to. At the moment, we're using the candle because it's not complicated, and we'll put something else in later. At the moment, you're going to your candle for protection, and later we'll change that, so you put yourself in a bubble perhaps, and it'll give you the same protection. You won't have to focus or meditate on it because it'll be in your head already. Once we get to that stage, the bubble will automatically come up and block it just like your candle was before your setback, and you can just get on with your life."

Harriet said, "If the negative spirits bring up the candle, I don't know if they would, but if they do..."

I said, "You'll know because it won't be the same as yours, there'll be something slightly different about it."

Harriet said, "Hmm, OK, it'll be different, like the image or when it comes up or the feeling or...?"

I said, "Any or all of the above. If you don't put the candle there or it's already there, then it won't be your candle unless it automatically comes up when you're under attack like before. But don't worry about that; just focus on your candle, and if you feel it's not right or going wrong, stop and start again."

Harriet said, "Should I always picture the candle that's on the ground that I normally picture?"

I said, "Yes, that's what you normally picture, isn't it?"
Harriet said, "The thing is it feels like they're bringing up the same candle. But I don't know whether it's me automatically doing it or it's them."
I said, "You're starting to doubt yourself. When you close your eyes you picture the candle, you're doing it. If when you close your eyes, the candle comes up before you picture it, then they're doing it. If, while you're picturing the candle and focusing on the candle, it starts to change, you're getting interference, so you need to stop and start again. That way you're in control. When I say stop, I mean open your eyes, and when the candles gone from your mind, then you close your eyes and bring it back."
Harriet said, "OK, thank you. I know they manipulate the candle changing colours and do all sorts to it."
I said, "This is why when you're focusing on the candle, you also make sure it's your candle. But as I say if at any stage you feel uncomfortable or you think something's not right then you stop and start again. If you're unsure, stop, take a break and then go back to it."
Harriet said, "I thought even if they bring up a candle, it would be a good thing."
I said, "No, because it would be their meditation, not yours, and if they're controlling your meditation, they'll give you all sorts of images and pretend guides. Whereas if you're controlling it, then you're blocking them from interfering."
Harriet said, "OK, so watch out for tricks. I've still got a long way to go."
I said, "You've come a long way, though."

Harriet said, "At night times, I try and focus on the candle, but when I go to sleep, I feel defenceless. I feel like I'm just supposed to let it happen."
I said, "Why do you feel defenceless because you're asleep?"
Harriet said, "Because I feel like I'm not controlling, I'm not thinking, I don't have free will to think of the candle or anything to distract me."
I said, "You have to remember that when you're asleep, your consciousness is asleep, but your subconscious is not, your subconscious is your spirit. Your spirit is still there, carrying on what it's supposed to be doing. That's why you meditate on the candle so often. It's to get it into your subconscious where it becomes automatic. When you go to sleep, picture the candle like you normally do and you'll drop off, and next thing you know, it's morning or you're having a dream. If you get a dream, just picture the candle, turn over and go back to sleep. A dream is just a dream; it may feel real, but when you wake, say that it was a dream and forget about it."
Harriet said, "Oh, OK. I thought when I get the voices out of my head what will happen then? Will I just have to focus on them not touching me? They don't do it much now, but I still feel sometimes they are touching me."
I said, "The touching will go at the same time as the voices because you'll have got rid of the negative spirits either by blocking them or removing them."
Harriet said, "Oh, I see, so getting rid of the voices stops that too?"

I said, “Yes, there’ll be no negative spirits around you who can interfere because you’ll stop them coming to you by putting up your protection.”
Harriet said, “So that means everything spiritual will be gone except for my spirit guides?”
I said, “Yes, but your guides won’t interfere; it’ll be like most people who are unaware of their guides. That way, they won’t confuse you into thinking the negative spirits have come back.”
Harriet said, “I thought if they want to speak to me after this, then because I can easily block the negative ones, they’ll be able to speak to me.”
I said, “You’ll just get the odd thought now and again when they’re advising you about something. Normally your guides advise you when you leave your body during sleep as you’ll often meet up with them to see if you’re still on track with your life’s path.”
Harriet said, “Oh, I see. Why don’t I remember?”
I said, “Because if they told things and you woke up thinking, I’ve got to do this, I’ve got to do that, they would be taking away your free will. They’re there to guide you, not tell you what to do; it has to be your decision.”
Harriet said, “I see, so we do talk.”
I said, “Of course you do, we all do, but not everyone remembers what’s said. Take meditation; this is when you’re consciously trying to tune in to your guides, and sometimes they’ll repeat something they said during your sleep if they think it’s important that you hear it. It’s still up to you whether you take any action or not. When you meditate on the candle, that’s a different

kind of meditation because you should be so focused on the candle that nothing else exists; that's how you control your mind. Once you can do that at will, then if you want, you can try a meditation to communicate with your guides, but I wouldn't advise that at the moment as you're not ready."

Harriet said, "OK, I'll wait till you tell me it's OK. I'll let you know how I get on with the candle during the week. I have a clearer understanding of whose thoughts and feelings I'm getting now. It's so much easier to tell the difference between mine and the negative spirits. So much so I'm a little depressed. I had no idea that the negative spirits had such control over my thoughts and feelings! It's like they have seventy-five per cent of my mind, where I have only twenty-five per cent of it. They seem to have so much control right now; it's scary. When focusing on the candle, it's tricky! They overpower me pretty much straight away! They play tricks. Like pretending it's me thinking it when it's them! I have to think three times as hard now, to work out who's me and who's them. I'm not complaining too much about it, as I now know the truth, but it's just a little frightening seeing the power they have over my mind! Which, of course, makes me way more determined to fight back. But the thing is, how? Every time I bring up the candle straight away, they attack, I'm fighting back as much as I can but still finding it hard. I don't know whether it's because I know they had that much control, or that the attacks are just stronger for some reason. Also, because I'm weaning off the medicine, could that be a factor? It's hard to pinpoint, difficulty sleeping being due to the spirits, and me being on medication. I know if I feel worse, they make me feel even worse, but I'm so confused about what's happening right now! When I come off the medication completely, will my concentration get any better? I hope so."

I said, "You'll be more alert and recognise things sooner."

Harriet said, "Ok thanks see you next week."

I said, "Hi, how're you today?"

Harriet said, "OK, it goes up and down, but I think I'm getting it under control now."

I said, "Good, because we're going to do something different today. I want to talk to one of the voices. What I want you to do is tell me what they say, nothing else, OK?"

Harriet said, "OK, but I thought you said to block them and try to ignore them."

I said, "Yes, but now it's time to change things a little. So, can you hear a voice?"

Harriet said, "It's silent right now."

I said, "Good here we go."

I said, "Why are you bothering Harriet, Charlie? She has asked you to leave her alone?"

Harriet said, "He said I don't want to leave her alone. I like talking to her."

I said, "Well, she would rather you left. What's the problem? Maybe I can help so that you can move on and be with your family?"

Harriet said, "He said it's none of your business, go

away."
I said, "So you enjoy it here, wasting your time instead of being free to do what you want rather than what you're told to do?"
Harriet said, "Said **** off and leave me alone."
I said, "OK, we'll talk again. Harriet, concentrate on another voice. Now I know it's a lady's voice you can hear. Hello, what's your name?"
Harriet said, "Nothing."
I said, "If you talk to me, I can help you. Would you like to go where it's warm and light and be with your family?"
Harriet said, "Yes, but I can't find the way, and they won't let me leave."
I said, "Who won't let you leave?"
Harriet said fearfully, "She said there are some men here who are stopping her from leaving."
I said, "OK, is there anyone else that wants to leave?"
Harriet said, "She says there are a few."
I said, "OK, I'm going to put protection around you and your friends so they won't be able to interfere. Now, I want you to open your eyes and look for a bright light."
Harriet said, "She says she can't see any light, but there are some people over there who are brighter than any others."
I said, "Ah, good, you can see them, that means the other spirits are trying to block out the light, so those spirits have come to take you to your families."
Harriet said, "She said, is it safe?"
I said, "Yes, go with them and I'll watch until you arrive in the light."

Harriet said, "The voices are fading, and I wondered who those bright people were, I saw them when you said about the light."

I said, "They're some of my guides."

Harriet said, "The ladies have gone now; there were three of them."

I said, "Yes, they were told to talk to you and shout at you until you gave up the candle; that's why the voices got louder."

Harriet said, "Can we get rid of the rest of them?"

I said, "We have to be careful; you've had lots of people talking to you for a long time. If we removed them all, you'd feel as though you'd lost something and start looking for what's missing. So, we need to go slowly, while your subconscious gets used to the change."

Harriet said, "Does that mean they won't come back?"

I said, "Yes, that's right, providing you continue to block and focus on the candle when you hear voices. We'll remove a few at a time. They were willing to go, but as you heard, some don't want to leave, so we'll deal with them when we need to, but they'll all go eventually, just be patient. We won't do any more today; we'll let you get used to the change and see what happens."

Harriet said, "Thanks for everything today, it really helped, but I was just wondering, the fact that I'm not going to be meditating every day, and only when I need to now, does that mean I'm progressing?"

I said, "You are progressing; that's why you only need to meditate when you get interference. But if you have trouble focusing, then you'll have to go back to meditating twice a day."

Harriet said, "Why did you decide to talk to the spirits now and not before? Is it because it was the right time too?"
I said, "Yes, you weren't ready to talk to spirits before now."
Harriet said, "I'm just confused a little. Am I still on the right path even though I'm not going to be meditating daily? I would love some confirmation to see if I'm doing well or not; it's so hard to tell now."
I said, "You're still on the right path; we wouldn't be talking to the spirits if you weren't ready. Let's not cheer too soon; we still have a way to go, but you're doing well."
Harriet said, "I know, now will be better, since fewer spirits are around. See you next week."

I said, "Hi, how's your week been?"
Harriet said, "Pretty much the same to be honest, nothing major. I stopped meditating on Tuesday, because I was feeling horrible from the tablets and I was in no mood, I couldn't concentrate, and I thought maybe I'll give it a rest for a bit and then speak to you and see how you felt about it. Nothing has changed since I stopped to be fair, it's kind of been the same. I still get that male voice in my head, very vocal and loud."
I said, "Do you get the other voices still because I was wondering whether after removing some last week you had noticed any difference."
Harriet said, "I was thinking it's the guy who you spoke to mainly that's talking to me. That's why I don't think I

hear other people's voices; I hear maybe just one."
I said, "Right so before last week, it was more than one voice?"
Harriet said, "Yes, but only when I started talking to you after that, it went to mainly this one person."
I said, "OK, so when you say talking to me, do you mean back then or last week?"
Harriet said, "When you started talking to the spirit that was with me, that's when I started hearing more voices, but after that, it's just been the one."
I said, "Right, so that means the other voices that were there were listening to me because they wanted to leave. Now that they've gone, the spirit who says his name is Charlie has filled up the space left by the others with his voice, hasn't he?"
Harriet said, "That's what it feels like."
I said, "That's good, so it would appear we just have the one to get rid of; this one is going to be difficult because he doesn't want to go."
Harriet said, "God, it's so stressful I feel like he's the main troublemaker of everyone that's been bothering me."
I said, "Well, that's progress; we now have just one to remove."
Harriet said, "That's good. I'm glad you helped those other spirits out as well. But do you feel like this is still the same guy that I had five years ago in Australia?"
I said, "There's no time in spirit, a thousand years is nothing in spirit. Now, if you're OK, we'll have another chat with him."
Harriet said, "OK, that's fine. I just knew it I knew it was

the same spirit all that time still with me. I know other spirits have been coming and going, but I knew it's the same one."

I said, "Were you hearing female voices as well?"

Harriet said, "When I was in Australia, I heard a female voice audibly, but as the years passed it came to just one voice, a male voice. It sounds like the same voice every time now."

I said, "Why is it stressful?"

Harriet said, "Because you said it's going to be hard to get rid of him."

I said, "No, I said it would be difficult. I didn't say we couldn't do it."

Harriet said, "Oh, OK. I just feel that once he's gone, I just know everything will just be hunky-dory, I think."

I said, "Well, let's see what happens."

Harriet said, "Yeah, thank you. I got the same kind of constant visions and feelings from this same person, which is similar to what I had in the past. But didn't you say they can look into our memories and copy them? Because if you cleared them when we first started, maybe someone else is doing it and copying the memories."

I said, "Yes, that's correct; the spirits can copy what someone else has done. It makes you doubt they can be removed. But clearing you originally was just to give you some space. I knew you would get others coming in because you had no control over your mind. Now you can block them, and you understand how they work, we have a better chance of removing them for good. It depends on the situation when people have had interference for a while, and it's removed, they'll feel a sense of loss. They'll then subconsciously try to find what's missing, and by looking, they'll invite another spirit to fill that loss. The incoming spirit will be aware of what's been going on, and usually they'll continue with the same type of interference to make you think they can't be removed. It leads to people giving up as they think the spirits are there for the whole of the person's life."

Harriet said, "I kept thinking all week that I just had a small group of spirits with me and that no one else can come in at all. I just get that feeling. The thing is I'm now getting shaken when I'm lying down; it's like a wave of energy."

I said, "How long does that last?"

Harriet said, "Not very long, maybe two or three seconds and then it goes, and I might just get touches; otherwise, it's OK. I just noticed it because it happened twice this week. It faded away, but it's come back again. I was just wondering what the cause is; I think it's the main spirit doing it. Other than that, meditating on the candle has got easier, though I have to admit, I noticed the difference. When I meditate, I feel like someone is sitting next to me. I can't see them, but they're very calm. I can't see their appearance, it's just light like the whole body is light."

I said, "How do you feel about that?"

Harriet said, "I feel great."

I said, "You say this individual is full of light and very peaceful, so it's not going to be negative spirit."

Harriet said, "So they wouldn't pretend to confuse

me?"
I said, "They might pretend, but they already tried interfering with your meditation and look how that turned out, they were discovered and stopped. I don't want you to take any notice apart from observation. Otherwise, it'll divide your concentration. Keep your concentration on the candle. They're just there to give you energy. How're your moods coming on?"
Harriet said, "Kind of up and down. The funny thing is I don't know if it's all spirit. It's hard to explain. I've been in a low mood, more down than normal. I'm doing different things, experimental stuff, not spiritual just other things in life. I don't know whether this is due to the tablets or not; I'm on the lower dose now."
I said, "Keep a close eye on how you feel; it'll probably take a couple of weeks to get used to a lower dose. If you're aware that you're suddenly going downhill, you might have to do something to change it. If it's sudden, then it's spirit; if it's gradual, it's you. Your arm's not hurting, is it?"
Harriet said," No, but I'm feeling a little panicky at the moment."
I said, "That's why we're taking it slowly, so it's not too much of a change, we'd expect to get some sort of reaction from your pills until you've got the higher dose out of your system. It may be slight withdrawal symptoms. Because you're taking the lower dose, it'll probably be mild, but you need to be aware of it."
Harriet said, "Yeah, I feel like I'm suffering headaches as well, so I feel that's part of it."
I said, "Work through it if you can, once you get past it,

you should settle down. We don't want even to consider reducing the pills any more at least for the time being."

Harriet said, "That's the lowest dose."

I said, "Reducing means stopping them, and we won't do that because you've been on them for such a long time your bodies used to them. We don't want to take away what your body's depending on until we've dealt with the spiritual aspect, and your mind is strong enough to cope. One thing at a time. How're you managing with work and going out?"

Harriet said, "It's ok working at the Red Cross and the sanctuary is great, and it gets me out. I've decided to put a Facebook page up and put all my artwork on there and just see what happens, just trying it out."

I said, "That's a move in the right direction."

Harriet said, "Yes, I think so. I feel like I'm being encouraged to do it, so we'll see where that goes. I've had a few responses, and it's only been up a couple of days. I don't know as many people now as I did when I was in Australia, but I've got some good responses, so that's good. It'll take time, but I'm sure it'll build up. I've just been dealing with the headaches, and the reduction in the dose has been a bit hard, just trying to ignore it and get on with things."

I said, "How will you feel when we get rid of this individual, and it all goes quiet? You're going to feel empty when there's nothing in the background."

Harriet said, "I won't be hearing the voices every day and won't have to worry about touching, not worried about dreams; I'll be better."

I said, “Of course you will. I’m just warning you, that’s all. You know what I told you last week, about taking too many off at once and you feeling a loss, you’ll feel a little empty like something should be there, but it’s gone. That’s what we don’t want to happen. We want you to be able to cope with everyday life without interference. OK, we’re going to talk with this individual again. So, what I want you to do is keep your eyes open, and I want you to tell me what they say.”

Harriet said, “OK, I’m ready.”

I said, “Hello, are you going to talk to me this week?”

Harriet said, “Hello”

I said, “What’s your name?”

Harriet said, “Charlie.”

I said, “You’re the same person we spoke to last week, aren’t you?”

Harriet said, “Yes, did you think I’d gone?”

I said, “I know you didn’t go; we took the others instead.”

Harriet said, “I hate you.”

I said, “Do you mean you hate me or you hate her?”

Harriet said, “Both.”

I said, “So why would you want to stay when you don’t like somebody?”

Harriet said, “I just... hate her.”

I said, “So why don’t you leave?”

Harriet said, “Why?”

I said, “Well, if you don’t like her, it doesn’t make sense for you to stay, does it?”

Harriet said, “Yes, and no.”

I said, “So somebody’s making you do what you’re

doing, are they?"
Harriet said, "Why do you care?"
I said, "Because I can help you."
Harriet said, "No one can."
I said, "Yes, they can. If you open your eyes, you'll see some people around you."
Harriet said, "OK."
I said, "I can take you to heaven if you want."
Harriet said, "Yes."
I said, "Open your eyes and tell me what you can see."
Harriet said, "Yes, I can see them."
I said, "They're friends of yours. Are you happy to go with them?"
Harriet said, "If I have to."
I said, "It's the best choice as they will explain everything to you. I've just asked your guides to take you somewhere safe. Bye Charlie. How are you feeling now, Harriet?"
Harriet said, "OK, I can't hear him anymore, has he gone?"
I said, "Yes, and you've got protection around you, so you're safe. Now forget all about it. If you think about him, you'll draw someone back who'll take his place, just forget about him. Now tell me about your drawings."
Harriet said, "Oh yeah I started a Facebook page, you can see loads of drawings on there. I've got other stuff on there too, so have a look. So, about Charlie, I know you're not supposed to think about it and what happened, but how do you feel things are going now, is there anything you want me to do?"

I said, "Carry on doing what you're doing. I just want you to forget all about Charlie. He's gone now, I watched him go with his guides. Try to forget about the voices. It doesn't mean to say you won't get some voices back, but they won't be the same spirits, and continue with the candle. As I told you last week, it's a gradual process. As we get rid of some, there will be others taking their place but not as many. We'll continue removing them until no more come in as your protection gets stronger."
Harriet said, "It's so creepy being in the middle telling you what he was saying."
I said, "You are in the middle but not for much longer. Didn't you tell me you saw a car you were thinking of buying?"
Harriet said, "Yes I saw this at a car sales place it looked nice, but I thought the price was too good to be true. I decided to leave it as it was 12 years old, I thought it was too old to be reliable. But I'm still thinking about getting a car. It's kind of got the ball rolling. To get me out and about more, and then I thought I would start to meet people. I know you said I shouldn't think about it, but it's weird every time I try to focus on anything or imagine things, it gets interrupted almost immediately. If I imagine a dog running in the park, it turns into something stupid."
I said, "When that happens, bring back the dog in your mind just like you do with the candle."
Harriet said, "Like I said if I imagine a dog running in the park, I get images of the dog being hurt or killed. It's just horrible. I get other horrible thoughts too, and it's

painful."

I said, "This is other spirits trying to control you, use the candle to block them. That's part of why you're doing the meditating on the candle, to control your thoughts."

Harriet said, "I do try to think about something else, but it's funny because I get these scenarios where I'm not in a relationship, but I feel like there's a guy always there, just like we're dating or something, and it's awkward when I'm working at the Red Cross. I get erotic feelings."

I said, "That's when you focus on the candle to block the thoughts."

Harriet said, "Even on that?"

I said, "Yes, because it's not you controlling it."

Harriet said, "I get that often, and it's creepy, and I don't like it."

I said, "You got that often, past tense, you don't get it anymore."

Harriet said, "Oh yes, got that often, got that often yes, OK, I understand."

I said, "We've got to think positive here."

Harriet said, "I now try to think positive, it's just hard because I just hate it, I feel like someone's got control over me and I can't do anything to stop it."

I said, "You mean someone's had control over you; we're getting rid of it."

Harriet said, "Someone had control over me, but that's in the past now, OK."

I said, "As I told you, it's going to be a gradual thing, it won't all happen in one go, don't look back, be positive and look towards the future."

Harriet said, "That was it really; it's just starting to make sense, that's all. It didn't make sense before, but now it does, so that cleared that up. So now I'm doing the Facebook page, I'm doing some tattoo designs and artwork and putting that up too, so that's good."

I said, "It's all good; you're starting to move forward now."

Harriet said, "I haven't been meditating for two days now, but you said to do it when necessary, is that right?"

I said, "Yes, when you get these thoughts, that's when you meditate to take control of your mind to block them out."

Harriet said, "What if I'm out and about, can I do it then?"

I said, "Yes, you can bring up the candle when you're walking along, can't you?"

Harriet said, "Yes."

I said, "The idea of the candle is that you're putting the picture in your mind, not somebody else. That means you're controlling what comes into your mind. If you fail, spirit wins."

Harriet said, "It's just hard because I know they copy the same image, so I have to be clever about it."

I said, "When you decide to bring up the candle, they're already trying to do something else, aren't they? Otherwise, you wouldn't bring up the candle. So, the negative spirits are putting thoughts in your mind, which is why you bring up the candle, so it's your candle because you brought it up. If you can focus and block them out altogether, you're in control. I know it's not easy, but with practice, you will succeed. If you start having difficulty with the candle, then you need to go back to practising daily."

Harriet said, "OK, I'll try my best. Do you think we'll be doing this talking thing next week?"

I said, "We're going to be doing it every week until we don't need to do it anymore. Each time we do it, we get rid of somebody, then it's working, and we'll carry on until we get rid of everybody, a piece at a time. We have to be careful that you don't feel a loss, that's why we're doing it slowly."

Harriet said, "It's funny. I've been more focused on my Facebook page than anything else, maybe that's a good sign."

I said, "It's an excellent sign; while you're busy with that, you don't get interference, do you?"

Harriet said, "No, that's what you meant when you said to keep my mind busy. Do you think this is quite quick all this happening?"

I said, "About average, I would think for this sort of problem. In some aspects, it's quick from where you started. But once we started talking to spirit, it has moved things along, but we couldn't do that until you were ready. As I said, we don't want to get rid of them all at once. We have to give your subconscious time to adjust to not having them around. Charlie's gone now, but you may get someone else who is a little less aggressive but pretending to be Charlie, but it won't be him – he's gone. If they can make you think we can't get rid of them, then they'll be hoping you'll give up. That's their plan, so accept they've gone. OK, any questions?"

Harriet said, "No, I think you've covered all my questions."
I said, "OK, see you next week. If, in the meantime, you have a query drop me a line."
Harriet said, "OK, bye."

I said, "Hi, how's your week been, the same, better or worse?"
Harriet said, "More or less the same, but last night it seemed to get a little bit worse. I don't know what happened, my bed shook and it scared the hell out of me; I woke up wide eyes thinking what the hell was that. I'd been in a deep sleep; it was like a violent shake of the bed."
I said, "What happened after the bed shook?"
Harriet said, "Nothing, I just remembered what you said, just ignore it turn over and go back to sleep, nothing else happened and next thing I knew it was morning. Before I went to sleep, I was having trouble sleeping, and it's like a common occurrence now. When I close my eyes to go to sleep, it's tough. It's like they're purposely trying to keep me awake and annoy me."
I said, "Are you aware of an individual doing that, anyone in particular?"
Harriet said, "Probably, the loudest voice I hear is the male voice again. I keep getting Tony for some reason."
I said, "Do you hear other voices as well?"
Harriet said, "A tiny bit, only sometimes when it's tranquil I can hear them but mainly the male voice. It's funny, you've been mentioned, it's like Mike this and Mike that, not in a bad way, but I don't know whose

saying that. It's been normal apart from the voice and chitchat just when I try to sleep. It's a constant bombardment of chatter. To the point now, where I just don't want to go to sleep."

I said, "So you're expecting it, are you?"

Harriet said, "I've only recently started to expect it, about two days."

I said, "If you're looking for it, you'll find it. What should you do to combat it?"

Harriet said, "I think of the candle."

I said, "Does it work?"

Harriet said, "I don't think so. I just keep thinking about the candle until I tire myself out and fall asleep."

I said, "So it is working, isn't it because you're controlling things by picturing the candle."

I said, "How are you getting on with the pills?

Harriet said, "OK, I'm still getting a migraine. I believe it's from withdrawal to a lower dose, so I'm just hanging in there and working through it. To be honest, I expected it to be worse, the side effects and coming off them, but I don't really see it, so it's pretty good, I think I'm doing alright."

I said, "How're you getting on with your website?"

Harriet said, "I've put my artwork on four galleries on Facebook, and I've had a few responses, so I'm pleased. It's a place where I can show my work and sell it too, and it's a cheap form of advertising. I didn't go into the Red Cross because I just felt awful, I was getting dizzy spells, and the headaches were nasty. It's difficult to tell, and I didn't want to jump to the conclusion and say it's probably spirit. That's why I want to get off the pills so I can determine what's causing it. Mum said to ask spirit to take it away, but I don't want to keep saying that if it isn't spirit."

I said, "When you say take it away, do you focus on the candle to block it?"

Harriet said, "I thought that was to block spirit from talking to me."

I said, "It's to block any interference from spirit, and also recognising the pain is not yours by denying it. You would be surprised at how easily people accept a pain that's someone else's. So, you didn't go to the Red Cross at all this week? How did you feel about that?"

Harriet said, "I felt bad, and I wasn't feeling good."

I said, "Did you feel better when it was too late to go?"

Harriet said, "You know what? I did feel a little better."

I said, "Tony has taken Charlie's place, and he is starting to exercise control. He's making it difficult for you to sleep and concentrate on your meditation. He's also giving you pain and making you feel ill. He's keeping you off balance as far as the effects of the pill are concerned too. So shortly we're going to speak with him."

Harriet said, "He's done all that, I know you said someone might take Charlie's place, but I didn't think it would be that quick."

I said, "We knew it was a possibility, but he's a lot more obvious than Charlie and not as strong, he doesn't have full control, and we'll remove him today, don't worry. Just remember if you decide to do something, do it unless there is a good reason that's out of your control not to. They'll make you feel sick and give you pains. You have to think whether you've done something to cause the discomfort, if not then it's spirit. It will go away once you do what you were planning, there's no point attacking you once you're there, is there?"

Harriet said, "Yes, that's true, but it's hard to tell, I didn't know whether it was the pills that were doing it. I was getting confused, but I didn't waste a day even though I was feeling down. I promised myself that I would go online and join galleries and I felt better for it. But I didn't know, I've felt rough this week."

I said, "Yes, you got to remember you'll get attacked by spirit a bit more because you're more vulnerable at the moment while your pills settle down. They'll take advantage of your confusion, but gradually you'll see things getting better."

Harriet said, "I'll be going in next week; they're not going to win. I feel a bit weak that they could get to me so easily. It's so muddy at the moment at the Red Cross, I keep slipping and hurting myself. Mum says to pack it in till it dries out, but I'm thinking what am I going to do in the meantime. I'll think of something. Still thinking about getting a car to get me out and about a bit. There's so much to think about."

I said, "Yes, but what you're thinking about is your future, you're thinking positive."

Harriet said, "I'm still trying, but I really want to get off this medication."

I said, "Don't make that an objective, controlling your mind should be at the top. It's not important at the moment. The fact that you're on the low dose is good, but you have to stabilise yourself before you reduce it any more. We can deal with that later. So now we have

Tony here taking over from Charlie."

Harriet said, "I've been getting Tony all week."

I said, "We know it isn't Charlie because he's gone. When did Tony arrive?"

Harriet said, "It didn't happen straight away; this was about two days ago."

I said, "Did you have less interference up until then?"

Harriet said, "Yes, I don't think I had much talking at all."

I said, "Then the voice came back?"

Harriet said, "I just started hearing the name Tony; it just happened."

I said, "What's happened is when we got rid of Charlie, your subconscious felt something was missing, which is no surprise. When you get used to something, it leaves a hole when it suddenly disappears, and you automatically try to fill that hole. Remember, I told you that if we get rid of them too quickly, you'd feel a loss. You see, Charlie was prominent in your awareness, and once he's gone, the gap was more prominent than you expected. Tony isn't as strong, and he's new, you won't feel the loss so much."

Harriet said, "So the more we do this talking to the spirits, the less effect they'll have on me, and the group of spirits will get smaller?"

I said, "We'll have to do it at a pace you're comfortable with because what you feel is important. If you feel something missing, you'll look for something to replace it. If you can't replace it with something positive, then something negative will come in. What do you do to protect yourself?"

Harriet said, "I just focus on the candle, and sometimes

I imagine a light around me when things happen, more the blue light than I do the purple."

I said, "Does that stop things from happening?"

Harriet said, "I think it does."

I said, "Can you use it more?"

Harriet said, "I can try."

I said, "When you go to bed, visualise the protection around you."

Harriet said, "It's weird, for the two days since it happened all I could think about was Tony this Tony, Tony, Tony, I couldn't make it up. That's why I try not to talk to them at all, but it was constantly hearing his voice. I don't know why it's like that. It's funny the night before I speak to you, I just get all that commotion, so they know what they're doing. They also know I'm going to be speaking to you, I don't know why they're doing it, that's all."

I said, "They're trying to stop you from talking to me and also trying to make you think we can't get rid of them."

Harriet said, "You know when you said Tony, is he part of the group that's with me or is he someone that's just come in? I was worried he might be new."

I said, "He's new; he came to take Charlie's place to keep up the pressure. Don't worry, are you ready to talk to him?"

Harriet said after a deep breath, "Yes."

I said, "Tony, you want to talk to me?"

Harriet said, "Yes, I do."

I said, "What do you want to talk about?"

Harriet said, "Harriet, I'm new."

I said, "Yes, I know you're new."
Harriet said, "How do you know?"
I said, "Never mind that, have you come to bother her?"
Harriet said, "Yes."
I said, "Why?"
Harriet said, "Because I like it and it's fun."
I said, "What if I have fun with you, would you like that?"
Harriet said, "No, of course not."
I said, "Then why would you do that to her?"
Harriet said, "It's easy."
I said, "It's easy for me to do it to you too."
Harriet said, "Lots of swear words towards you, Mike, sorry."
I said, "So Tony, why are you doing this, never mind about it's fun, who's making you do this?"
Harriet said, "Ha, Ha, Ha, wouldn't you like to know?"
I said, "I already know, but do you know who's manipulating you?"
Harriet said, "I do, and it's none of your business."
I said, "It is my business because you're disturbing Harriet, and you shouldn't be there."
Harriet said, "Harriet likes me."
I said, "No, she doesn't. She doesn't even want you near her."
Harriet said, "Mike, I didn't even know he was here."
Tony was silent.
I said, "Tony, we can take you to where you'll be safe and at peace if you want."
Harriet said, "Come on, then do it; let's see if you can."
I said, "No, you have to be willing. If you're not

interested, we'll have to remove you."
Harriet said, "Why are you wasting your time? I'm not leaving."
I said, "I'm not wasting my time, you are because you won't be staying for long, one way or the other. The choice is whether you go willingly or forcibly. Think about it, it's your choice."
Harriet said, "All I can hear is quiet chattering like other people talking to each other."
I said, "Yes, he's stepped back thinking about the trouble he's got himself in. Are you frightened, Tony? What are you frightened of?"
Harriet said, "I heard he's gone."
I said, "Tony stop pretending, I know you're there, you didn't make all that effort to get here just to run away when I talk to you. If you think by being silent, I can't deal with you, you're wrong."
Harriet said, "He says to think of the spider Harriet, no horrible nights. I didn't tell you that I had some nightmares."
I said, "Don't worry about them; it's just this idiot playing games. So, Tony, you've decided you don't want to leave, is that right?"
Harriet said, "Make me."
I said, "Very well, just take a look around you; see those people?"
Harriet said, "Silent."
I said, "Can you see those people there? They've come to collect you. They'll take you away and put you in the custody of your guides. You can go now. Goodbye. So, Harriet tell me more about your Facebook page again."

Harriet said, "Oh, did you have a look?"
I said, "Yes, I had a look; it's looking good."
Harriet said, "Oh, OK, so basically I did different albums, one to show off my work that I did for tattooing and different clients I had. I did another album for selling, and that's the one I put on the galleries, it's going pretty good actually. I got a few friends out of it too, which was good, and a few artists who invited me back to their page to look at their work, it's been excellent. It's just nice to branch out and see other people's way of working; it felt good. It's so exciting to get up in the morning and check Facebook and see who added me, and who's looked at my work, it feels like I can do something meaningful."
I said, "Which you are, aren't you?"
Harriet said, "Yes, I know, but sometimes it feels like it's not enough, like so many people do such great things in the world, and I don't."
I said, "A little bit at a time, you can't do it all at once; you need to be patient."
Harriet said, "I know. I was thinking about getting a job too."
I said, "Are you ready for that?"
Harriet said hesitantly, "Yes, sort of."
I said, "OK, that's good."
Harriet said, "Oh, really, OK, good. I think so, once I'm off the tablets and I find out how I'm going to be, then I'll be fine. I'll be left alone to do my own thing. I know it takes time, but that's why I'm a bit worried, I know I shouldn't worry, I'm too focused on it really, I know I should just calm down."

I said, "Just pace yourself, tell me this; what can you hear?"

Harriet said, "It's quite quiet."

I said, "OK, don't focus anymore, Tony's gone."

Harriet said, "I see, wow."

I said, "So don't look for anything. Just carry on as normal as though nothing has happened."

Harriet said, "It's just so hard, you know when you've lived with something for years, and it's gone just like that."

I said, "It feels like there's a gap, something you're used to has gone. Don't look for what's missing because if you look for it, you'll bring someone else in. You've just got to forget all about that now, and we'll deal with the next spirit if they come along."

Harriet said, "It's so frustrating because I want to move on and get a job and do all this and that. Am I ready to do that? But if I don't, I'm going to be focused on what's going to happen next with the spirits, and it's not good."

I said, "When I spoke to you about a job a little while ago you were totally against it, you weren't ready. Now it sounds like you're ready, so go for it. It'll get you into the world, it'll focus your mind on something else and so less time to focus on spirit. You've still got a little bit of chatter there, haven't you?"

Harriet said, "Yes, in the background. How do you know?"

I said, "Because I'm a medium, so I'm going to talk to them now. Come and talk to me. I'm here to help you."

Harriet said tentatively, "Hello."

I said, "Hello."

Harriet said, "Hi."
I said, "Hi, what's your name?"
Harriet said, "Sofie."
I said, "Hi, Sofie, nice to meet you. Do you know where you are?"
Harriet said, "No, we've got no idea."
I said, "Is it dark there?"
Harriet said, "It's pitch black."
I said, "Do you know what's happened to you?"
Harriet said, "No."
I said, "What's the last thing you remember?"
Harriet said, "Falling."
I said, "What did you fall off?"
Harriet said, "I fell over."
I said, "When somebody falls, what happens to them?"
Harriet said, "You can get injured or die."
I said, "And where you are means that you died, so we need to get you and your friends together and take you to heaven where your families are."
Harriet said, "Somebody's crying."
I said, "Are you in pain?"
Harriet said, "No."
I said, "Why're you crying?"
Harriet said, "Harriet's nice."
I said, "Yes, but Harriet has got a life to lead, and we want you to live your life with your family and your friends."
Harriet said, "We hated what happened. It wasn't an accident."
I said, "Well that's in the past now. We need to look to your future, so what I want you to do is have a look

around you and tell me what you can see."
Harriet said, "There are people here."
I said, "Yes, can you see the light?"
Harriet said, "No, we can only see those shiny people."
I said, "Good, they're friends of mine; they're going to take you into the light."
Harriet said, "Awesome, thank you."
I said, "Can you see that light?"
Harriet said, "Yes, we can now."
I said, "Go into the light with my friends, and you'll be with your families."
Harriet said, "It's gone quiet. I can't hear anything."
I said, "OK, so tell me what sort of car you're looking for?"
Harriet said, "I don't know, I like the Astra car or Vauxhall Corsa might be nice. 2008 model upwards. I'm just looking around. I've got some money saved up for a car. I used to drive all the time in Australia, but now, I know, I'm not thinking about the past."
I said, "If you get a car, it'll get you out more, and when you look for a job, you'll have more scope."
Harriet said, "Exactly, I have the urge to get up and go now. I've never had this before. Like I said to you last week, I felt renewed. It's like someone is encouraging me to do this. It's just weird, maybe not weird maybe it's my guides helping me."
I said, "It is your guides helping you because they know that once you get out there and get a job, your mind will be occupied, and you'll be able to rebuild your life."
Harriet said, "That's true. OK, I'll start looking for a car, this is crazy, but I can to do this."

I said, "Of course you can."
Harriet said, "Yes, I know, and I shouldn't think of the past, but it's been so long since I drove."
I said, "How do you feel now?"
Harriet said, "Well someone's shouting at me in the back,"
I said, "Ignore them and bring up your candle."
Harriet said, "It feels quieter, though, it feels a lot better; that's awesome."
I said, "What qualifications do you have?"
Harriet said, "I've got A levels, but I didn't do my degree because I was ill. Tattooing I did, I might have to go back to school for art and design although I did it in A level's and I went to college and did that for a bit."
I said, "So what about doing something in the computer industry like designing websites or something like that? Google jobs in art and design and see what comes up."
Harriet said, "If not, I wouldn't mind a driving job where I can be out and about, not indoors, I can go where=ever the job takes me just to get me used to getting out and working. I was thinking of looking for local galleries as well to put my work in; I'll look into both and see what comes up and see what feels best."
I said, "Are there any cafés or restaurants near you where they might hang your work up for sale for ten per cent?"
Harriet said, "I can ask. There's a café in mind I can try and there's also the restaurants on the seafront. Yes, I'll give that a go. I'd better do more artwork then."
I said, "You've got to produce more pictures, have you? That'll keep you busy and keep your mind occupied."

Harriet said, "I know I should get out of this, but when I do something, and I get backlash, I get so much hate."
I said, "No, that's what you got before when you were getting interference."
Harriet said, "What do you mean?"
I said, "When you were getting interference from spirit, you got all those negative moods and emotions, and now, we're getting rid of them, you shouldn't get that, and if you get a bit, you can use the candle to block them."
Harriet said, "Yes, I see what you mean. But I'm always scared to do different things because if I fail at something, I always get the voices laughing at me and saying you failed, you're useless."
I said, "Yes, you used to get interference, but you're overcoming that, so let's be positive."
Harriet said, "Yes, right, move forward; forget about the past."
I said, "Yes, don't think you won't get the odd voice, for the time being you will, and we'll deal with it when it comes up."
Harriet said, "OK, yes, there's a lot to do this week then."
I said, "Well, you haven't got to do it all in a week, pace yourself."
Harriet said, "I'll get some work done before I speak to you next week."
I said, "If you're busy, it'll keep your mind occupied, and that's a good thing."
Harriet said, "Yes, it'll give me something to do. I'm getting bored easily. I just want to get out and about

now. I don't want to be hanging about indoors."
I said, "Well you've got choices. You can look for a job or look for a car, you can do more pictures, and you can visit the restaurants and also post on Facebook in the galleries. You've got lots to do, but don't rush things, start by doing a bit of art and looking for jobs. Don't try to do everything at once. If you want to extend your ability to get a job, the car would be one of your first priorities."
Harriet said, "Yes, I understand what you mean. OK, I'm going for a walk tomorrow and have a look and see what's about."
I said, "Good, this is the start in you getting your life back."
Harriet said, "As for meditation, I'm doing it when I need to like every other day, at least. So, do you want me to keep that up?"
I said, "Yes, I think so, just for your peace of mind. It'll be there if you need it then. What I want you to do now is not focus on spirit at all."
Harriet said, "No, I try not to, but it's so hard when they talk so loud."
I said, "We're getting rid of them as we go, sometimes we'll bounce back, and then we'll move forward quicker, but we'll stick to it until they're all gone. At the moment, the spirits are quiet because there's just a few that are lost; they won't bother you, but they help fill the space Tony was in."
Harriet said, "Oh, OK, right, I'm definitely going to look for a car so here goes, everything is happening so fast, but it's good, I want this."

I said, "Right is there anything else you want to ask?"
Harriet said, "Just the dreams that were annoying me, but if I do that protection, I'll be OK. I won't look for it, other than that I'm good."
I said, "OK, so if you get a dream, just turn over and ignore them, everybody gets dreams, just put them where they belong – in fantasy world. If that's it I'm going to let you go. If you get any problems let me know, otherwise we'll talk next week. Bye for now."
Harriet said, "Bye."

FEBRUARY 2020

I said, “Hi, how’s your week been?”
Harriet said, “It’s been OK. I’ve been looking for a car. I looked at one last weekend, but it wasn’t in great condition, so we decided to leave it. There’s another one we’re going to check out on Saturday, which I hope will be better. So, I’m having a good week what with looking for cars and being online with my artwork, and it’s kept me busy focusing on other things. I also went to work this week, which was great. The only thing is I feel a bit run-down, feeling ill, so I’ve been getting that sorted out with the doctor. Besides that, I’m doing my meditation as well, just keeping on top of it. It’s funny because I’ve been so distracted trying to find a car. I almost forget to meditate. I don’t know whether that’s a good thing or not.”
I said, “That’s a good thing because if you forget to meditate because you’re too busy, you don’t need to. What about the voices?”
Harriet said, “Yes, they're pretty loud still.”
I said, “OK, have you heard another name?”
Harriet said, “David, I think, but it’s not bothering me during the day. Another good thing, I went to the café, and she agreed to put my work up on her wall.”
I said, “Did she? That’s brilliant.”
Harriet said, “She said yes that would be fantastic, she said she would be happy to help, so I’m going to see her tomorrow. She’s redecorating the café, so I’m going to take a picture of it and put it on Facebook, so it’s been excellent. I’ve been getting out and about trying to do

things."

I said, "That's good. While you're doing all of that you're not getting the voices are you?"

Harriet said, "No, and if I do, they can be very loud, but I just ignore them, and they go away pretty quickly."

I said, "So you're getting them under control, aren't you? If you get the voices, do you bring up the candle?"

Harriet said, "Not as much as I should do, to be honest, I try, but it's very hard."

I said, "You must keep using the candle; we want it to be automatic, so when you need it, there's no effort, it just appears."

Harriet said, "I know, I know. At night I try and do it the most. I'm getting insomnia now. I'm not sleeping as well as I used to. I don't think it's spiritual, I think it's due to the tablets I'm still on. I try to think of the candle, but it's so hard to concentrate, that's why I'm trying to meditate a bit more this week because I just thought it might be helpful to have the candle stay in my mind a bit longer. It's been a bit of a struggle because I'm getting interference, but I do remember to do it, then next time I'm like, ah, make sure I do it, make sure I keep getting that practice in."

I said, "How often do you practise?"

Harriet said, "I do it every day when it gets to a point where I'm really distracted I do try to bring it up, but not when I'm at work or anything; it's just like when I'm quiet on my own it comes up a bit more, and I try and do it then."

I said, "What does that tell you?"

Harriet said, "I don't know, to practise meditating

more? I'm not sure."

I said, "What it tells you is that spirits isolated you so they can have you to themselves, which means they can get at you anytime they want. What you're doing is you're counteracting that by getting on and doing things, and you're keeping your mind occupied so they can't get in. What that's telling you is the more you keep yourself occupied, the less interference you'll get. It's when you're not doing anything you get the voices, isn't it?"

Harriet said, "Yes, OK, so I need to keep myself occupied and do something."

I said, "As you practise the meditation for 20 minutes in the morning and afternoon or evening, then you'll keep that with you, and it will, as you've already found out, come up automatically when you need it."

Harriet said, "You think I should go back to doing it in the morning and afternoon then?"

I said, "Yes, it was helping, wasn't it?"

Harriet said, "Yes, definitely, OK."

I said, "Are you still getting touched in bed?"

Harriet said, "It's not so obvious. Sometimes I think it's happening, but it's so faint, I'm not always sure."

I said, "If you've got to think about it, then you're not, which is good. So, stop looking and try to forget about that and move forward because it's in the past. Do you still put that cat behind you?"

Harriet said, "Yes, I do, and that seems to stop it."

I said, "Now we'll have a word with David, shall we? OK, David, let's have a chat."

Harriet said, "Hi."

I said, "What are you doing?"
Harriet said, "Making her life miserable."
I said, "Why?"
Harriet said, "Because it's fun."
I said, "It's not fun for Harriet; it's nasty."
Harriet said, "It is, but who cares."
I said, "I care, and we're not going to allow you to stay, you have a choice you can go by yourself, or we'll remove you."
Harriet said, "It's horrible what they're doing to her."
I said, "That's not David, who are you?"
Harriet said, "Hanna."
I said, "Hanna, do you know where you are?"
Harriet said, "It's a miserable place; this is miserable."
I said, "Are you lost?"
Harriet said, "I think so."
I said, "Do you know what's happened to you?"
Harriet said, "Died, hopefully, died."
I said, "Yes, you did. Where're you supposed to go when you die?"
Harriet said, "I don't know, is this hell?"
I said, "No, you're just lost. Most people go to a place we call heaven where your family is. We can take you there if you want."
Harriet said, "People keep bothering me."
I said, "Yes, that's because you're in a place where you're vulnerable; it's not a safe place. You're on your own, aren't you?"
Harriet said, "Yes, I'm alone."
I said, "OK, open your eyes, and tell me what you can see."

Harriet said, “I can see lights.”
I said, “OK, one light is very bright.”
Harriet said, “There’s a huge light.”
I said, “Right we’re going into that huge light. That’s the entrance to heaven, don’t take any notice of these other people they can’t hurt you. Just come with me, and I’ll take you to heaven.”
Harriet said, “OK, thank you. Will Harriet be OK?”
I said, “She’ll be OK, yes. What can you see now?”
Harriet crying said, “I’m scared.”
I said, “There’s nothing to be scared of; that’s where your family is. Now we’re coming into the light, and you should see something, what can you see?”
Harriet said, “I can see people.”
I said, “Good, do you recognise any of them?”
Harriet said, “There are some of my relatives; there’s my grandad.”
I said, “You’re safe now. Do you want to stay with them?”
Harriet said, “Yes, thank you so much.”
I said, “You’re welcome. David, I need to talk to you. We can help you if you want. Do you want help?”
Harriet said, “Don’t need help.”
I said, “OK, your intent on staying, are you?”
Harriet said, “I’m staying to keep her miserable; it’s fun.”
I said, “Right, David, you’ve had your chance. I’m putting you in the custody of your guides who’ll help you sort yourself out. You will not be able to come back or leave your guides until they say so. You can go now.”
Harriet said, “Let go, leave me alone (swearing); let go

of me."

I said, "Goodbye."

Harriet said, "Hm, it's gone quiet."

I said, "OK, there's somebody called James there, shall we talk?"

Harriet said hesitantly, "Hello, where am I? I was coming home, I don't know where this is, I thought I was going to heaven."

I said, "You got lost; it's very dark where you are, isn't it?"

Harriet said, "Random people here, all sorts, with weird clothes."

I said, "Yes, don't worry about them. Do you know how you died?"

Harriet said, "I felt a pain in my side and then nothing."

I said, "You know what happens when people die, they go to heaven."

Harriet said, "Can you show me the way?"

I said, "I can take you to the light so that you can be with your family."

Harriet said, "I can see a bright light, is that heaven?"

I said, "It's the way to heaven. We'll go now; you'll feel it getting warmer as the light gets closer. I can see your father there. He's holding his arms out to you. Go and stay with your dad."

Harriet said, "Sorry, Harriet, I didn't mean to cause trouble."

I said, "It's OK, you're safe now. Harriet take your focus off him as though you've closed a door, he's gone now. What do you hear now?"

Harriet said, "Nothing, he's gone."

I said, "OK that's another one safe."
Harriet said, "Yes. There was something else that happened this week as well; I wasn't sure whether to mention it. When we've finished, I can talk about it?"
I said, "We've finished for the moment."
Harriet said, "Basically, I don't know if it's me, but I've had such a bombardment of voices lately because I've been looking for a car and all the other stuff. I'm doing walking and visiting art galleries, talking more and just trying to get my life together. I did notice an increase of voices. Then I thought it didn't feel like guides, but I felt there were other people in the mix trying to help."
I said, "Yes, there are."
Harriet said, "It was really like, wow, where did that come from? They were trying to support me saying don't listen, try and ignore them, which was nice I just got emotional. They want to speak to you every time."
I said, "Yes, there are other spirits around who are on your side trying to help."
Harriet said, "Yes, I didn't understand that before, I just thought that was so nice. I felt sorry and felt a rush of emotions and felt like crying, I don't feel upset or anything I just feel emotional. I feel that some of their emotions do come through their frustration, anger definitely, and feeling scared, and a lost feeling as well comes through. It's good to know that we can help people, but it's very distracting. I don't want to be feeling it at all. It's just scary picking up people's emotions all the time. I don't want to cry, but I feel like crying."
Harriet was talking so fast and getting upset that she

couldn't stop what was happening.

I said, "Stop, just relax, calm yourself down. We can stop the voices that are not necessary. We're going to ask your guides to take those people that are not involved but attracted to what's going on around you away. They won't be talking to you anymore, so you can tell when it's interference and fight it. We need only to deal with the ones that are bothering you, those that aren't bothering you can be met by your guides and diverted into the spirit world."

Harriet said, "It makes sense where it was coming from, but now I don't want to focus on them at all."

I said, "We need to help the lost souls so we'll ask your guides to stop them coming to you, but to help them on their way."

Harriet said, "I honestly thought they were, but it didn't seem it this week. I don't know what happened."

I said, "What we're trying to do now is stop them from talking to you so that you won't be aware of them. You don't need to be aware of those people because your guides can take care of them if they're asking for help."

Harriet said, "Why do my guides allow that to happen?"

I said, "It's a lesson. Your guides are teaching you that there are a lot of people in spirit that aren't nasty and they're showing you."

Harriet said, "I thought I was trying to be mean, but I was trying to avoid speaking to spirit at all."

I said, "That's the best thing you can do."

Harriet said, "I wasn't assuming that all spirits are negative. It was just that if I thought they were all negative, it would be easier to manage and deal with because I could get rid of them easier. If I knew they were people who wanted help, then, of course, I'd want to engage in trying to help them."

I said, "You treat all the spirits that you hear and feel as wrong, and you push them out, get rid of them, ignore them, block them. We're not going to decide who's good and who isn't, that's up to your guides to sort out. You stop everything from coming in, you don't need to be bothered by people who want help or by spirits that are annoying you. You need to be getting on with your own life. It would be too confusing to be helping some and not helping others. Just rest assured your guides will help all those looking for help."

Harriet said, "This is a lesson, then?"

I said, "Yes, they're teaching you to defend yourself against the negative spirits. By explaining to you that not all spirits are nasty, they're showing you and letting you make decisions, and the decision that you've just made is that all those that are innocent don't need to come through you. We only need to deal with the ones that attack you."

Harriet said, "Because that's my lesson I need to learn. That's horrible, and it's so difficult."

I said, "No, it's good actually because now you know that there are spirits that need help, and your guides can help them."

Harriet said, "That's true, but I was thinking I guess I don't do it automatically then because people who don't know they have spirits around them, whether good or bad, their spirit guides don't take the good people away at all?"

I said, "They don't need to, they're not bothering them, any spirit that asks for help will get it. People who aren't aware of spirit who get interference think it's themselves, and there's something wrong with them. But the process still goes on in spirit with their guides trying to get through to the lost souls so they can take them to the spirit world. It takes a bit longer, but they will get through to them in the end, and then they'll take them to heaven. But it's not your job."

Harriet said, "So why is it everyone talks to me."

I said, "You're a bright light in a dark place, and they're like moths to a flame. They come because they see there is light here. Now we have your guides redirecting them to their guides who'll sort them out, and that leaves you free to deal with your problems, which are the ones that are attacking you."

Harriet tearfully said, "I don't know why, but I just heard someone say thank you so much. I wondered what my purpose was to do with this. It just seemed so random this happened to me. It's good that it's helping other people, I suppose. It's nice to know."

I said, "Well, it's helping you as well, isn't it?"

Harriet said, "Knowing that I'm helping them, yes; I suppose it is."

I said, "No, I mean, it's helping you to understand the difference between the good guys and the bad guys. I can't see why they need to teach you that because we don't want you to work spiritually anyway. But then we don't know what your life plan is; maybe you'll get involved working with spirit later on in your life."

Harriet said, "It's confusing what you said was maybe I

was in the wrong place at the wrong time. It wasn't as though it was my path or anything, right?"

I said, "Not necessarily, you were in the wrong place at the wrong time from your point of view. But from your life path point of view, you might have been in the right place at the right time. If you hadn't been getting the problems you've been getting, you wouldn't understand as much as you do, would you? Maybe it's a lesson you need to learn so you can pass it on to someone who's having problems that you meet later in life. What we want to do at the moment is for you to get rid of the voices that are attacking you. The benevolent spirits who come around you won't bother you because you'll block them out anyway, that's the idea of the candle."

Harriet said, "I see, so when I do get that blocking effect with the candle, would it just automatically happen? How will it block them out?"

I said, "It will automatically come to mind and will block them out once you've practised your visualisation during meditation. You'll be blocking spirit out altogether from your conscious mind. It's a process you need to perfect because we don't want all these innocent people bothering you as well, that's not your job. All we're interested in is getting rid of the negative spirits that keep annoying you. We've got rid of a few today, and we're not going to remove any more because we don't want to leave you too empty, so to speak."

Harriet said, "OK, thank you. So, I just do the meditation twice a day and take it from there."

I said, "Yes, you sound a bit apprehensive. What's

bothering you?"
Harriet said, "It's been a rough week. It's good on the other hand because I'm getting on and looking for a car and looking for galleries and stuff."
I said, "You mean today?"
Harriet said, "The past few days, I think."
I said, "It's like I said, it's a process we need to go through, and it's going to go backward and forwards. When it gets heavy, then you bring up the candle more, or you do something to keep your mind occupied. Now you've been to one café, and you've got some pictures to hang up there, are you going to try another one?"
Harriet said, "I did ask around, and there are some priced galleries, but I didn't have enough work to hang in them. I was hoping if I get this car on Saturday, I'd have more time to go out to art shops and pick up canvases and stuff. I can get loads of things done."
I said, "You can't go out to art shops unless you've got something to show them."
Harriet said, "I've got four pieces, and the lady in the café said there are a few cafés that do the same thing. The galleries' prices are quite high though, it's about £100 for a week."
I said, "Oh no, I'm not talking about you paying to hang your paintings, you don't pay them. I'm talking about hanging them for free and giving ten per cent when you sell one. If you've only got four pictures, you need more, so pick up your brush."
Harriet said, "OK, I keep trying to draw something."
I said, "Don't force yourself because if you force yourself, you won't be happy with what you produce.

You've got to get in the right frame of mind and be inspired by what you see around you."

Harriet said, "Overall this week, I guess it's been something new, something I needed to learn for some reason. I guess I'll just move on for now and deal with the normal negative ones."

I said, "Just try to block the voices with the candle meditation, all of them, nothing's changed. Before you were getting people that were lost around you as well, but they weren't talking; they were just observing."

Harriet said, "It's stressful."

I said, "Don't look at it as stressful. Look at it as improvement, you're doing very well. You're going to look at a car on Saturday, and you're going to get more art stuff, you're going to do some more paintings and drawings. You've found other places to display your work, seems to me you've moved forward a lot."

Harriet said brightly, "Yes, I have. I didn't think of it like that."

I said, "Is there anything else you want to talk about?"

Harriet said, "No, I think that covers it. Thank you. See you next week."

I said, "OK, bye."

I said, "How're you this week?"

Harriet said, "I've got a car, and it works fine. I'm thrilled with it. I'll be able to get about more easily now. I'm still a bit scared to drive it, but with a bit of practice, I'm sure I'll settle down."

I said, "What else have you been doing?"

Harriet said, "Going to the Red Cross. They're happy

with my work, and they're happy to have me there because I've sold a lot of things. That makes me feel more positive looking for a job. I'm going to start looking for work soon, just need to get a bit better, and I'll be fine, I think."

I said, "How do you mean you need to get a bit better?"

Harriet said, "Just dealing with the candle meditation. Trying to maintain that focus, it's kind of hard. I feel like doing it every day is beneficial. It's just when I'm quiet; it's difficult to block out the voices. It's getting easier to block out the images they send me, but blocking out the voices is hard. I struggled with that this week, especially when I'm going to sleep. I'm trying to focus on the candle, and I'm blocking out the visions that they send, but it's the voices that seem to have come on top of it. It's like, I imagine the candle. The voice is there, so I'm not sure I'm blocking it out properly or not, it's hard to determine if I'm doing it right. So, I don't know."

I said, "It sounds like you are because you're blocking out the visions now, aren't you?"

Harriet said, "Yes, a lot better."

I said, "So you're progressing, we just need to take it a piece at a time. You're quite impatient, aren't you?"

Harriet said, "I know, but I was thinking if I'm going to work, I don't know how I'm going to block out all the shouting."

I said, "You just said when you're quiet, you hear the voices, but when you're not quiet, and you're busy doing something, you don't hear them?"

Harriet said, "Yes, that's true, I guess when I'm distracted through work and driving it's fine now. I don't know, when it's just the visions, it's fine, but when it's the vocal stuff, maybe I'll get a sign, and I'll get to know whether I'm doing it right with the vocals."

I said, "It'll get less and less. For instance, have you heard somebody new this week?"

Harriet said, "Possibly, I'm not sure, I was going to ask you. I'm not sure how this works, is there a person there forcing other people to do something to me?"

I said, "Yes."

Harriet said, "I thought so, because I do have someone new, but the person who is mainly in charge, he's not doing anything besides controlling other people, is he?"

I said, "Correct."

Harriet said, "Oh, Is, that because you can see it?"

I said, "Yes, I can see the person that's doing it."

Harriet said, "Oh, so it's like you said in your book, it's like an organisation forcing different people to attack me."

I said, "Yes, when we remove these individuals. We've spoken about somebody who's in charge, haven't we?"

Harriet said, "Yes, we have."

I said, "That's the person that we need to remove. When we've removed them before, you've noticed that I've changed the subject."

Harriet said, "Yes, yeah."

I said, "The reason for changing the subject is to take your mind off the individual, that helps you to let go and block them out. What I want you to do is ask your guides to remove Kevin and place him in the custody of his guides."

Harriet said with surprise, "You want me to?"

I said, "Yes, just ask them to remove him."
Harriet spent a moment concentrating.
I said, "Right now, just forget about him. Once you've had him removed, you know he's been removed, and you have to have faith that your guides will do as you ask. We've done it a few weeks between us, haven't we, so now we need you to learn to do it by yourself. Now anytime you get an annoying voice, you just ask your guides to remove them."
Harriet said, "Right, OK."
I said, "And believe it. Once you've done that, you just get on and do something, so you refocus your mind. That will help you to put the spirit out of your mind. How are you doing with your protection?"
Harriet said, "Pretty good; it's only honestly just been the voices."
I said, "The protection has also got to stop the voices."
Harriet said, "How would that do that?"
I said, "Just by putting up your protection."
Harriet said, "OK, gotcha, I keep forgetting to do that. I'll have to remember to do it."
I said, "You need to do that in the mornings when you wake up and at night when you go to bed."
Harriet said, "It's scary, though, because it seems they're supposed to be there to do this."
I said, "Not necessarily, you need to be focusing on getting the mechanics right with you and the ones you're aware of, then we'll tackle the lady in charge. She's been attacking you herself since you removed Kevin, but it's not affecting you, is it?"
Harriet said, "Not really, no."

I said, “No, because you’re busy talking to me, and you’re automatically blocking her. You see how easy it is to distract yourself?”

Harriet said, “Oh, I see, I thought it’s quite easy not to do what they say and just do what you want.”

I said, “We’ve said that all along if you decide to do something, do it.”

Harriet said, “It’s stupid. For instance, I decide I don’t want to go for a walk, they start saying I’m just lazy, but then if I go for a walk, they keep saying don’t do it you might see someone who hates you. It’s like I can’t win whatever I do.”

I said, “Whatever you think, they’ll try to persuade you to do the opposite.”

Harriet said, “I decided to do what I want and be happy. It seems to be going well. I’ve found I’m more distracted just doing whatever.”

I said, “Since last week you’ve had a lot more to occupy your mind. You’ve been doing your pictures, your Facebook, looking for places to hang your pictures and looking for a car, so you had a lot to do. While doing all that, you didn’t get any interference, did you?”

Harriet said, “No, only when I stopped.”

I said, “As you know, they try to isolate you and get you in a situation where you’ve got nothing to do, and you get bored, which makes you an easy target. But what you’re doing is counteracting that by keeping yourself busy. For instance, if you had a full-time job, you’d have your mind on what you were doing all day. So, they wouldn’t bother you because they wouldn’t be able to get into your mind. When you go to the Red Cross, you

don't get any aggravation, do you?"
Harriet said, "No, none at all."
I said, "Maybe when you're sitting on the till and you're bored because there's nobody there and things get quiet, then you get a little bit of aggravation, don't you?"
Harriet said, "Yes, exactly."
I said, "So you can see what you need to do to stop it."
Harriet said, "Yes, I see, but the thing is it's good to be distracted and doing loads of stuff, but sometimes I just want peace. Just some time to myself, but I can't do that right now. I have to keep myself busy, and it's just stressful thinking I have to do so much stuff to try and keep on top of it, if that makes sense."
I said, "It does make sense, but it'll become a natural thing for you. Remember, you've had four to five years where you've been isolated, with nothing to do, so they've been the most prominent thing in your life. Now, because you're starting to do things, they're not as prominent as they were. At the same time, we're getting rid of them, and we need to stop any more from attaching themselves to you. So, we're putting protection around you, wherever you go, you'll have this protective bubble around you, which should stop them from getting in and bothering you."
Harriet said, "OK, so just keep thinking about the bubble around me, and I should be protected?"
I said, "Yes, you should be protected."
Harriet said, "But I have to think about it for it to work?"
I said, "You only have to think about it if you start to get interference. You're only going to put protection

around yourself in the morning and evening, if you get any interference in the meantime, you just reinforce the protection."

Harriet said, "OK. Something else I wanted to ask. They can change their appearance, can't they? Especially the main person who is doing this and she's not showing herself as a woman is, she?"

I said, "Sometimes she doesn't because she wants you to think there are others here as well."

Harriet said, "So, sometimes she doesn't, and sometimes she does. Oh, OK because I'm not getting that image. You're right, I think she's just trying to confuse me. I need to stop thinking about it. It's hard just knowing all this, but I'm trying, I'm hoping I can get on with it and think about other things."

I said, "Right, would you like to get rid of the lady?"

Harriet said a bit surprised, "Um, yeah. Not because I want her to hang around or anything, I was thinking if she goes who else is going to come in."

I said, "Once she's gone, there shouldn't be anyone else come in because that's what the protection does. Then all that's going to be left are the minions that she's been controlling."

Harriet said, "OK, but won't they be free as well after she's gone?"

I said, "Some of them will move on when they realise, they're free. Some will want to stay because the spirits are more comfortable here; they're the ones we have to ask our guides to remove."

Harriet said, "Why do you want to remove her now?"

I said, "Because I think it's time."

Harriet said, "Oh, OK, that's cool, yeah. So, do I ask my guides?"
I said, "No, I'm going to talk to her in the same way as before with the others. What are you getting at the moment?"
Harriet said, "I'm just getting a lot of thank you."
I said, "OK, so Matilda, we need to have a chat."
Harriet said, "I know she can hear you, but she's just not answering."
I said, "Yes, I know, she wants us to think she's not there. You're wasting your time because I can see you."
Harriet said, "Something about hating my race, whether she means it, I don't know."
I said, "She'll say anything to try and upset you, just take no notice. Matilda, why do you hate her race? You have no reason to hate Harriet; she's done nothing to you. Why're you attacking her?"
Harriet said, "No, she hasn't done anything."
I said, "So why're you here, what made you come to Harriet?"
Harriet said, "She's easy to control."
I said, "Not so easy now, is she?"
Harriet said a subdued, "No."
I said, "It's going to get harder as Harriet gets stronger so you would do well to leave now."
Harriet said, "I'm a strong woman."
I said, "You may be a strong woman and control others. I'm going to take them all away from you if you don't leave. Why are you pretending someone is controlling you? I know you're in charge, so stop playing games."
Harriet said, "I thought I'd got you then."

I said, “No, are you prepared to go willingly, or do I have to remove you?”
Harriet said, “Why be removed when I can stay?”
I said, “You can’t stay; that’s not an option. I take it by your silence; you think you can stay. As you won’t go willingly, we’re going to remove you and put you in the custody of your guides. It means you’ll no longer be able to control anyone. Your guides will look after you.”
Harriet said, “Why should I go?”
I said, “You’ll have noticed our guides who keep us safe, they’re going to take you and introduce you to your guides who’ll take over your rehabilitation. We’ve finished with you now so you can go. Right Harriet now take your mind off Matilda, then you won’t hold her back. By putting her out of your mind, you’re putting her out of your energy. How’re you getting on with your pictures? Have you done any more?”
Harriet said, “I have to be honest. I just need to think of what to do. There’s a gallery that charges ten per cent. It’s perfect because it’s a gallery and I think it might be better to do that than to do the café, so I’ve got options.”
I said, “Why can’t you do both?”
Harriet said, “That’s what my dad said to do both, so I just need to focus on getting some ideas and start drawing again.”
I said, “Matilda has gone now, hasn’t she?”
Harriet said, “I not aware of her, so yes, I believe she has.”
I said, “Believe it.”
Harriet said, “Yes, she’s gone, so thank you so much. Do

you think she was there at the start?"
I said, "Yes, she was, she's been building up the interference gradually while she got her claws into you until you couldn't ignore it. By which time she had you double guessing everything and not knowing whether you were coming or going."
Harriet said, "Yes, how do you know?"
I said, "It kept going pretty strong until we started talking, and it faded a bit. Then Matilda counter-attacked to try and keep control of you. You remember you had a bad week?"
Harriet said, "Yes, I did."
I said, "Now, it's quietened down a lot as you exercise more control."
Harriet said, "Yes."
I said, "That's because you've worked hard to get on top of it by protecting yourself."
Harriet said, "It's good to get confirmation that I'm doing it right because I sometimes question myself. I want to put your teachings to good use, and I pray that it works in the end. It's so hard when I don't get that confirmation during the week, and I don't want to annoy you by email all the time."
I said, "You won't annoy me; just believe in what you do, have confidence in your ability, you're as strong as they are, you just haven't known how to beat them."
Harriet said, "Yes, definitely, yes."
I said, "What sort of car have you got?"
Harriet said, "A Peugeot 209. It's a smashing little car, great for what I need."
Harriet went quiet for a while.

I said, "You're quiet."
Harriet said, "Yes, I was thinking it's going to be so strange, but how am I going to manage when I don't hear the voices. I know that time is coming, and I'm just thinking it's going to be so different."
I said, "Don't be fearful. If you fear you'll look to see if you're clear. In looking, you'll attract the negative spirits. That's why we have to go slowly, so you don't feel the loss. You'll cope just fine; you'll be free."
Harriet said, "The spirit guides are looking after the lost people as well?"
I said, "Yes, they are. You haven't heard voices this week, have you?"
Harriet said, "Only pretend voices, but no."
I said, "Exactly, they're trying to undermine what we're doing."
Harriet said, "Yes, they're saying there are loads of children now, I know there aren't. It's like learning how they work and recognising the tricks, they play, I'm thinking how did I fall for this as it's so obvious sometimes. I'm not trying to be cocky; it's just I have more confidence now."
I said, "Unless you know what game they're playing, you become part of it so you can't observe what's going on from a distance. It's tough to get out from inside when you're stuck in the middle. Now that we've got you outside of the game, it's easier to see what's going on. Now that we've got rid of the main person who was causing the problem, things should start to ease up."
Harriet said, "OK, thanks, see you next week."

Harriet wrote, “I'm really sorry to bother you, but I'm still having problems. I'm off the Cymbalta, I'm happy about it, realising now how much it poisons the body. Glad I'm not taking it, so I've a hundred per cent made this decision to come off it because I genuinely believe it was for the best, so don't worry, I'm not blaming anyone. However, I'm having strange symptoms that aren't improving and are starting to become scary. I'm having a tight chest and difficulty breathing, so much so I had to go to A&E. They couldn't find anything! Had tests done with no problems coming back, it's really worrying now because it's interfering with my life. I'm planning on going to the doctor again on Monday. I can't keep going on like this. But I want to rule out something if you don't mind, please, can you see if a spirit is causing this? I'm asking spirit guides to help, but it’s still pretty much the same. I know they're helping, but it seems something else could be the cause, something of which I’m not aware. But don't worry, I'm doing everything I can on my behalf! I'm not relying on my spirit guides for everything, the opposite actually because it feels more real then spiritual, but I just want to rule it out, if I can.”

I wrote, “It sounds like side- effects from coming of pills. If the hospital didn't find anything. You went to the hospital last week, and they said you were OK. Now you've been twice and still got the all-clear. I'm going to clear you tonight and will contact you in the morning at 9.00. Just try to relax and don't panic. You haven't had breathing problems before, have you?”

I said, “How are you feeling now?”
Harriet said, “I’m a lot better; did you do something?”
I said, “Yes, I removed some negative spirits last night. You weren’t ill, just had a lot of interference. They tried to make you think you couldn’t do without the medication.”
Harriet said, “That was difficult, it felt so real, I was going to the doctors tomorrow to see if there was anything else because I thought it might be withdrawal symptoms. I’ve read horror stories about it, and they stuck in my mind.”
I said, “That’s one of the things we need to be careful of; if you go to the doctors and say you’re feeling anxious, they’re going to put you back on them. You don’t need it; you’re doing fine, three weeks on a reduced dose now, you’re nearly clear of them, stick at it.”
Harriet said, “Three weeks, yes I know, that’s what I was scared of too because I was thinking oh my god you’re panicking or maybe depressed or you’ve got the high anxiety and I have to go back on them. I was like I don’t, and I don’t want to try anything else either.”
I said, “What’s happening is spirit is taking advantage of your vulnerability and trying to panic you so they can get back control of you. The way to do that is to get you back on a higher dose, so you’re dependent.”
Harriet said, “Yeah, I don’t want to do that. I’ve got a strong feeling not to do it.”
I said, “You’ve done very well so far.”
Harriet said, “I just want it to end, want to feel better. I feel like I should be doing more finding work and stuff.

I've been doing my CV and everything, but it feels like since this happened, I'm frightened if I get a job, I'm going to get interference."

I said, "All in good time, do what you can, and things will come together. Don't sell yourself short. If you think about it, you've not had a breathing problem before, have you?"

Harriet said, "No and funnily enough it only started now, it didn't start in the first week I reduced the pills."

I said, "I think if you look back, it came on suddenly, didn't it?"

Harriet said, "I think it did, yes, I think so."

I said, "When something happens, think about how you were aware of it. If it's sudden, it's not yours, and you're far too young to be having a heart attack, so it's not that."

Harriet said, "That's a load off, thank you. I honestly don't want to go back on them."

I said, "Forget about them, move forward. That's in the past now. You're getting control of the situation. The spirits are trying to throw all sorts of things at you like depressive moods, anger tantrums, anxiety, pain and fear. If they can get you back under their control, they'll isolate you again, and you've beaten that, and you can do it again, each time it gets easier."

Harriet said, "I noticed I've been angry at the moment, irritable, and don't want to talk to anyone, and I've been rude."

I said, "They're trying to isolate you again."

Harriet said, "I just didn't know what was wrong."

I said, "Well, if the hospital can't find anything wrong

with you, then there isn't."

Harriet said, "I know, and that should be a good thing, and if there's nothing wrong, it must be interference."

I said, "There's nothing wrong with asking your guides to help; I do when I'm working. You have to recognise your part of a team and work together."

Harriet said, "I won't go to the doctors tomorrow. I don't feel like it's anything serious."

I said, "It's not, there's nothing wrong with you. These are classic attacks if you think about it, you've had them all before at different times. Ok see you next week."

I said, "Hi How're you?"

Harriet said, "I've been horrible this week like I've been stabbing at everyone."

I said, "Well, you're going through a process, and you know what the side effects of the withdrawal symptoms of Cymbalta are, it's not going to go away in a couple of days. You're halfway there, just work your way through it. Remember, you're not just fighting the medication; you're fighting spirit too."

Harriet said, "That's the thing, I'm going through the symptoms of withdrawal, but it could be spiritual too, or it could be both attacking me at once."

I said, "The withdrawal symptoms are a chemical reaction which can be enhanced by the negative spirits. If you deal with the spiritual side of it, then you'll find the withdrawal symptoms won't be half as bad."

Harriet said, "Yeah that's true, I'll have to stop getting paranoid because it's getting so bad, I was thinking maybe they're bad, the symptoms, and I go online and look at other people's experience."

I said, "That makes it all seem worse, doesn't it? You don't need to look. It's like somebody who has pain, looks up the possible ramifications of the pain, and they discover they've got the worst problem they can find when it is just indigestion or something."

Harriet said, "Yes, my mum told me to stop looking, so I stopped. I was just looking for ways to manage it and to deal with it. I bought supplements and stuff; I believe that'll work. But it was weird, I was getting the reverse affects when I started taking the supplements, now that I think about it. It makes sense."

I said, "What you've got to think of is, is what you do now working. If you start on something else, you've got to start at the beginning, and it's going to interfere with what we're doing. If it's not spiritual, it won't work because what you're getting is spirit interference, which is the mind, not your brain, so not chemical. How long did they say the medication would take to get into your system?"

Harriet said, "About three weeks, I think."

I said, "It's going to take a bit longer to get it out of your system for two reasons. One because things have been a bit intense for you, and you're not just dealing with the Cymbalta. Two because you're getting everything enhanced, even when you've got rid of the withdrawal symptoms and moved past that. They're still going to keep throwing stuff at you, and that's what's happening now. You're getting to the end of the withdrawal symptoms, and they've increased the pressure on you. I said earlier how they would make you moody; anxiety

is a mood."
Harriet said, "Yes, I just have to reinforce myself. I know it's not me. I know it's them, but I can't shake the emotion off."
I said, "Once you've got the medication out of your system, you'll have full control again."
Harriet said, "It's good because right now, I'm going on a detox, and I'm flushing all the toxins out of my body. I'm not eating, so it's been so hard to try and not listen and just get on with it. I'm doing it safely, drinking lots of water, and my mum's supervising. It's been tough to stay focused; my mind's felt a bit scattered, and I think it's been worse because of that. So, I prepared myself for it and managed, which was good. I wasn't tempted to call you or frustrated to the point that I needed some answers. I was at the point where, you know what, just deal with it and keep thinking of the candle and just manage. I've been doing that, it's hard, but it seems to be paying off. It's like it's a challenge, it's harder, but that gives me more practice in putting the candle to good use. I keep doing it, make it a habit, and just keep doing it and doing it, and I'm realising now that the images I keep getting over and over again are about my fears. There's a huge candle in front of it, and it's blurring out the background, and I focus on the candle, and it goes. Before, the image would stay in my mind so long until it bothered me and I'd get fearful, and I wouldn't like it, but now every time I get a fearful thing, or they bring up a negative phase that happened in the past, I put the candle there and have the background blurred. It would then fade off, and I'm just thinking of

the candle."
I said, "The candles working, isn't it?"
Harriet said, "It seems like, yes, it is. It is finally, and I just need to keep that going."
I said, "Now, you've got half your life back because you're halfway to beating the voices."
Harriet said, "It's funny. I don't know whether this was Kaz or not, but I got a vision of half an apple. I wondered if he was saying I was halfway there. It felt positive.
I said, "It is positive you're halfway to getting your life back."
Harriet said, "It does feel that way, it really does."
I said, "Now we need to keep the momentum going, so you get the other half back by putting some of your drawings out there. You'll be looking for a job, and once you've done that, you'll find your mind is more occupied, and then you'll have most of your life back. Once you start going to work, you'll start meeting people and become part of a social circle and have people to go with if you want to go somewhere."
Harriet said, "Yes, that'll be good."
I said, "It's a slow process, so don't rush it."
Harriet said, "It feels like I have to rush it to get my life back, and I feel pressured by it, but I know I have to do it, and I will do it. I just feel like if I don't do it, I'll just be reverting backward, and I don't want to be doing that. I know I have to take it at my own pace as well, you're right I can't rush it, but at the end of the day, I need to do it. It'll be good to get back to normal."
I said, "The thing about all of this is that it's taken four to five years of doing nothing but suffering. It's taken us

six months to be proactive and achieve what you have. Instead of being the pawn pushed around, you're now the queen regaining control of your life."

Harriet said, "Yes, definitely, I realise how much control she had; it was scary, even manipulating my thoughts, mimicking my voice, pretending it's me. I recognise it so quickly now that it's not me. Move on, don't think about it, and say what you want to say, and don't be scared to speak as well. I felt scared to speak. I felt I was speaking negatively, but it wasn't me speaking I felt like I was all this evil stuff they were telling me I was. When I speak to people, I'm a social person, but when I'm alone, it's horrible, completely different, everything goes out the window. It's like you said, when I'm isolated, it's the worst, and I'm not myself, I'm horrible."

I said, "Don't isolate yourself, spend more time talking to family or play music."

Harriet said, "The thing is while we're playing music, would that block out the candle?"

I said, "No, because when you started meditating with the candle, you were listening to music as well, it didn't block it out, did it? If you're reading or something and playing music in the background, it won't stop you bringing up the candle if you want to."

Harriet said, "So I can do both. I was thinking it must be so hard to do both, especially at night time when I'm trying to be quiet, and I just want to sleep, but I know I have to focus on the candle. But if I focus on the candle, I'm not sleeping, but I need to block out what's coming in. Hopefully, if I'm thinking about the candle, I will eventually go to sleep. I don't know. It's so hard to try and sort it out."

I said, "What happens when you're not focusing on the candle when you're trying to go to sleep?"

Harriet said, "When I'm not focused on the candle, I'm bombarded with so much stuff."

I said, "When you do focus on the candle, what happens?"

Harriet said, "It does cut it out, I admit, it does, which is good. I'm not surprised because I'm refocusing, but it's just, erm, they push harder, and I have to learn to try to overcome them."

I said, "They're at the edge of the cliff now, you're about to push them off; they're going to fight harder."

Harriet said, "That's true, they're going. It's like for the first time this week I thought, what am I going to do if I don't hear these voices. That never happened before. I never got that question come up because I thought it wasn't possible before. I don't know, it's just that they haven't got that control anymore, it's going to be freedom, but it's going to be worrying too. I'm just hoping I'm not going to be that evil person they're making me out to be and speak all those horrible thoughts about people, and I don't want to be like that at all."

I said, "Stop, listen to what it's going to be like when you don't hear the voices – normal. You can choose what you think about, what you do and when you do it without interference."

Harriet said tearfully, "You have no idea how different it'll be. I don't know if you've experienced this, but every day, I get horrible thoughts, and I just pray that

I'm not going to be like that, not like them – hateful and spiteful and horrible."

I said, "Of course you're not, you're not that kind of person, you understand now why we've been doing it gently and not quickly, you're starting to bring up fear now of not hearing the voices. We need to get past that to not being fearful, of not hearing the voices but being happy that they've gone. You've got to put this fear away; it's not something that will do you any good because it's going to undermine you. There's nothing to be fearful of, and it's your right to have control over your thoughts. It's not the right of others to control your mind."

Harriet said, "Yes, OK."

I said, "We've been removing them slowly so that you get used to the loss and the feeling of space. Now we've got rid of the main player it doesn't mean to say they've all gone, there are still a few stragglers there. We didn't want to remove all of them at once because you'd feel a sense of loss, once you get comfortable with the space, then we'll remove some more. But those that're left shouldn't cause you too much problem, providing nothing else gets in."

Harriet said tearfully, "Is that why this week I've thought I can think what I want to think now. It's so weird, like I said I never thought about not having the voices in my head before this week. The fact that I can think what I want to think now, it didn't occur to me before because I've been blocking my thoughts and restraining myself not to think certain things because they manipulate them all the time. I don't know how

I've got this far. It's been like a living hell, how they can mimic me and pretend to be me and just act like it's me that's been horrible. Now I've just realised this week that, you know what, I can just do what I want now, no worries, don't need to think about what other people think. If I want to imagine, then I can, which is good, and talk the way I want to talk, and just be happy. Thank you so much, they're happy tears. I promise it's such a relief that it's nearly coming to an end. I don't know, I've never had this before, I thought I'd be living with this forever and thinking how am I going to manage."

I said, "Are you worried about when it's all sorted out, when it's all gone?"

Harriet said, "I'm not sure why I'm worried. I'm scared that you're just going to go, and I just don't want to be left alone again. That's another thing as well; I realised this week I don't want to come home. I get the feeling I don't want to be left alone in my bedroom anymore. I was driving in my car for ages, and the spirits were making me fearful of coming home."

I said, "You've got to overcome that."

Harriet said, "I felt there was something else, it wasn't that, how to explain this, I was driving in the car, and I didn't want to come home, so I thought why don't I stay out in the car and enjoy myself. And I did, I drove around and didn't care what the spirits were saying I did what I wanted to do. I wanted to drive around town, see places and people, pop in and say hi, and just be the social person I was before."

I said, "That's getting your life back, isn't it? Remember when you're out enjoying yourself, you're out because you want to be out. If you want to go home, then you go home, don't be fearful of anything in your room. They might try to attack you differently, like making you fearful of going home. if you get thoughts of not going home because you don't want to be in your room, ignore them because they're just trying to find a way back to you."

Harriet said, "Yes, OK, thank you."

I said, "You'll be a target for a while, they'll try and drag you back to where they had you before. We're going to have to fight a little longer yet till we get rid of the spirits."

Harriet said, "Yes

I said, "The more you can do yourself, and the less I do, the more independent and the more in control of everything you'll be."

Harriet said, "Thank you, it's such a relief to know the boss has gone, and I can just deal with the minions now."

I said, "Don't even worry about the minions. Deal with them if they interfere, don't go looking for them."

Harriet said, "No, definitely not, I try as much as I can to avoid them and block them out and everything and just to refocus. But they're pushing hard now, so I know it's coming close to the end."

I said, "You can push just as hard back."

Harriet said, "I know I've been doing that this week."

I said, "The way to do it is not to push hard and make them go away but to remove them. If you push, they'll just push back."

Harriet said, "That's another thing I want to speak to

you about. I thought I could do this, but I feel like I have to be doing this my whole life just pushing them away and managing it. I want them just to go, and I don't have to deal with it."

I said, "That's right, and that's what we're aiming for."

Harriet said, "Thank you, I needed to know, I don't want to be doing this, fighting them constantly every single day. As soon as I wake up, it's a constant fight until I go to sleep."

I said, "Well, it's not constant right now is it? Right now, you're not fighting, are you?"

Harriet said, "This week, but not now."

I said, "No, what I mean is that even during the day all this week, you've had times when you haven't had attacks, and you're not trying to block them out because they're not bothering you. When you're busy doing something, you're not getting interference, are you?"

Harriet said, "No, you're right."

I said, "What I'm trying to do is teach you to remove them yourself, rather than just push them away, delete them, and know when you've removed them. If someone starts nattering to you, just ask your guides to put them in the custody of their guides."

Harriet said, "I can do that, right?"

I said, "Yes, you can because you've done it, you did it last week, and you did it the week before, we did it today."

Harriet said, "That was you, though, wasn't it?"

I said, "No, that was us, I can remove everything that you've got with you, but if you don't want them removed, you'll bring them back. I'm only guiding you; it has to come from you. We have to do it slowly so that you're comfortable with what you're doing. Now you're starting to become a little fearful of having no voices, aren't you? And you've got to get past that to a stage where that's a good thing, that's normal. You understand when you're reading, there's a voice saying the words when you're reading to yourself isn't there?"

Harriet said, "How did you know that? Yes, there is."

I said, "That's normal when I read. I talk inside my head, that's my inner voice; it's your inner voice when you're reading. If you read *Mary had a little lamb*, in your head, you're saying *Mary had a little lamb*, aren't you?"

Harriet said, "Yes, that's right."

I said, "That's your inner voice; it's nobody else's voice. It's your inner voice. When you think, you talk to yourself inside your head, don't you?"

Harriet said, "Yes."

I said, "That's your inner voice, and you need to recognise the difference between that and interference, and you'll notice that the inner voice will only follow your thoughts. When it's interference, it's going against your thought, and that's not your inner voice."

Harriet said, "Right, I'll have to get used to that. I thought, is there someone inside here with me? It sounds like me, like when I agree to something, and I get, yeah, go for it."

I said, "That's your thought."

Harriet said, "Oh, I see, why is it clearer now than it was before?"

I said, "Because you haven't got so much interference now so you can recognise one from the other."
Harriet said, "Oh, OK, wow, that's amazing, thank you, OK."
I said, "When we finish today, look up inner voice, and it'll tell you about it. Everyone has an inner voice. What are you going to do this week?"
Harriet said, "I'm not going to the sanctuary, for the time being. It's too muddy; I'll go back when it dries out a bit. I've got to get some canvasses so I can start drawing again. I might visit the gallery and see what the possibilities are of hanging some drawings. Do more stuff with my sister and mum; we'll probably visit family now. I've got my car. I've got in my head a few times this week to do stuff that makes me happy. Then I keep coming back to the voices, and I can't think that way."
I said, "No, you can't. You've got to forget about them, you're moving on, just deal with them as and when you have to and don't push them away, you remove them. Just ask your guides to help you remove them and put them in the custody of their guides."
Harriet said, "When I do remove them, do I just ask my spirit guides to remove them, please?"
I said, "Yes, then put them out of your mind and concentrate on what you're doing. You see, if you ask your guides to help remove someone and you look to see if they've gone, you'll invite other spirits in because they're still in your mind. If, on the other hand, you just dismiss the very thought of them, they can't come in because you've put protection up by dismissing them. You only need to do it when you get major interference.

Otherwise, you'll be looking for them all the time, and that's an invitation. So, when you would normally put the candle up, try removing them as well. Then change your focus onto something other than spirit."

Harriet said, "Is this every time I hear a negative voice?"

I said, "No, just when you feel you need to bring the candle up, the minor interference you can deal with by just changing your thoughts."

Harriet said, "Although I can hear the voices, it's when they're getting to me. Then I do it?"

I said, "Yes."

Harriet said, "OK, I was thinking I'd be doing it every second otherwise."

I said, "We don't want you to focus on spirit; just get on with your life and deal with the major interference, as I've said. I'm a little confused you said you don't get the voices as much and then you said you get them all the time."

Harriet said, "It's hard to explain. It depends on how bad it is. Because sometimes they put emotions and feelings into it too, I've got so used to hearing them I don't register it sometimes. But I do when they're shouting at me or pushing me, and it's hard to tell. That's why I was asking when to do the candle and the spirit guides because I can hear them in the distance saying certain things, and I just get on with it, but sometimes they're really loud, and I just have to take notice."

I said, "OK, when they're in the distance, you can block them out, can you?"

Harriet said, "Pretty much yes I can; it's when they're

really pushing, they disturb me."

I said, "That's when you need to remove them because you ignore the distant stuff?"

Harriet said, "Yes, that's right."

I said, "By ignoring the distant stuff, gradually that will disappear."

Harriet said, "I have to admit that is getting easier too, ignoring the distant stuff because before I was noticing it and thinking not again, but now, I'm just uh again."

I said, "Consider this; the distant stuff is not necessarily negative, is it?"

Harriet said, "I'm not sure."

I said, "There are spirits all around you, some negative, some positive. The positive spirits that are lost are confused and distressed, and they will be talking to each other, and you're picking up their conversation and think they're talking to you. For instance, if you hear a voice saying 'it's horrible here, I want to get away', that's a conversation a spirit's having with another spirit. It's nothing to do with you, but because you're so tuned in, you'll pick up the conversation. When you get distant conversations, and you block it out, you're then controlling your space. Suppose you're in a crowd and you hear a conversation between two people over there, they're not talking to you. When you speak to the person you're talking to, you block out the other conversation by focusing on what you're saying. Well the distant voices are the same kind of scenario."

Harriet said, "I see."

I said, "All you need to do is deal with the ones that are attacking you."

Harriet said, "Honestly, I think I probably do recognise it. I don't pick the negative stuff up as much as I did. As soon as I hear negative stuff, I know instantly it's caused by a spirit. But I rarely think I might be picking up a little bit more, hearing that tiny bit more, maybe more 'help' and 'thanks' and 'hellos', I'm not sure."

I said, "You need to block those out as well; you don't want to be having conversations with any spirits."

Harriet said, "That's what I thought. I know that it's rare that it happens. I hear other people's thoughts and feelings because there's normally just one person saying it. I was getting that, same voice, same thing over and over again, and I wasn't getting anything else. I knew someone was there controlling this person, or it was the main person doing it. That's what I figured out this week, I thought I was so slow, but it came to me this week."

I said, "How do you think you got that information, your guides?"

Harriet said, "Yes, probably, I wasn't sure because it's sometimes hard to determine. I know the negative spirits try to trick me. I was just trying to think about it a bit more, and how it made more sense the more I thought about it – putting things together from how I was getting things in the past and wasn't clearing anyone else. I thought if I've got lost people wouldn't they be speaking to me too? I knew someone was trying to control them to not speak to me, or blocking them out and just having one person saying negative stuff to bring me down. The goal is to make me snap and to bring me to my knees. I knew that."

I said, “So really, we need to ignore those voices and allow them to fade away and focus on the ones that come in to attack you and just remove them. If you have any trouble with any of them, call me.”
Harriet said, “So I bring up the candle when I get that main one pushing hard, and I’m not ignoring them as much by distraction and focus and ask my guides to help me remove them and just know they do it and believe it. Then dismiss all thought of them and get on with something. It’s challenging because I can’t see what’s physically happening. I have to believe they’ve removed them.”
I said, “Look at it like this. When we removed those last week, you knew they’d gone, didn’t you?”
Harriet said, “Yes, pretty much.”
I said, “How did you know?”
Harriet said, “I don’t know.”
I said, “But you knew, when we removed Matilda, you knew she’d gone, didn’t you?”
Harriet said emphatically, “Yes.”
I said, “How do you know, because I tell you?”
Harriet said, “Because I feel it inside. OK, so believe it and go with my gut instinct and just know.”
I said, “Also, don’t forget there’s nothing to fear about not hearing a voice.”
Harriet said, “OK, yes. Also, I’m getting like yeah, she’s gone, I don’t know where that’s coming from.”
I said, “Ignore it. It’s right, but ignore it; just go with your gut instinct. That’s the spirits talking to each other, they’re glad she’s gone.”
Harriet said, “Oh, I see. Something else I realised this

week; I don't need to hear the good spirits because I know they're being taken care of, so I'm trying to not focus on them now, and I don't need to worry about them. Also, other people can go like that other woman was going to her family. That's a good thing."

I said, "Well, yes, it frees them as well, doesn't it?"

Harriet said, "I'll try not to be angry with my guides. I know they're just trying to help."

I said, "It doesn't matter if you're angry, it shows emotion. But if you get angry it's a negative emotion, isn't it? That negative emotion you produce could draw someone to you. You need to be as calm and peaceful as you can be."

Harriet said, "OK, but it's hard."

I said, "Just count to ten and take a few deep breaths. Now you've got the car; you can get out a lot more."

Harriet said, "I'll try not to think of spirit at all this coming week."

I said, "Is there anything else you want to talk about?"

Harriet said, "I think that's it for now. See you next week. Thank you so much for your time."

I said, "Hi, Harriet, how have things been?"

Harriet said hesitantly, "OK."

I said, "Are you telling the truth because I can't help you if you don't tell me what you're experiencing. You still hear the voices, yes?"

Harriet said, "Oh yeah definitely, it's complicated. I came off Cymbalta a weeks ago, I just wanted to see how I would do without it."

I said, "You came off Cymbalta, I thought you were still

on the lowest dose, and now you've weaned yourself off completely."

Harriet said, "Yes."

I said, "How are you feeling?"

Harriet said, "I feel fine. I just have to deal with the withdrawal now. There's a lot of things that can happen when you come off it. So, I was a bit worried about that for a while, and I've had horrible experiences. I'm not blaming the spirits more because I thought it's more the physical symptoms, I didn't think it was spiritual at all. I've had horrible insomnia and headaches, and concentration is terrible. I try to concentrate on the candle and I can't do it for long, it feels like it's not even spiritual this time it just feels like it's me. I'm doing it still just to keep practising, but it's tough, and I've been getting horrible symptoms, and I just had to go to the hospital and get checked out. I was just getting paranoid with it."

I said, "When did you go to the hospital?"

Harriet said, "Yesterday."

I said, "And what did they say?"

Harriet said, "Pretty much everything was fine, I was having pains in my abdomen and stuff like that, and I thought I had appendicitis. I'll start from the beginning. When I started having the symptoms, I felt they were persistent, and I started showing physical signs. I was getting a fungal infection and stuff like that, so I knew it couldn't be spiritual."

I said, "Is this originally or just recently?"

Harriet said, "No, this is recently, this was when I started coming off it, and when I started seeing physical symptoms, then I started to worry because you told me that spirit couldn't give you physical symptoms. I looked into it a bit more, and it said about Cymbalta withdrawal syndrome and how it can give you yeast infections. How it can do this and that, it's horrible coming off it. It's addictive, your brain can't manage without it, and it can give you all sorts of symptoms, that's when I started to panic a bit."

I said, "It's a mind-altering drug, isn't it?"

Harriet said, "Yeah and it's like poison to the body. I thought, oh my god, maybe the spirit guides were right. I remember you saying about coming off it because it just seemed horrible what people are going through on it. I started a diet, I fasted, and I'm detoxing my body because that will get it out of my system faster. I didn't eat for three days, but I was drinking water. I started feeling worse, but I thought that was because I was detoxing. I started to get more symptoms like bloated abdomen and pains. They were physical pains, and the doctor was pressing on my stomach, and I could feel pain, and I thought, oh god, it's definitely not spirit. It must be something more. I had to go to casualty because I was in pain, I was uncomfortable, and I was fragile. It was hard because I didn't know if it was due to the diet I was on or due to the Cymbalta. It could have been both at the same time. It was getting so confusing, so I thought I might as well go to the doctors and get checked out, and the doctor said to go to casualty if it doesn't get better. She thought it might be my appendix. I thought I would be in more pain if it were, but I didn't want to exaggerate and think it was worse. I knew if I did that, the spirits would have a field day. It was so hard not to think of the worst and to try and keep calm through it. I went to the hospital and had all the checks, which took about six hours. They gave me painkillers and anti-nausea medication and fluids, but they couldn't find anything wrong with me. I got angry and stressed out at the same time, and I thought if there's nothing wrong with me, then why am I getting these symptoms, physical symptoms."

I said, "Spirit can give you physical symptoms."

Harriet said, "They can?"

I said, "They can give you pains, can't they? Don't you remember we talked about this? You said you had a yeast infection; they can't give you an infection, but they can give you the pain that you would get from an infection."

Harriet said, "Right, OK."

I said, "If you have an infection, that's something else, and that's physical. If you're getting just pains and no reason for them, that can be spiritual. So, from what I understand, you've come off these now for about a week?"

Harriet said, "It'll be a week in two more days."

I said, "Do you remember when you first went on them, and they probably told you it would take a few weeks for them to get into your system, didn't they?"

Harriet said, "They did, yes."

I said, "Conversely, when you're coming off them, it's going to take a few weeks to get them out of your system. If you think of it like that, the longer you go without retaking them, the easier it's going to get. If you've got some kind of infection, then you need to see the doctor. That make sense?"

Harriet said, "Yes, I'm just curious, since I came off the Cymbalta is it possible to know if it was made worse by mental and physical symptoms apart from the fungal stuff I can see?"

I said, "Mental is not physical."

Harriet said, "Sorry, I meant focus and concentration, has it affected it in any way?"

I said, "It shouldn't have done when you're focusing or concentrating; that's a mental thing, not a physical thing. So, if you've got a physical problem, that's what it is, if you have a rash on your hand that's physical, spirit can't make that happen, but they can give you an itch that you scratch which can then develop into a rash."

Harriet said, "I see."

I said, "Basically, if there's nothing wrong with your hand and it starts itching, you'll scratch it. If it irritates you a lot, you scratch it more, that will create the blemish on the skin which could, depending on how irritating, become a sore or even bleed. Therefore, spirit can cause physical effects, but they will need your help by scratching the itch to produce the end result. But if you have a persistent itch, you'll do something about it long before that. Going back to my question, have the voices faded at all, are you in control of the voices?"

Harriet said hesitantly, "Yes, I think so, it's kind of hard, yes and no. I say yes because I've been more focused on just dealing with all this stuff that's been happening these last few weeks. I'm not noticing them much at all.

I still hear them, but it's not interfering as much as it was. Because I'm too focused on dealing with this and everything else, I didn't even think about them. I still get them, and they still annoy me, but I think it's because I'm sticking up for myself a bit more and ignoring it and just getting on with it. I decided I've got more important things to think about than them."

I said, "That's part of the process to get you occupied, so you're not sitting around thinking all the time, and while you're distracted, of course, it's more difficult for them to get in your head. Do you still have fears of the time when you don't have any interference?"

Harriet said, "I do, I feel like it's quieter sometimes, like I'm thinking oh my god it's peaceful when I'm lying in bed or just doing nothing. It's just not hearing this constant shouting. I'm getting longer moments when it's quiet."

I said, "So that's progress, isn't it?"

Harriet said, "I think so yeah, it's surprising it's so quiet, and I'm expecting to hear something, I know I shouldn't. I know, I know that's just a thing with me I'm paranoid I think oh my god, it's quiet, something's going to happen. As soon as I think something is going to happen, something does."

I said, "Yes, because what you've done is you've opened up again. What we need to do is when it's quiet, just forget all about it. It's when you get the persistent and constant shouting that you need to remove the spirits."

Harriet said, "OK, I can do that."

I said, "Now, have you tried removing anybody this week?"

Harriet said, "Yes, I have, I think two people, I think I removed."
I said, "And they've gone and not come back?"
Harriet said, "I don't think so, that's the thing, I genuinely believe it, they did go, didn't they?"
I said, "Yes, they did go. Positive thinking."
Harriet said, "This is so hard when you can't see it. You just have to believe, and I really believe I know."
I said, "This is when they talk about faith and trust."
Harriet said, "I'm pleased though they took two people that were annoying me, one during meditation and one out of meditation."
I said, "When you went back into meditation, you had no more interference?"
Harriet said, "No, it was fine."
I said, "That should tell you straight away that they've gone because you're not getting interference anymore, and when you weren't meditating, and you got interference, what did you do?"
Harriet said, "I was just watching TV, do you mean what did I say?"
I said, "Yes, what did you say and do?"
Harriet said, "I brought the candle up like you said, focused on that and said to my guides, 'Can you please remove the one that's shouting the loudest, the one that's distracting me the most right now?" I just said, 'Can you please remove them from me?' I remembered what you said afterward to think of something else and focus on that and just try to change the subject. So, I focused my thoughts on the car and just pictured the car."

I said, "And it went away, did it?"
Harriet said, "Yes, I think it did, yes."
I said, "You've just learned a valuable lesson. You see, one of the problems that you've had and people in your situation have, is that you're so focused on spirit being there, so you're looking for them subconsciously. When you get rid of somebody what's happened in the past is, you're looking to see if they've gone and if you look to see if they've gone, you tune back into them, and you hang on to them. What you've just learned is you can change your focus completely, just forget about them. When I do it, I just dismiss them entirely, and they've gone from my mind and can't come back. You've got some progress going there, and you've been busy doing other things I take it?"
Harriet said, "Yes, definitely."
I said, "You've had no interference while you've been doing that?"
Harriet said, "No, not at all."
I said, "The point is, as you get your life back and you occupy yourself more, there's less opportunity for them to get in. If they do get in when you're watching TV or when you're meditating, you were able to remove them. Now you're getting control of everything. There's always going to be the odd episode where you're sitting quietly, and you get attacked or maybe when you're going to sleep. Gradually that'll stop as well because when they attack, you'll just remove them, alright?"
Harriet said, "OK, yes. So, keep focusing on the candle as well and keep doing that."
I said, "Yes, it's good to keep practising; you saw what

happened a few weeks ago when you weren't meditating as often. It's your backup now; you're working with your guides to remove them when they come and interfere with you. It's when it gets a bit overwhelming that you need to bring your focus in to help you to block them."

I spoke to Harriet's mum, and she was saying how Harriet doesn't always remember, so she listens to our conversation sometimes so she can remind her of what's been said. She says Harriet needs reassuring and that she is getting better but lacks belief in herself and her ability. She says it's always been an issue with Harriet, and she has to keep reinforcing that she's doing OK, and she has to believe in it, and it will happen. "That's where Harriet is a little weak, but she's improving. When we were at the hospital, Harriet had practically no interference at all, and we were there for six hours. So that shows she's making progress. I keep telling her that, but for some reason, Harriet needs to hear it all the time for it to sink in. It's been nearly a year now since she started all of this. She's taking one step forward at a time; she hasn't regressed at all, so she's getting stronger. I have been monitoring Harriet as she has reduced her medication and also her diet, and I think she's done well, not over but well on the way."

Harriet said, "This week I know they're going, and are on their way out, I believe that more now and that other things are affecting me more than spirit. I don't know whether it's well-timed, but it seems like perfect timing for me to be focusing on my health and detoxing and getting better. It's dramatically changed my mind how unimportant the spirits are, and how important it is to focus more on my health and going out and doing more stuff. It's like I needed that to see that I can cope without them."

I said, "It's like them being in the background because your mind is full of other things, and when they come forward, all you need do is remove them. Your life has been focused on interference. But now it's revolving around your life rather than spirit."

Harriet said, "Yeah, this is such a dramatic change, they're not important at all, they're going they're gone. Now I need to get a job, I need to sort the car, I need to get my health in order, I need to do this I need to do that, it's just like normal stresses. Everyday stress which I wanted. It's like I envy other people who don't have the spiritual stuff, I'd rather have the normal stresses of life. This week I realised they're not the main focus any more, it's as though they're gone, now I can do what I want and be happy. It's a subtle change, but it feels good, I know it would stress out most people, but I like the new stresses I get because it's not focused on the spirits anymore. I don't want to be thinking about them anymore."

I said, "That's what normal is, but remember they aren't going to give up that easily. Negative spirit could counter-attack in ways you're not expecting or haven't experienced so far, so be aware."

Harriet said, "It's what I think normal is. I just want to have a normal life, do what I need and get on with it."

I said, "How will you feel when there are no voices at all?"
Harriet said, "When I said there had been more peaceful moments, I started to think, wow, is this how it's going to be? Oh my god, it's scary at first, it was just so quiet I thought, is this what it's normally like. Not having anyone shouting or screaming or random things coming through your head. I have to admit it's like being alone, but hopefully, I'll get used to it but not in a bad way."
I said, "It's not alone so much, it's that you've got space, don't think about it as being alone. I was a bit concerned about your fear of not hearing a voice because you're so used to it. It's habit forming, once you get interference continually, you get used to it, and you expect it. Now we're working the other way you're getting rid of the interference, and you're expecting nothing to be there."
Harriet said, "OK, yes, I realise it's become a habit."
I said, "Well, it's a habit in the sense you've got so used to it happening."
Harriet said, "Yes, definitely, yes."
I said, "Now you're on the other foot where you're saying your expectation is, you're not going to get attacked. But at the same time, you've got the knowledge to deal with it if you do. It's good that you're not focusing on spirit so much because that's what we want, we want you to get it out of your system altogether. Then you can get on with your life and forget about it, that's the plan."
Harriet said, "Yes, I'm just starting to realise it's coming

to an end, it's good, but with me, I worry so much, I get paranoid I feel like it's too good to be true. I know I worry too much, and I need to focus and let it go and not be scared."

I said, "There's nothing to be scared of; change is good change will give you your life back. So, what about when you go to bed at night and go to sleep, do you get a lot of interference then?"

Harriet said, "Yes, I do, but I haven't noticed it much this week because I've been sleeping better. I think because I'm getting the withdrawal symptoms out of my system a bit more, I know I've been sleeping better, so I'm assuming it was that which was causing it. I don't listen; I do try to bring up the candle, but as I was saying, my concentration was a bit off. I don't know. But I don't engage with them or anything, I just ignore it and try to go to sleep and try to think of the candle as much as I can."

I said, "Well, are you using the protection?"

Harriet said, "Oh, when I do the protection, do you mean the bubble?"

I said, "Yes."

Harriet said, "I do it when I meditate, I do the bubble, sometimes the bubble comes around me. I think it's working."

I said, "Don't think so, know, so, believe it."

Harriet said, "Yes, it is working, and I do imagine it at night too. I've just reminded myself yes, I do it at night as well as the morning."

I said, "So you're getting to sleep better without so much interference?"

Harriet said quietly, "At the moment, yes."
I said, "Good, that's progressing as well. Are you having problems thinking of what to do with yourself?"
Harriet said, "What, to keep myself busy? Not really, to be honest, my mind is full of stuff I need to do."
I said, "That's normal."
Harriet shouted happily, "That's normal. I know," laughing happily. "Oh my god, that's normal, that's right. I'm not scared to have quiet moments anymore. I was really terrified, thinking the quieter I get, the more I'm going to hear, and it's harder for me to ignore. I normally have a distraction at first, but now I've learned to be quiet. I went to the library and got a few books to read. I know I can read them and imagine what I want now without any restrictions. It's a kind of peace now when I'm reading."
I said, "Did you look up about the inner voice I told you about?"
Harriet said, "I did, and yes, I'm hearing that a lot more, definitely hearing that so much more now. It's crazy it's like me, I speak a lot of sense to myself, like ignore them do this do that. Telling myself what to do and saying it positively and I'm thinking, yes, you're right I should be doing this, telling me to do certain things like distract myself, do this, plan stuff to do in the future, really positive stuff and I know it's from me. I can definitely tell the difference between me now and spirit. I know they mimic me as well, but I know it's them and ignore it, and my inner voice confirms that."
I said, "When you say your inner voice confirms that, what does it do? When you think there's somebody

there, does it tell you there isn't?"
Harriet said, "Yes."
I said, "That's not your inner voice."
Harriet said, "It's not! No, oh, OK."
I said, "Say to yourself, I, 2, 3."
Harriet said, "1,2,3."
I said, "Not out loud in your head. You hear what that sounds like?"
Harriet said, "Yes."
I said, "That's your inner voice. You see if you get a voice telling you to do something you haven't thought of, that's not you. When you talk to yourself, you'll say something like, I think I'll go and do so-and-so, what do I need to go and do that, and you're saying this inside your head. For instance, you decide to go for a drive; right, I need to put my shoes on. That sort of thing."
Harriet said, "Oh, yes, I know what you mean."
I said, "If you get a random voice or thought saying that's the right thing to do or you're doing the right thing, or don't do that, ignore it because that's not your inner voice. The spirits can be very subtle, bear in mind they're now losing their grip on you. So, they'll fight harder to stay, and they're going to try different tricks. At the moment you're withstanding their attacks, and you're overcoming them. We need you to continue to progress in the same way, so don't accept anything. You ignore any other voice except your own. If you're not sure it's your voice, then ignore that too. As you said earlier, you recognise the difference between you talking inside your head, and someone else, so believe that."

Harriet said, "Yes, I definitely will practise that and just be mindful about that too."
I said, "At the moment, you've got one voice that keeps coming back to you, haven't you, a female voice."
Harriet said, "I'm not sure, I know there's someone still there definitely, but I just do my stuff and get on with it. Sometimes it's hard to tell when to take them away and when not to because I know when they go, and I know someone's jumped in straight away. I feel I'd be saying it all the time to my guides 'take it away, take it away', that's why it's hard to keep asking them to do it all the time."
I said, "Yes, all the while, they're not bothering you ignore them. The female is not as forceful as the others, so I'm not going to remove her at the moment, simply because you can do that when you need to, and better the devil you know than a stranger. The idea is that if I do it for you, you won't build up your strength and ability, whereas if you do it, you'll be more confident in what you do. Don't worry about these individuals; if they get too much of a bother, we can soon deal with them. At the moment, I want to coast along as we are, and allow you to progress yourself, getting rid of the side effects of your medication, which will make life a lot easier. I'm a little bit concerned about the paranoia. Are you paranoid about what people think?"
Harriet said, "What do you mean?"
I said, "Originally, you were worried about going out. You had a bit of anxiety then."
Harriet said, "Oh anxiety yes."
I said, "You said earlier you were a bit anxious last week,

why was it about whether the spirits were still there?"
Harriet said, "No, I know they're going. I'm worried about it happening again; that's the biggest thing."
I said, "How can it happen again, once we've got rid of them, you'll be protecting yourself, and if you become aware of interference, you'll automatically deal with it."
Harriet said, "I truly believe they're going."
I said, "Well, you've had the experience of them being removed, that's a fact, and you can't deny it."
Harriet said, "No, I can't. It's like you said last week, when this is all over, I'm paranoid it's going to happen again."
I said, "Well, don't worry. If I did all the removals you would still be defenceless wouldn't you? We're doing it this way, a bit at a time so you can cope with the space they're leaving behind, which you can then fill with your own thoughts. You're also building up your ability to reject them anyway so that it won't happen again. We just have to get to the end of the road this time. You'll find once you get your life back on track, you'll be so busy thinking about other things there'll be no room in your mind for spirit."
Harriet said, "I'm just scared of letting everyone down; it's like I've worked so hard to get here. I just don't want it to happen again."
I said, "Well, it's not going to, you have to let go, fear breeds fear and they'll use that. Any fear you have will be jumped on and enhanced by them. So have no fear, there's nothing to frighten you. Apart from being normal."
Harriet said, "Yes, OK, so just know it's coming to an

end, OK. I was also a bit worried about coming off my medication, to be honest, because I thought they were helping me deal with my moods. It feels better, I feel fine, but I was so paranoid about it because I thought I was getting extra help with the pills to help me deal with this. And now I'm off them it seems to be going OK so far. I'm just hoping it'll get better."

I said, "It will get better. If you get a headache, you take a pill; it's just a headache. Are you getting on better with your sister now?"

Harriet said, "Yes, a little bit. She's got her own things to deal with, she's training to be a detective, she's got a job and I've got nothing, I can't really do anything."

I said, "You've got determination, ambition and courage and you don't need to compete with your sister. Just be you. If you're happy that's all that matters."

Harriet said, "Yes, thank you. Don't you find it scary for yourself that other people in spirit know you're doing this?"

I said, "No, all people have an energy around them. It depends on what's attracted to them; some are clairvoyant, many are healers, I just do something a little different."

Harriet said, "There's another thing, I have a problem with my guides, I understand they're there to help you when you have problems?"

I said, "No, they're there to guide you."

Harriet said, "Sorry, I meant they're not there to interfere."

I said, "They're looking after you and guiding you in the right direction to find the help you need. Your guides won't do it for you, but they'll help you once you make an effort. When you ask for help in removing someone, they're removed, aren't they? Therefore, your guides are helping. Now, what was your question?"

Harriet said, "I don't know, I know I shouldn't see them as scary, but I kind of do, to be honest."

I said, "What your guides? They're the best friends you've ever had, just because you don't see or feel them doesn't mean they're not there. These are spirits you chose to look after you while you're here, and they'll be with you until you return to the spirit world. There's nothing to be scared of, although it's difficult to understand how they work sometimes."

Harriet said, "It's just scary, I know there's probably no pressure, but it's like you have to do certain things for them to help. I do understand, but I feel there's pressure to do it, and I don't like the pressure side of it."

I said, "They're not pressuring you to do it, but if you want help, you have to ask for it, and how do you ask spirit. If you make an effort to achieve whatever it is, you're showing intent, and your guides will assist you to a satisfactory conclusion all the while you're doing your bit. You'll notice when you make an effort, you've had more success than when you've just given up fighting back. You're working much harder at protecting yourself so, you're getting a lot more help. They know you can't do it all at once, but to help you to build up your ability, they let you learn. I know it's the hard way, but you don't forget. Sometimes when you've run out of steam, they'll take the pressure off to give you a break. You don't need to know your other guides; just know that they're there. We don't want you to get hung up on what your different guides feel like, it's not necessary."

Harriet said, "No, it's kind of the opposite. I just don't want them to show themselves or talk to me in an obvious way. I'd rather they did what they do and help me when I'm in need. I just want to get the idea of spirit out of my head so that I can live an ordinary life. I know the reason they're there, but I'd rather not know about them I just want to get rid of the interference."

I said, "There's one thing I don't think I've asked you, how did all this start?

Harriet said, "I was in Australia on an average day, my fiancée was going to work, and I went to bed, had no spiritual experience before. I was laying there, and suddenly, I couldn't move except for my eyes. I felt as though I was paralysed. I was half asleep and half awake. I could see my bedroom, but it was blurred, and I knew where I was. I looked to my side and saw this tall apparition of a dark skinny figure like a skeleton person, completely black, standing to one side. It looked demonic with long sharp nails and quite frightening. I didn't know what it was, but I felt a pressure on my stomach, there wasn't anything there, but it felt like someone sitting on me getting heavier. Then the apparition appeared in front of me on me, and I was saying to it 'Go away you're not welcome here, leave me alone'. I don't know why that was the first time I'd encountered anything like this. I was apprehensive, of course, and it was making a hand gesture towards my throat. It was reaching towards my throat, and I was adamant in saying go away and leave me alone. Then it stopped in response to that; it went back a bit, then for some crazy reason, it leaned down and kissed me. I saw this as if I was outside my body, it was weird. I was standing in the corner of the room watching it happen as well as feeling it happening to me. I was terrified, it wasn't for long, and it felt real too, I remember thinking what's happening and I really wanted this thing to go. Then it just vanished, and I woke up, and everything was normal again, and I could get out of bed. The weird thing was I saw the door open and close. That scared me because it must have been something more than just me dreaming; it just happened; there was no draught or anything. I knew a little about ghosts before this happened, that's why I said go away you're not welcome here. My gran can see spirits, so it's in the family, but it didn't happen to me.

"When I was young, I thought I saw the fridge magnets move, and in my teenage years, I felt someone in the corner of my bedroom just standing there watching me entirely in black. I used to hide under the covers and slept like that. I was so paranoid, it got so bad I would run into my mum's room and sleep with her. I couldn't stand being in that bedroom; it felt haunted. Then we moved to eastern England, and I was so glad to get out of that house. The new house was quiet to start, and I felt nothing wrong, but sometimes the door would move, and no one was there. I heard people walking, other than that nothing happened until it started when I was in Australia, and everything went downhill from that day, everything was horrible. It just got worse and worse, my partner and I started arguing all the time, it was like there was some rage in the house and anger. I'm usually a bubbly person, but I was completely different. I was shouting, angry, paranoid, scared and things were moving around the house. My engagement ring kept going missing, and this is why I thought it could have been an incubus. I couldn't think what else it could be. When I looked it up, they were talking about spiritual husbands; I thought maybe it was that. I didn't realise it was just human beings. That's when my paranoia started growing that it was demonic and other beings coming into my life. I wasn't in control of myself. I did stupid things like strip naked and ran outside, and I was threatening my partner with a knife. I was a completely different person. That whole house changed everything. When I was outside the house, I was fine. I wasn't doing stupid things only when I was in the house."

I said, "When you finally arrived back in England, were you OK for a while?"

Harriet said, "A few things happened while I was in Australia that I might just mention; first, I had just done a course in spirit keeping, and that's when it got worse because they were playing on them, and I believed it was the spirit keepers. I thought they were good spirits; that's why I started listening to them."

I said, "To be clear, before anything started, you did a course on spirit keeping?"

Harriet said, "Only after I saw that spirit in the bedroom, I didn't do it before that."

I said, "So you opened yourself up to spirit, and that's

when it got worse."

Harriet said, "I believed I had good spirits around me, so I listened to them, and that's when I realised that was the biggest mistake ever."

I said, "There are so many things on the internet that can ruin your life if you don't know what you're doing and all they're after sometimes is your money."

Harriet said, "I thought if spirits do exist, then I thought maybe other things exist too, I was just bewildered."

I said, "Imagination is a wonderful thing. For me, it's straightforward – you're a dead person or you're a live person. I've got a good imagination at the moment. Why should it change when I die? There are those in spirit that manifest things to frighten and control the living, and as you've seen, they do it for fun. That's why you got that tall thin man with the long fingernails."

Harriet said, "Yes, I thought it was a man. Is he still here, or have we removed him?"

I said, "I removed him when I first cleared you right at the beginning. To bring us back up to date at the moment you've got things under control, although there's a couple there. They're not bothering you too much, if they step it up you'll need to remove them. Simply, ask your guides to help you remove them and put them in the custody of their guides, then dismiss any thought of them."

Harriet said, "I feel silly for believing it to be honest, I kind of feel weak, and I don't like seeing myself as weak."

I said, "You shouldn't feel silly for believing it. People can be persuasive, and if you don't know any different, why shouldn't you believe it? You should hear some of the things I hear. Sometimes I wonder where their head is. If things seem too good to be true, then usually they are. What have you got planned for the rest of your day?"

Harriet said, "I'm going to do some research into a new diet, maybe play a few games with my sister Charlotte, then I'll maybe read a bit and do a bit of drawing. I've got a lot of things to keep me busy now. I'm panicking now because I've got so many things to keep me busy. I'm wondering how I didn't notice all this before. It should have been brought to my attention a long time ago about keeping busy, but the spirit stuff got in the way. Now I just push it aside and get on with what I want to do and get healthier and get a job and do whatever."

I said, "That's the thing about all this, first thing spirit do is isolate you, and you have to fight to come back from that isolation and include others in your life. It's hard to do that if you don't know what's happened, which makes it a difficult step to take, especially when you're feeling panic attacks and anxiety. When they talked in your assessment about socialising, they were right in that you need to keep other people around you to interact. But they were wrong in how they were trying to do it because they were forcing you without considering your feelings. They weren't trying to understand why you felt isolated, and they didn't have any idea what caused it, they just wanted you to conform to their programme."

Harriet said, "That's the thing, they didn't sit me down

and talk me through it. Or talk about what I was feeling, what my problems were, or why I wasn't socialising at all. It was just like being pushed to do things I didn't want to do. Until I figured out what was happening in my head, I thought I couldn't socialise too much because I needed to talk to someone who knew what was going on with me. But I didn't get that, so all I could do was go along with it."

I said, "That's in the past now, but we understand it, don't we, is there anything else?"

Harriet said, "No, I think that's about it for now."

I said, "OK, talk again next week."

I said, "Hi, how're things?"

Harriet said, "It's confusing I've felt run-down all week, and I feel like I can't do anything."

I said, "Why would you be run-down? You've been sleeping OK, haven't you?"

Harriet said, "I have been, yes."

I said, "So what makes you run-down? If you're sleeping OK, and you haven't been that busy, this is not you; this is interference making you feel lethargic, you just have to believe in yourself."

Harriet said, "The last thing I want is to go back to how it was."

I said, "An alternative medication is only good if you have a physical problem, and you don't, so it wouldn't work anyway. What you're doing now is working. You're a lot better than you were, and you're off the pills, believe in what you do."

Harriet said, "I'm feeling spirit is constantly attacking

me. Does that mean I have to call on my guides every two seconds to stop them from doing stuff to me?"

I said, "Are you still hearing the voices all the time?"

Harriet said, "Yes, and I do ask my guides to help me take them away, and it goes."

I said, "So that's working OK, are you putting protection up?"

Harriet said, "Yes, I find I'm doing that a lot more recently."

I said, "You only need to do it twice a day."

Harriet said, "Just twice a day?"

I said, "When you wake up in the morning, and when you go to sleep at night if you get attacked. You can use the candle to get control of your mind and ask your guides to remove them. If it's just slightly annoying, then ignore it; just go and do something. The thing is you have self-doubt."

Harriet said, "It's like I'm not sure how much pain they can give, I believe they can, but it's hard to explain, I don't want to believe they have so much control. It's as though if I can't sort it out myself, I don't want to believe it. It's kind of weird, the fact they can hurt me and do certain things like that to me, so I can't avoid the situation, because I can't deal with it. After all, I don't know what to do."

I said, "You are dealing with it, and you do know what you're doing; you just need more confidence. You're removing the spirits as well as defending yourself each time you ignore them or block them. As far as the pain is concerned, yes, they can give you nasty pains that you think are yours, and the pain can feel real, and you'll suffer. It can make you think there's something drastically wrong when there's nothing wrong. Consider this, if somebody in spirit passed away in an accident, and they had a massive trauma to the head, initially, they'll still feel that pain. If they come close to you, then you'll feel it depending on how sensitive you are. Because you're particularly sensitive, everything is category ten rather than category one. You need to slow yourself down when you get this sort of thing, breathe slowly and keep yourself calm. Then think to yourself, did this come on suddenly, yes or no; if no, then maybe you've got something wrong; if yes, then it's spiritual, providing you haven't just done something to cause the pain you're feeling. Either way, deny it, throw it out; just tell yourself this pain is not mine. If it's a headache, for instance, and it doesn't go away, take a painkiller, then you've got it covered, and forget about it."

Harriet said, "When I do get the pain can I say 'Guides, can you take the pain away if it's not mine or don't believe it's mine, please take it away'? I don't know how to word it, what should I do."

I said, "Just say 'This is not my pain, go away' If it doesn't go away then you ask your guides to help you remove this interference. What you're doing is telling spirit that you know it's them, there's then no point in them continuing. By being positive, you're letting negative spirit and your guides know that you're aware of what's going on."

Harriet said, "I also noticed removing certain spirits; they do go, which is great. I don't know how to phrase it, sometimes I don't know the gender, and I don't want

to be asking them and getting into a conversation."
I said, "The gender doesn't matter; all that matters is, 'Can you help me remove this person that's causing this problem and place them in the custody of their guides?' Then dismiss them from your mind and move on."
Harriet said, "I knew they would make use of my withdrawal, but I didn't think they would go that far. I didn't think it would be so bad that I would have to go to A&E, it was horrible."
I said, "Knowledge is power, now that you know how far they'll go, you can deal with it."
Harriet said, "Yes, and they've been trying really hard to grab me back into their control. I have been noticing now everything they've been doing; it's silly things like Archangel Michael is telling me, and I know he's not involved in this at all. They keep bringing that in and also get a necklace for protection. I'm like, why would I need that if I just think about it logically, why would I need a necklace. It'll take the focus away from the candle, and what you've been teaching me, so I knew it was wrong."
I said, "When you get stuff like that, just tell them to go away."
Harriet said, "It's so annoying, they think I'm so stupid and expect me to believe that again. I just want it to stop. I can't wait till this is all over."
I said, "Be patient, know that there's a process to go through, and we're making progress. You've made an awful lot of progress."
Harriet said, "Really?"
I said, "Well, of course you have, you now understand

what's happening and why it's happening, you know you can deal with it and stop it, you're not getting things as badly as before. When you do get it, it's more severe, and the harsher it is, the more obvious it is, the easier it is to decide and deal with. It's only since August that we've been doing this, and I did tell you it could take a year or two, but it's not going to take that long in your case. Just keep yourself busy doing what you want to do, if you want to go for a drive then go."

Harriet said, "That's another thing, they've been trying to put me off driving."

I said, "Of course they will, that's your escape, your road to freedom. I know it's been a stressful week you've had your high points and your low points. We need to get more high points than low points, and we will."

Harriet said, "I notice when I'm driving or working, trying to do the candle at the same time as calling my guides is really difficult."

I said, "Yes, the idea of the candle is to exclude everything else from your mind but the candle. You can't do that when you're driving or working because you have to be aware of what's going on around you. So, transfer the power of the candle to your protection you put around you in the morning. That will keep you safe if you believe in it."

Harriet said, "I definitely believe in the protection and the protection I do. It's just that this week has been particularly hard. I knew it would be hard because of a few things. I'm still recovering from this chest infection, and I feel it's making me vulnerable to them constantly attacking me. It got to the point when I was at work, I found they were just shouting to stop me from concentrating. It felt more noticeable. I don't know whether it was because I was feeling a bit weak, and I couldn't fight them all the time, and they knew that so they were just pushing my buttons."

I said, "They're trying to wear you down."

Harriet said, "Yes and I can't be talking to the customers and thinking of the candle as well as shutting them out and calling my guides all at the same time. It was so difficult, I wanted to get it right."

I said, "You have to accept the candle has brought you this far; you know you can control your mind with the candle now. You can control your mind by dismissing the spirits because they can't get in through your protection. I did say we would need to transfer the candle at some stage. If you ask for and put protection around you in the mornings, try to forget all about spirit for the rest of the day as best you can. And put protection around yourself before you go to sleep, the protection will do what the candle does, only you won't have to concentrate on it. It'll be more in a subconscious way than a conscious way. You must believe in your protection, and it'll protect you."

Harriet said, "I don't ask my guides to protect me when I do the protection, I just do it. Is that OK, because I'm just finding every day, I'm asking my guides five times or more to remove spirits."

I said, "That's fine, but you're focusing too much on spirit now, you need to focus more on the physical than the spiritual."

Harriet said, "I knew that was the case because I was

feeling ill, but I didn't want to stay indoors and focus on spirit. I don't want to be thinking about it, so I went to work trying to shut them out. I was on the computer and I was trying to read what I needed to do because I was doing a course online. Even during the quiet times, I couldn't read at the same time because of the interference. I just couldn't focus I'm trying so hard to ignore them. I tried loads of things to try to ignore them and not think of spirit at all. What they're trying to do is ask me questions and pretend to be me, and I think it's me, and I answer my own questions, thinking it's just me thinking. It's so hard trying to trick them and avoid what they're trying to do."

I said, "So you're getting frustrated, a bit upset, and you're getting annoyed. First, we need to deal with those, and to deal with those we need to count to ten and breathe slowly. Know that you're winning. Spirit wouldn't be trying so hard if you weren't winning. Now you've had in the past periods of peace, haven't you?"

Harriet said, "Yes, I have."

I said, "So you're improving. You just need to find that peace again."

Harriet said, "It's funny, even though I said it's getting worse, I still have those moments of peace, and I feel like it's so contradictory. It feels like it's a lot worse now, but then I get those moments of peace as well."

I said, "That's because you're getting the highs and the lows; the highs when it's peaceful and the lows when they're attacking you. Gradually what'll happen is that peace will last longer, and the attacks will be less. When you get attacked, just try to ignore them and dismiss spirit from your mind. Focus on what you're doing; if you're driving, focus on driving."

Harriet said, "I'm trying so hard to go out driving and doing all these things and just forget spirit, but they just keep bringing it up all the time, and I can't seem to block it out. Even when I'm driving, I want to focus on driving and what I'm doing today and stuff, but it's constant. It's like they're trying to shift my mind, and I can't control it."

I said, "Remember you've had this going on for so long it's second nature to you, it's almost a habit. We've got to try and break the habit and to think of something else. I know it's difficult, but we will do it."

Harriet said, "It's a good thing too in a way because I'm starting to realise now how much control they had over me. I know I keep saying that, but it just feels each week, it becomes more obvious how much control they had over me. Which is a good feeling too, as I said before, I won't say I wasn't bothered, but I thought I was managing it whatever happens."

I said, "You know impatience is a mood. If spirit can make you impatient, then you get frustrated, and when you get frustrated, you give up or get angry. You need to take a few deep breaths, stay calm and don't react."

Harriet said, "When I'm driving, which is great, I love it. I get dangerous images and visions of me crashing the car. Of course, I know it's spirit, and I try to ignore it, but when I'm trying to get rid of them with the candle and calling on my guides to help, I'm finding it a bit dangerous because I'm focusing so hard."

I said, "That's exactly why we're moving away from the

candle so you can focus on what you're doing. You've got to bring your conscious mind into the physical world away from the spiritual world. The way to do that is to be aware of what you're doing all the time and forget about spirit. I know it's hard, but with practice, you can do this. You want to try the advanced driver's technique which is to have a running commentary of all that you see on the road and pavement as you drive."

Harriet said, "I've tried that and other ways to distract myself, and it helps. Then I remember you said to bring the candle up and ask your guides to take them away, so I'm thinking so hard on it."

I said, "We're changing that now that you have more control."

Harriet said, "I just want to get it right now so I can just get it done."

I said, "Yes, but you need to be patient, keep calm and focus on what you're doing. That means when you're driving, follow the advanced driver's technique because while you're thinking about that, your mind is on your driving and nothing else. When you've tried that over the past week, you've found it's not been so bad, haven't you?"

Harriet said, "No it hasn't, and I did do it this week, I wanted to practise parking, and I thought I would just ignore everything, don't bring the candle up for a bit and just try and focus on driving because that's still a distraction, I thought. So, I went to the car park and started practising parking, and I did great because I was focusing so hard to get it right and not do anything else. It was good because I managed to stay focused on what

I was doing and no voices. Yes, I thought I would just get on with it, but it's just annoying that they give me visions and images, and I can't seem to get rid of them."

I said, "You will, just stay positive, look at what you've achieved so far."

Harriet said, "Instead of the candle method, are we just going to do the protection in the morning and at night?"

I said, "Yes, only do the candle now if you're sitting down and meditating or if you get so much trouble and you're overwhelmed just make sure you're not driving when you focus on the candle to block. While you're doing that, ask your guides to help remove them."

Harriet said, "I try to think of the candle when I'm sitting down meditating, but I don't know whether I can just think of one in my head."

I said, "Of course, you don't have to have a candle in front of you."

Harriet said, "So the only time I bring up the candle is when I'm sitting down safely. So even during the day when they're really pushing everything, I can bring up the candle and the guides as long as I'm not doing anything."

I said, "You can do that, but why don't you just reaffirm your protection? If you imagine the centre of your body, there's a peaceful place where all your energy is. Then you expand the protection until it surrounds your body, and as you do, you push all the negative energy out of your aura. Then ask your guides to maintain it and forget about it knowing that it's doing its job. The idea is to dismiss the spirits from your mind. To do that, you need to dismiss the thought of them. It's not important what you say as long as you make the request."

Harriet said, "So, only think of the candle when I'm meditating, and when I do get interference during the day, just think of the protection around me."

I said, "Have you got someone in particular annoying you at the moment?"

Harriet said, "It's hard to say because it feels like there's always someone there, to be honest."

I said, "Yes, there is always going to be someone there at the moment, but there's nobody that stands out is there?"

Harriet said, "You're right, I noticed that too. That's funny because that's one of my questions. I was going to say it doesn't feel as organised as it did."

I said, "No, because we've taken away the boss, haven't, we?"

Harriet said, "Yes, it feels like they're shouting and pushing and shoving to get my attention. It feels like now they know I know the truth. It feels like the battle is getting harder, and they're trying to put more fear into it now. They seem to be trying to emphasise that fear."

I said, "The important thing is there is no particular individual in control, so you've moved forward, and your protection is stopping anyone else coming in for the moment."

Harriet said, "I thought, it doesn't feel organised, just people pushing and shouting randomly. It feels like more voices now, and I notice there are more women's voices."

I said, "OK, we have a lot of lost souls asking for help, so we're going to ask your guides to remove all those that want help and take them to spirit world. I'm going to let you ask your guides to do that."

Harriet said, "OK."

Harriet closed her eyes and silently asked her guides to take them to the spirit world.

I said, "Now, the chatter should subside, and you'll feel peaceful."

Harriet said after taking a moment to check, "Peace, it's all gone quiet. Another thing, some of them were shouting at me just to get attention. It was like spirit were using it as an excuse to get my attention to get my guides to take them away, and I thought, why was I thinking that?"

I said, "Because that's what was happening. We're going to ask your guides to set up a way-station so those looking for help go there, and they can take them to where they need to go rather than keep disturbing you."

Harriet asked her guides to do that.

I said, "What did you hear?"

Harriet said, "Very peaceful and quiet."

I said, "Well, that's what we want isn't it? Now you've got to learn to forget about it. What are you doing, looking to see if there's anyone there?"

Harriet said, "Oh, sorry it's so weird, it feels so foreign. So, not to think about it, that's cool, but I'll still do the protection just in case."

I said, "Of course, most mediums do that every day."

Harriet said, "You know I said they seem to influence my dreams, or I feel like they do. It's hard to tell, of

course."
I said, "They do definitely."
Harriet said, "What me in particular or everybody?"
I said, "Everybody, you see, it's your subconscious working, and they can implant pictures and thoughts into your subconscious, and it comes out in a dream. Normally what happens is your subconscious puts into order what's happened during the day and files it away so that you can remember. But sometimes you get dreams where you're doing something, that dream might start with a memory of your own, but spirit can twist it. It's like if you have a meditation and your meditation takes you to a garden, the garden that you take yourself to is a garden you chose. If, after a couple of minutes, that garden changes into something else, it means spirit has influenced your imagination, and they've taken control. If that's the case, then you must always bring yourself back and open your eyes, because you're no longer in control of the meditation. It's the same for dreams. Only you can't always bring yourself out of a dream. But when you wake up, just tell yourself it's just a dream, turn over and go back to sleep. If the dream bothers you, then they've got you where they want you. There's no point giving you bad dreams if you're taking no notice. It's the same if you get a pain, you say take it away, I know it's not mine, there's no point giving you the pain because they know that you know it's not yours. So, what have you been doing this week?"
Harriet said, "Just going to the Red Cross. Oh, I went to the library because I wanted to start reading again, but

I can't read any fantasy stuff, can I?"
I said, "You can read whatever you like; why is it a problem?"
Harriet said, "Because you know when I said about spirit keeping? That's part of it because that's fanciful, it's not real. I thought if I start reading books based on that, then they're just going to play on it again as they did in the past."
I said, "Are you talking about spiritual books?"
Harriet said, "No, not them, just fiction and fantasy, that sort of thing."
I said, "Yes, that's just like a dream, isn't it? You read it, and it's their story, follow the story, and at the end, it's just a story. Just a dream, just a story, same category, but it's a distraction."
Harriet said, "I thought about getting a book that's good to practise my quality time. It annoyed me at work, and I was reading the computer online and just kept getting bombarded with things just talking to me and shouting, I couldn't focus on the questions, and I thought maybe reading might help build up the resistance, I don't know."
I said, "Try it. When you're reading your mind gets into the story, and you follow the characters, and that's a distraction which is a good thing because you're controlling what's going into your mind. I'm not quite sure what you're worried about if you go into the story and follow the storyline."
Harriet said, "Oh, I see what you mean. I imagine a lot of things, and because I had a lot of creatures and stuff visit me before which are human, I'm worried they

might play on that again."

I said, "You're worried they're going to play with your imagination?"

Harriet said, "Yes, definitely, yes."

I said, "Let's just say, for instance, you imagine that you're walking down a road and two people are coming towards you. That scenario can change in an instant. They could be two people you know, so you have a friendly meeting and conversation, or it could be two total strangers who walk straight past you. Or it could be two people who are still strangers, but they accost you for money or something or try to mug you. All those scenarios are possible, it depends on what the storyline is, you follow the storyline, and when you're not reading, you just dismiss it, because it's not real, it's fiction. Are you worried about spirit bringing that up in your imagination?"

Harriet said, "Yes, definitely."

I said, "If they're bringing that up in your imagination, just dismiss it, it's just a book. Just say out loud 'It's just a book; it's not real'. What you're doing is talking to spirit and saying I know exactly what you're doing, go away and stop wasting my time."

Harriet said, "I'm so scared of going back to what I used to be like, that I'm avoiding stuff I like."

I said, "In this way, you're talking generally. You're not talking to an individual. You were talking to an individual before, weren't you? You're not picking anybody out. You're talking to everyone who is listening. You're saying to your guides, negative spirit, loved ones and lost souls. I know what's going on, don't mess me around. When you do that, all those negative spirits around you think there's no point as she knows what we're doing. For instance, when you trotted off to the hospital, you were confused, being negative, and you were unsure. You need to be sure. The way I put it is if you're wrong, be confidently wrong. If you're feeling depressed and you say 'Right, I know you're trying to mess my moods about so go away', if it's you, it'll lift you, if it's them, then there's no point in continuing."

Harriet said, "It'll lift me?"

I said, "It'll make you feel better and lift the depression a bit because you're positive. If its spirit doing it, then you've caught them out and it'll stop. So be positive and trust your instinct."

Harriet said, "I was getting frustrated this week about the fact they're still here. I was calling them on the crap they were giving me, so I understand. I get a bit confused too. It's so hard not to feel like I'm engaging with them when they're always there."

I said, "If you're saying something out loud for everyone's benefit, it's also for your benefit, but you're not engaging with an individual. You're not attracting; you're rebuffing them."

Harriet said, "I'm not speaking to anyone in particular, I'm speaking to all of them. I just don't want to be focusing on one person as though they're important."

I said, "No, you don't; you don't care about them; they're not important enough; they're just an irritant."

Harriet said, "I realise that a lot now, I'm just doing what I want now as much as I can when I'm not ill. It's like I

want them to listen to know that I know now as well."
I said, "That's the point you're trying to get across that you're not the mug they thought you were, and you're not such an easy target now. Because of the knowledge you've gained, if you need to, you can deal with them, look at how you've just got rid of all those people shouting in the background. Last week I cleared you because you were having so many problems, but I don't normally clear you, I let you do that yourself, because I want you to build up your strength and ability and your confidence. And you can only do that by doing it. You've come a long way because you don't get the individuals shouting and yelling at you anymore, do you?"
Harriet said, "No, I don't. I just get the odd shout from different people."
I said, "So you know the one in charge has gone, and now that we've helped those asking for help, it should be quiet for a while. What's likely to happen is someone's going to try and take charge. When that happens, you just remove the spirit and place them in the custody of their guides."
Harriet said, "While I do that, should I think of the candle at the same time?"
I said, "No, just ask, and picture them going away, then dismiss them. By dismissing them, you're taking them out of your mind, and you've dismissed the spirit from your consciousness. They don't exist anymore, that's what you should have in mind whenever you dismiss them."
Harriet said, "It could be just me, but I feel like some of them now they know I realise what's going on, are

giving up and saying they're going. I could be wrong."
I said, "You're not wrong, but remember it could be a trick. Why would they let you know they're going? They don't care about you. Don't acknowledge any thoughts or voices; just ignore them. From what you said earlier, you haven't been as busy as in the previous weeks."
Harriet said, "I've been more distracted because I've been doing other things, yes, you're right; I was doing more last week."
I said, "I know it's a pain, but you need to keep yourself busy."
Harriet said, "That's what I thought too."
I said, "We just need for you to keep your mind occupied. If you're occupying it, they can't. So, by following the storyline, you're controlling your mind thinking about the story, and thinking what's going to happen next. Don't have any fear about reading books, but don't read spiritual books."
Harriet said, "No, in fact, I gave them all away this week, I didn't want the constant reminder of seeing them on the shelf, and I've got rid of my crystals and everything to do with spirit. The only thing I didn't get rid of was the religious stuff because of mum, that's her stuff, that doesn't affect me. I'm looking for a job, which is getting me out more. I've got an appointment at 12 o'clock today. I'm going to see someone about employment, and I'm looking forward to seeing what's about."
I said, "That's great; are you going to an agent?"
Harriet said, "Yes, I don't know what I want to do, and they said they'd help. Funnily enough, they're people who helped me when I came out of the mental

institute. They're there to help when you're ready to start work."

I said, "That's another step forward, you'll take a step back occasionally, though, but that's good because going over old ground just strengthens and reinforces things."

Harriet said, "Like remembering what happened in the past?"

I said, "Yes, if you get attacked again as you did before, you'll remember how you dealt with it, that reinforces your confidence in your ability to resolve it. The attacks will become fewer as you're more able to deal with them until you may just get one occasionally."

Harriet said, "That's what I was going to ask you. I'm confused, I don't know where I'm going with this. Is it going to be that I wake up one morning and nothing, or is it going to be that I walk through life putting the method in motion and pushing the interference aside? I just don't know."

I said, "Where it's taking you now is, you'll get a bit of peace and a bit of interference; at the moment there's not as much peace. Gradually there'll be more peace than interference. In the sense that you had trouble finding peace to start with, you'll find it easier to find peace, and because you have control, you'll get little or no interference. As I said, it won't happen all at once; it'll gradually build up. At the moment it's about half and half, isn't it?"

Harriet said, "Yes, it's hard to explain. I do get bad weeks, but I learn from them."

I said, "Of course you do, you don't learn from the good

weeks, but you can see your progress."
Harriet said, "Good because I've got a life to live, I need to find a job. I need to sort my car out I need to do things."
I said, "While you're doing all this, they're not in your head, are they?"
Harriet said, "No, I've got a calendar now, so I don't forget what I've got to do. I've got things to buy for the car, and it's good to worry about new things instead of old things. I feel I'm starting to move on a bit now. I want to ask you one more thing, you know the tablets I'm off, have you noticed any difference since I came off them?"
I said, "It's going to be difficult for me to notice the difference in an hour once a week, but if you want to ask that question of your mum, she'll be able to answer you better as she's been monitoring you. What about diet?"
Harriet said, "I've stopped doing it for the moment. Mum said I have to change my eating habits for a long-term solution. I'm laughing more about the way they're doing things now. I know their methods, and I'm thinking, not that old chestnut again. I'm not falling for it. That's new this week."
I said, "That's good because you're not fearful anymore, but don't challenge them to do better."
Harriet said, "No, I'm not engaging with them. I nipped that in the bud because I don't want to communicate with them. I thought that's just stupid, think of something else. It's tiring; it just feels like I'm fighting all the time."

I said, "That's what life's about – fighting to do this to get that to survive."

Harriet said, "I didn't want to admit this, but I hate that it's happening. I notice when I get the quiet moments, I'm so paranoid I'm going to hear someone say something abusive to me, that I automatically say it. That's what I'm worried about. I didn't want them to affect me in that way."

I said, "You mean you didn't want to have that expectation. Accept the fact that you've got the peace and enjoy it rather than worry about it. By you looking to see if anyone is going to disturb your peace, you're inviting someone to do just that; subconsciously you're looking for trouble. You need to accept that the spirits have gone. That's why it will take a while because you have to tip over into acceptance, rather than the fear they're still there."

Harriet said, "It's like you're saying they've left an imprint that I can't get rid of."

I said, "Yes, but the imprint is getting fainter, you can program your mind to do whatever you want it to do. You need to believe things are getting better because they are, you've only got to look back over recent months."

Harriet said, "If I take anything from this, it's think of the candle when I'm meditating, and use protection in the morning and night. Should it be a specific colour?"

I said, "Whatever you feel is nice for you. Another thing that you need to take away from this is when you're driving, keep your mind occupied with what you're doing by doing the advanced driving technique."

Harriet said, "Even when I do have the moments when the voices are very distracting, I just imagine anything like there's more energy, so it covers me and just ask for more protection?"
I said, "You can ask your guides to help you with the protection and help you remove those that are being a problem and put them in the custody of their guides. You know what to say."
Harriet said, "I know, I so want this over. Sometimes it's like I don't trust my guides at all. I do, and I know they're the good guys, and I know they're my friends. I thought I couldn't trust them or rely on them to let that happen."
I said, "You've had the experience, but you're still alive, aren't you? We have these experiences for a reason. It may not be clear to either of us at the moment why, but there'll come a day when you'll understand. I know it's difficult to trust someone you can't see, but you've experienced the effects of their help. Though you think things are nasty, they could be worse if they weren't there. You could have been possessed, meaning you would have no control over your body or your mind. Just remember your guides work together for your benefit, whereas the negative spirits don't, so your guides will always win. The weak link is us, so it's up to us to hold our end up."
Harriet said, "I think the new method of the light thing is so much better in the long term. I had difficulty focusing on the candle this week."
I said, "That'd be because you've had so much on your mind. You've been practising, haven't you?"

Harriet said, "Yes, I try so hard to focus, but my mind keeps racing through; it's not even spirits, it's me."
I said, "You need to slow down. Don't get frustrated with yourself. Just stop and start again, then you're exercising control."
Harriet said, "I've been rewinding the music and doing it again and again."
I said, "Try different music, just nice calm stuff, OK? Anything else?"
Harriet said, "That's all for now, except I'm a bit worried about the Cymbalta withdrawal symptoms. I want to keep going without it. I really don't want to go back on it."
I said, "You're nearly out of that now. I think you seem OK but just check with your mum if you're worried. But you don't need to, you haven't seen any difference have you.? You've got no noise at the moment, have you?"
Harriet said, "No, it's pretty peaceful."
I said, "Then, I'll leave you with your peace."

MARCH 2020

Harriet wrote, "I'm having a bit of trouble at the moment. The voices and attacks seem to be a lot more, than usual. I'm placing the methods you mentioned, like the candle, including the meditation. Also, the added protection, by imagining the ball of energy starting from within and completely covering me. Doing these methods is OK. I'm able to put them into place a lot better, but it seems I'm just being bombarded daily with constant attacks! And I'm not sure why it's hitting me so hard recently. Ever since the way-point was set up, it just seems to have gotten harder to handle.

"I'm still keeping as busy as I can while still ill, but it doesn't seem to be making a dent. I feel I'm always asking my guides to remove each so-and-so, and just finding it hard to recover, without some other 'idiot' jumping in afterward. I'm surrounded by spirit, who're continually attacking all at the same time. I'm not removing a specific individual, more like one or 2+ at a time, it seems, because it feels quicker to do that than one at a time, and I'm not sure if that's right. I'm trying so hard to distract myself, plan for the future and focus on everything but spirit, but because the voices and attacks are so frequent and so loud, it seems worse than before. I'm not sure why this is happening. I feel like spirit is just wandering in and just attacking me, and there's no barrier protecting me. It's at the point I need to figure out what's going on and why it's affecting me so severely. I can't even talk to people without this happening now. I had this before, but again it seems worse: loud chatter, emotions, feeling ill, visionary tactics, images, thoughts all attacking me at once, and it's overwhelming. I can barely think now. I thought It was terrible before, but It seems extremely distracting now, like a shift change. Instead of one person, it's multiple people all attacking me at once. Which shows no one is in charge. Different ways and different techniques but all at the same time!

"I hate to vent, but I'm not a medium or a miracle worker! There's only so much I can do! If I'm placing all the methods, including meditation, what else can I do? I feel useless like I have to deal with this, and it's hugely upsetting because I can't simply walk away. I'm calling my spirit guides. I know they're helping with my request. I'm not saying they aren't, but all their work seems pointless if I'm just getting a few seconds later, someone else jumping in. I'm keeping busy, but nothing seems to be lessening the effects of their attacks. Now getting death threats which have pushed me to ask for help. I just don't know what the spirit guides want me to do. It's frustrating. I'm not aiming my frustration at you, just feeling crappy right now. I got so many things to do, car, life, etc. I can't be dealing with this for too much longer."

I said, "OK, I'll clear you now, just try and relax."

I said, "Hi, how're you since I cleared you?"

Harriet said, "You don't know how much better it felt, like a lot was cleared. I feel so much better. I couldn't believe the difference, it was instant. One minute I'm up to my neck in it, and then it all disappeared."

I said, “It’s been a busy week, hasn’t it?”
Harriet said, “Yes, it’s been horrible.”
I said, “How was work today?”
Harriet said, “It was good, but it was bad at the same time. I was busy, and I was staying focused and getting on with work and just dealing with it. But then I was getting bombarded so heavily again, and I was trying so hard to focus on just doing my work, and I felt like I was struggling. I was calling for help too, and I was trying to remember to focus on the candle as well sometimes. I know you said not to do it except in meditation, but I felt like I was using the candle to block out the images as well. I could put a candle in front of the image. It helps, I don’t know, I just felt I was struggling and I don’t know why.”
I said, “When you wake up, what’s your first thought?”
Harriet said, “In the morning, I don’t know.”
I said, “Do you hear voices when you wake up?”
Harriet said, “Oh yeah, I get ready for the day and focus on what I need to do during the day.”
I said, “Right, so when do you put up your protection?”
Harriet said, “Oh my god, I do forget sometimes. I do it during the day, but I keep forgetting to do it in the morning. I normally do it at night, but I don’t do it in the morning. Ah, that’s what it was.”
I said, “Put up the protection in the morning, then forget all about it until you go to bed at night unless you get heavy stuff, then just reinforce it. Your focus is not entirely on everyday life; it leans heavily towards spirit, doesn’t it?”
Harriet said, “Yes, quite heavily.”

I said, "That's part of the reason you get attacks. When we were talking the other day, you were saying how you're worried about if you get some peace. You're worried that someone in spirit would say something abusive to you."

Harriet said, "Yes, though, I'm trying my best, but it's so hard not to think about it."

I said, "When you have the peace, you're worried about it getting broken, aren't you? So, you're looking to see if anyone is going to come and spoil it for you. You've got to try and enjoy the peace. The more you can convince yourself it's not going to get interfered with, the less it will."

Harriet said, "I'm finding out as well how true it is because they're quite aggressive and trying to talk to me all the time. I get self-conscious about it because I don't want to be talking to them. It's tough to determine whether it's them or me and just trying to ignore it and put up protection as well at the same time. They do all sorts to try and engage me in conversation, and I'm trying so hard not to speak to them, but it feels hard not to. I feel like I do it subconsciously in a way that I don't recognise or just answering back when they're asking questions."

I said, "You don't do it subconsciously. If you do it you do it consciously, it's almost automatic. Someone says something, and you answer without thinking just like everyday life. It's very similar to this, isn't it?"

Harriet said, "Yes, it is."

I said, "The thing is, because you've got so used to it over the last five years, it's become second nature."

Harriet said, "Yes, it is, it feels like someone's standing there talking to me constantly all the time, and I can't shake them off at all."
I said, "What do you do to try and get rid of them?"
Harriet said, "I keep busy. I did a lot of stuff today, and I just call on my guides to remove them."
I said, "When you're keeping busy, did that help?"
Harriet said, "Not today, and I was trying so hard to keep busy, but it's so hard."
I said, "While you were keeping busy, you were also listening to what they were saying, weren't you? Then I suppose it's difficult not to."
Harriet said, "It's so hard not to, but I know what you mean."
I said, "OK, have you got a particular individual there at the moment?"
Harriet said, "Um, maybe a guy, I'm not entirely sure."
I said, "When I cleared you last night, and you felt a difference, was it all clear?"
Harriet said, "Yes, all clear, everyone was gone."
I said, "For how long?"
Harriet said, "Maybe a few hours."
I said, "What did you do when more of them came? In other words, how were you aware of more coming in?"
Harriet said, "I think it was just talking I heard."
I said, "So all of a sudden someone started talking?"
Harriet said, "I think so, yes."
I said, "What were you doing before that? What were you thinking?"
Harriet said, "I was thinking how peaceful it was."
I said, "Were you worried about getting interference?"

Harriet said, "Possibly, yeah."
I said, "There's your invitation. What I would like you to do is when you've got a peaceful time, don't focus on it. Just let it last as long as possible. If it goes and you get interference, will you write down what you're thinking at the time so we can understand what's going on? Now, if you just close your eyes, ask your guides to help you remove these individuals and put them in the custody of their guides (short meditation) and watch them go (silence). Open your eyes. Tell me how you're getting on with your car."
Harriet said, "Yes, good, it's got a chip on the window, and it made me paranoid, I just got so worried about it."
I said, "What, a stone chip?"
Harriet said, "Yes, I thought, oh god, there's so much money going into the car. I booked a service too. I've been driving around a lot more, which is good."
I said, "How did you get on with that appointment last week?"
Harriet said, "Sure Trust is an agency that helps people with mental health problems to find work. They gave me an assessment and seemed quite happy that I was OK, but they didn't have anything that I wanted at the moment. They offer training as well, which is good."
I said, "OK, so you want to be away from that because you don't have mental health problems, do you?"
Harriet said, "That's what I was thinking because she was asking me all these questions."
I said, "If you go to another agency, one where they don't know what's been happening, they're going to treat you as just someone looking for a job."

Harriet said, "I'm on Indeed.com, and that's good. I've been applying for jobs on that. I'm more focusing on finding a job myself to help me move on than having to rely on them. With the mental health thing, it was just an assessment. She wasn't going to bring it up each time I went to an appointment. It was more like if they could offer me anything else for mental health, and I said no, so they're just going to focus on me getting a job. I said I'm fine. I'm not on anything. I'm OK and I don't need any of that help. I just want to find work, and they said 'Yes, that's fine, you don't have to have any of that mental health stuff'."

I said, "As far as I'm concerned, you're normal. Those voices have gone now, haven't they?"

Harriet said, "Yes, it's all quiet."

I said, "You see how easy it is to do it?"

Harriet said, "It is easy."

I said, "But you don't want to be doing that every five minutes, do you?"

Harriet said, "No, definitely not, that's what I was worried about. Am I doing this too much? I don't want to keep calling them all the time."

I said, "What you want to be doing is like we just did, you just cleared yourself, and then we changed the subject. That's what you need to do to put your mind onto something else, and it helps you to dismiss the spirits."

Harriet said, "I've been trying to focus on something else and not think about it. I'm trying so hard to move on now."

I said, "Don't be impatient; just take it one step at a

time. Did you ask your mum if she's noticed any difference now you've come off that Cymbalta?"

Harriet said, "I completely forgot. I'll ask her tonight and see what she says."

I said, "Are you getting angry still?"

Harriet said, "Slightly, but I can manage it a lot better, it doesn't last long and goes quickly. I seem to have that under control. It's so different now, I realise when it comes on, and I nip it in the bud. It just goes straight away. I don't even have to think about it."

I said, "What about your moods?"

Harriet said, "It's hard to tell because I know they put emotions on me all the time."

I said, "Do you feel happy most of the time?"

Harriet said, "I think I am."

I said, "OK, you got your moods under control; then, you don't get depressed very easily, do you?"

Harriet said, "No, I get frustrated but not depressed."

I said, "That's because you want to be doing it right, and you're worrying you're not. Well you are."

Harriet said, "I know this is probably stupid, but the guides said I was a being of the light."

I said, "Yes, you belong to the light."

Harriet said, "I don't know why I just feel they're getting to me a little bit, the voices, I feel useless, like I'm not doing enough."

I said, "This is a slow process, one brick on the wall at a time. Don't be impatient, and don't knock yourself either. You're doing a good job."

Harriet said tearfully, "I just don't want to let anyone down."

I said, "The only person you ever let down will be yourself. If you feel a bit down, just think of how far you've come. You've dealt with the pills and the moods and the anger, you're dealing with the spirits, you're getting a bit more peace. You've got a car, and you're looking for a job, you're keeping yourself busy, and you're getting out more and talking to people. These are all pluses, aren't they?"

Harriet said, "Like when you said they stopped me from going out, they were purposely getting under my skin this morning. I was so close to thinking what's the point, I might just as well go to bed, but I pushed myself to get out and get on the bus, and I felt so much better for it. It felt terrific getting on that bus."

I said, "Why didn't you drive?"

Harriet said, "It's difficult to park, and it's only one-way in town. Hopefully, I can get a job where I can drive more, and hopefully, depending on the hours, I can still work at the Red Cross. I know you said it's a slow process, but I don't know, this week has been eating at me, this whole spirit thing; it's hard to explain."

I said, "Look, they've spent five years working their way into your mind. It's been a gradual process and got gradually worse, hasn't it? So, it's going to be a gradual process and get gradually better. We can't do it too quickly because you won't be able to cope with it. At the moment, you're coping with getting rid of the spirits and having a little bit of peace, but then you feel lost, don't you, because you can't hear the voice."

Harriet said, "OK."

I said, "You're worrying about the voice coming back,

and because you're paranoid about it, you're looking to see if it is. That's an invitation, and sure enough it does."

Harriet said, "Yes, definitely."

I said, "It takes six weeks, they say, to change a habit, and the voice is one small part of a big habit. We can only change one bit at a time. Don't give up on yourself; you're doing fine. To give you an example, I went to clear someone's house of negative spirits. The lady was happy that they were gone. Then her father, who dabbles a bit, went to see if they had gone, and in looking for them, he invited them back. If he'd minded his own business and stayed away, she would have been fine. So, I have to go back and sort it out again. What I'm trying to show is you're not the only one. At least you're starting to believe, and you try, and you know you've got backup if you need it."

Harriet said, "I don't feel it's wrong to ask my guides. I try to prioritise what I need them to do. When I get voices or imagery, I try to do that myself, but when they're shouting and getting in my face, then I ask for help."

I said, "It's when you can't cope; that's when you ask for help. If you can manage, then do so because you're building up your strength."

Harriet said, "I don't want to keep calling them. I want to be able to do it myself."

I said, "That's what we're learning to do. You did it just now, didn't you?"

Harriet said, "I thought that was you."

I said, "No, it was you. I just directed you."

Harriet said, "Oh right, I did say it to myself."

I said, “Have you got any background chatter?”
Harriet said, “No, nothing.”
I said, “OK, so the way-station’s working, isn’t it?”
Harriet said, “Can you explain that to me a bit more?”
I said, “Imagine the way-station’s a gate into the field where you live. Anybody attracted to your light will have to go through the gate first. Your guides are at the gate, they’re the security and help those who are lost. Because your guides deal with their problem, they don’t need to bother you. Does that explain it better?”
Harriet said, “Yes, it does. I’ll explain why in a second, but before that, can I ask if my guides are at the gate? How are the negative spirits getting in?”
I said, “Negative spirits come in through the fence, and your guides don’t stop them because you don’t. Your guides can’t go against your free will; this is what we’re working at, you learning to stop them. When you have that peace, you look to see if anyone is coming in. That’s an invitation, and that’s what you’ve got to learn to stop doing. Your guides know what’s going on, that’s why they help when you ask, they know you’re trying to do it.”
Harriet said, “I know they help because it feels calm, which I notice regardless of how short it is. I still notice it. It’s funny you said about the gate because I keep getting this feeling of seeing a door and I was trying to figure out what was happening, why were the negative ones coming in. It felt like they were coming through another way. I don’t know if the spirits are showing me that or something else. It’s so hard to trust what I get. I don’t want my guides to tell me stuff like that because

I don't want to misinterpret that as negative."
I said, "We've asked them not to, so any thoughts you get like that are not going to be from your guides. That way, you know what you have to deal with."
Harriet said, "You know the waypoint, what was the difference between now and before, because they were helping the lost souls. Now they've got a waypoint does that mean they're strict as to who comes in?"
I said, "No, it means they're still helping the lost souls, but they've moved them away from you, so you don't get the chatter confusing you. They're not helping the negative spirits unless they ask for help, you've got your own battle to fight. They're there to help you; they're not there to do it for you."
Harriet said, "Do your guides help the lost souls too?"
I said, "Everyone's guides do if asked."
Harriet said, "I know this is going to sound bad, but it's not attracting a lot of spirits to me. Is it because of this phenomenon?"
I said, "No more than before, you're just more aware of them."
Harriet said, "Can the spirits go through my memory?"
I said, "Yes, that's how they know what's happened before."
Harriet said, "I ask because I keep getting old memories brought up which they try to use against me. I know better and try to block it out, I just wanted to confirm it so I know I'm doing the right thing."
I said, "Your memory is what makes you, you. It's part of you and you can't change it, it's in the past. Just leave it there and move forward. We've all done things wrong

in the past. That's how we learn; it doesn't matter what you've done as long as you learn not to harm others; it's part of your growth. Just keep doing what you're doing because you're winning."

Harriet said tearfully, "You know what? I feel like I am; they've been pushing so hard this week I must be getting somewhere, definitely."

I said, "That message you sent me yesterday, it was almost as though that was the end for you, but you came through it, didn't you? You always will; sometimes it's a steep learning curve."

Harriet said, "I know this sounds horrible, but I get death threats all the time, and for some reason, it snaps something in me. I'm trying so hard now. It just feels constant. I know when I got on the bus this morning, I felt deep down no spirit influence, that was a good thing, I did a lot of good things this morning."

I said, "You succeeded, then, didn't you? You took control and made a decision. How are you feeling now?"

Harriet said, "Good, splendid, Red Cross tomorrow, I just do four hours and the funny thing now is it's harder. I'm putting into practice going to work and putting the methods in because I know when I'm going to be at work. I'm still possibly going to have the voices, and I'm trying to put into practice how to deal with it. When I'm on the till, I try to act like they're not there, but they're there. It's tough to comprehend how to work it out. I feel in between like acknowledging they're there and just act like they're not there. I'm doing that and practising remembering numbers on the till and chatting to customers longer. Trying to build it up slowly, so I'm putting the techniques in hand like the candle, thinking that my guides are there and making sure I remember what I said to the customers. I'm not listening to the voices I'm listening to the customer."

I said, "OK, it sounds like you've got a plan, well done. Is there anything else?"

Harriet said, "No, that's it for now. Talk Thursday again, OK?"

I said, "OK, bye."

I said, "Hi, is it better or worse after we spoke?"

Harriet said, "Hi, better, much better. I'm noticing the quiet more, which is awesome."

I said, "You're getting more of it?"

Harriet said, "Yes, I feel like I am; definitely, I'm accepting it now, and it feels longer. I started to realise the trigger points you said about when I hear the voices. It's when I question whether I'm experiencing the quiet or if they're being quiet or just doubting myself or what they're saying. I can't hear anything. As soon as I say that, I hear something straight away."

I said, "It's important to recognise what the trigger points are so you can avoid them."

Harriet said, "That's true, I know it's going to be a habit for now, for a while just realising that, but I'm trying so hard not to think about it. It's tough to focus on not hearing them."

I said, "It seems to be working a bit, though, doesn't it?"

Harriet said, "Yes, it does. Meditation has been easier as well, and I'm finding I'm staying more focused on the candle now and realising what's going on. I'm just ignoring it and pushing it straight away and just focusing. Dreams, they're kind of expected, but they're just dreams, but I feel like I'm having a conversation with someone, and I can't stop that. I have to try and push it out of my head as fast as I can or try and get up and do something. It feels peculiar. I don't like the fact that I've been talking to someone and waking up and having them carrying that on and being annoying and angry all the time."

I said, "When you wake up to do your protection that will focus your mind and take it away from the conversation, then you can get on with life and forget about it. Because you know the protection will work. Again, it's all about belief. Have you spoken to your mum yet?"

Harriet said, "About the tablets, yes I did, but I wasn't quite sure what you meant because she did say I was happier since I got off them and less moody. She said there were fewer mood changes."

I said, "Back to normal, then?"

Harriet said, "I suppose, it's hard to remember. I've been on them for so long, it feels like they're out of my system now."

I said, "So what happens is you or spirit now, if you get moody, it's either you or spirit causing it."

Harriet said, "That's true. I'm noticing my thoughts are more predominant than they were before. I'm more talkative in the sense that I thought stuff to the point that my mind's racing because it doesn't calm down a little bit, and I realise that's a change. It's not the slow

pace it was before."
I said, "Now, your mind is occupying itself, isn't it?"
Harriet said, "Yes, definitely, even if I'm just watching TV, it's as though it's blocking out the voices on its own."
I said, "When your mind is racing, you don't get the voices do you?"
Harriet said, "I don't hear them or feel them, no."
I said, "No, and that's normal; you're starting to get it under control now."
Harriet said, "I think so, I mean, I know so. It's a bit scary now because everything I think now is genuinely just me, and that's what's scaring me the most."
I said, "Why's that?"
Harriet said, "I'm so used to hearing negativity, I know it's not me. I knew it was from spirit. But now I know it's from me, it's just my head and my thoughts, and I think, do I think that way?"
I said, "We all have thoughts we don't talk about; they're called private thoughts."
Harriet said, "I'm noticing my flaws a lot more now than I did before."
I said, "If you recognise them you can do something about them, can't you? The thing is you've had false impressions for so long it's difficult to know what's you and what isn't. Now you know what you're dealing with."
Harriet said, "Yes, it's just that I have to deal with all that as well as concentrating on getting my head sorted."
I said, "We all have to do that, welcome to the real world."
Harriet said, "I know, but it doesn't help when I get the

emotions and stuff, they're sending me, it's annoying, I wish I had my own feelings now."
I said, "They're getting less and less, aren't they, so progress in the same way. When you get an emotion, is there a reason for it? If there's no reason, then it's not yours."
Harriet said, "I am getting through, my guides help me a bit when it's all too much, when it's just a little I try to sort it out myself. When it's really annoying me and affecting me, I ask them for help because it can be a bit overwhelming, and it helps a lot."
I said, "You're progressing nicely at the moment, and you're starting to figure things out and deal with them as they come up, which is making life a lot easier for you. You're now in the real world and moving forward. Have you had to get rid of any of them since Monday?"
Harriet said, "A few, yes, and they're gone. When we put the spirits in the custody of their guides, what happens? Do they just talk and go to heaven afterward?"
I said, "Their guides explain what's happened to them and help them to understand by showing them their true pathway. Often the guides will bring a loved one forward to meet them. That usually convinces them. The spirits can't leave until they realise their errors and are ready to go to the spirit world."
Harriet said, "I am noticing the guides' help is more obvious. At first, I had to believe it, but now it's easier to accept that they're helping me. It's showing a lot more because I feel it; I feel protected."
I said, "You don't need to worry about anything, your

protected, but they can only protect you so far; you've got to do the other little bit yourself. That's why when you invite someone in, it'll be allowed. It's when you reject spirit, you'll get assistance."

Harriet said, "I don't know if this is a bad thing or not, but when you said about the fence and them coming in, I started to make a dome to stop that."

I said, "Good for you. Did it stop it?"

Harriet said, "It feels a little less, I wasn't sure if it was a good thing or not, I thought I'd check with you. I didn't want anything aggressive, just a dome with me being inside it and the gate where the guides are."

I said, "That's fine."

Harriet said, "One more thing, you know I said I woke up this morning and I felt like I had a long conversation with someone, I wasn't sure who? It's difficult to trust anything; I started to feel what they were feeling in the sense of the negative spirits and not to be so harsh on them. I tried not to, and I got a sense of where their pain and frustration and hatred is coming from."

I said, "Now, you're starting to sympathise with them, aren't you?"

Harriet said, "Is that a bad thing?"

I said, "Yep, they're not important; they're nothing to you."

Harriet said, "OK."

I said, "You've got to keep it that way, no emotions or thoughts about them at all. Just they're there, they shouldn't be, remove. They'll get the compassion and help they need elsewhere the same as those who're attacking you. They don't care about you, do they?"

Harriet said, "No, but you said not to judge."
I said, "You're not judging. You don't have any opinion at all. The negative spirit shouldn't be there. In a sense, it's a case of you don't care. You care about those who want help, or those suffering and those who're lost. But you don't care about those who invade other people's space."
Harriet said, "So it's OK to be like that? If they're wrong, it's OK to say they're wrong?"
I said, "If you say they're in the wrong, then you're judging, aren't you?"
Harriet said, "Hmm."
I said, "All you do is remove them; you don't think about anything else. Once you've removed the negative spirits, you forget about them and dismiss them. There are plenty of others who will look after them."
Harriet said, "They can go where they want, can't they."
I said, "When you remove them, you get your guides to take them to the safekeeping of their guides; that's why you're putting them in the custody of their guides."
Harriet said, "They have the choice to leave; they're not stuck here."
I said, "No, that's right; they had the choice in the first place not to come here. If you just remove them without putting them in the custody of their guides, they'll attack somebody else. You're protecting other people, defending yourself and helping them."
Harriet said, "Blocking out emotion, the candle, can I block those emotions out with the candle and then concentrate on something else? When I notice I get angry; even if I'm less down I still notice it sometimes. I

also notice they put the fear on me all the time; it's constant."

I said, "That's the problem, isn't it? It's the fear of what they're going to try next and the fear that they're going to be able to do something at all. That's what you're worried about, isn't it? Like for instance, you're worried about what to do if you get an emotion that's not yours; just remove it, it's not yours. A soon as you recognise it, you change your focus, say 'That's not mine, go away' and do it calmly then dismiss it. If you get excited or depressed about it, then they'll have either pushed you down or pushed you up. You need to try and stay level with your emotions."

Harriet said, "When I ask the guides what kind of protection they mean, and I know they mean worse things can happen, I know that's not going to happen. But when it comes to emotions, I'm a bit worried because it feels like I can't block it out, and I just have to deal with it myself."

I said, "Do it yourself. You need to stop worrying about it because that's fear and that will feed them. It's the same as looking to see if anyone's there, it's an invitation, so you have to forget about it and if you're a little bit prissy one day, then so what? You're allowed to have emotions, too, you know."

Harriet said, "I do ignore it. It's just when it comes on out of nowhere, I just feel, oh not again, I just want it to stop now."

I said, "Well, when it comes on out of nowhere, you know it's not yours, don't you?"

Harriet said, "Oh, I know it's definitely them; it's just the fact they can do it."

I said, "You know they can do it, and they will do it anytime they can get through, you've got to counteract it as soon as they do it. You'll notice negative spirit don't do it as often as they did, that's because they can't because you're defending yourself."

Harriet said, "I see, and I know better."

I said, "Yes, and as you get stronger, it will be less and less."

Harriet said, "Oh, of course, it's the same thing with anger. If I get a sudden mood change, I just take a few deep breaths and calm myself."

I said, "What's important is you recognise when it's not yours, so it's harder to fool you, isn't it? You'll be normal in no time at this rate."

Harriet said, "I just want to be normal. It's good, but there are other stresses to deal with now, but it's good stresses, I suppose."

I said, "Yes, that's what life's about."

Harriet said, "I just have to deal with the stress of life as well as the spiritual stuff, it wears you down. I don't need the extra hassle, but I accepted that life was hard, but then I got thrown into another world entirely, and I thought why? I thought I was here to learn earthly things, not spiritual. I know it's all connected, so I'll just have to get on with it."

I said, "All you've got to do is be positive, that's all. When you do things in life sometimes, they go as you've planned and sometimes, they don't. People can get in the way, and sometimes they're argumentative, and sometimes they go along with what you're doing, that's

the way things are. You've just got to go with the flow."
Harriet said, "I was thinking if I had problems with someone and they were threatening, or really bad to me, I would be able to walk away or call the police. I can't do that with spirit because it's always there."
I said, "Ah, but you can, you just need to understand how."
Harriet said, "I can now, yes, but before it felt like I had no help whatsoever with this. I had no idea how to deal with it. I'm starting to understand it now, just realising that it's spirit."
I said, "The enormity of it is that you realise now how much control they had over you, and that can be a little frightening, but they don't have that now."
Harriet said, "That's true; they don't. It's so horrible knowing that someone purposely wants to stay behind and do this. I understand people being lost or hurt, that's a bit different, but when someone purposely wants to get at you and do horrible things to you, that's just awful."
I said, "You have to realise there's evil in this world, what with wars and genocide. The people that perpetrate these atrocities don't become Mr Nice Guy when they get over to the other side. You also get other people that are sort of nice, but not really. When they get over there, they find they can do things and not always get caught. It's only when someone like me comes along and catches them out they get caught and have to pay the price. If you imagine how many people around the world are hearing voices and have interference and don't know what's causing it, there's a

lot of people suffering. It's them we need to concern ourselves about, not the negative spirits. There are millions of people misdiagnosed, through the lack of understanding in this world, and destined to spend their life on drugs or marginalised."

Harriet said tearfully, "I just don't want to fail."

I said, "You're not failing, far from it. Look at what you've achieved up until now, how can you be failing? A large part of my job is education. If I can teach you, the knowledge you get helps you to deal with the situation, so I'm not doing it, you are. I'm just guiding you, and the only time I step in or my guides step in is when you're being overwhelmed.

Harriet said, "Now the guides are maintaining the waypoint, and now that I ask them to help me, that's progress?"

I said, "Yes, because you've set up different departments when you ask for help. You don't ask the guides on the way-point, they've got their job. You have a lot of guides with you, and you've got certain guides that are with you looking after your well-being. They're the ones that when you request help, they'll deal with it. You don't need to think about guarding the gate. They've got their job, you've asked them to do it, they'll do it."

Harriet said, "Because I've put effort into doing all this, now they're doing this?"

I said, "Yes, you've shown them, by your actions, you don't want this interference. The difficulty for spirit is people say, can you do this or that and don't try for themselves. Spirit says if you're not going to bother, why should we? If you work hard, then they're going to be there to help. The other day when we cleared you, you could have cleared yourself, but because you were bombarded, from all sides at once, it was a bit overwhelming. That's why as soon as you're aware of something, you deal with it. That way you keep yourself clear."

Harriet said, "It felt like I was surrounded, and everyone had their technique for bringing me down. Some were going for memory or putting thoughts in my mind, and others were making me feel pain, all at the same time. I just couldn't pinpoint who to take out individually, but I was worried my guides wouldn't take all of them away. I thought they were only allowed to take one at a time and not a group, so I wasn't focusing on asking them to take the whole group."

I said, "It's not your job to decide who to take. You just ask for help to remove those who are causing you problems, and they'll remove them. If you specify who you want help with, then that's all they'll take."

Harriet said, "I thought I had to pinpoint the main ones to get rid of."

I said, "In one sense you do because you've got to try and stop them yourself and control them. Sometimes when the spirits are too strong, your guides will add their strength as required. You don't want to spend all day removing them, so the important thing is that you put protection up in the morning then forget about spirit. It's important to put them out of your mind, and do the same in the evening. At the moment, about fifty per cent of your day is spirit-oriented, and fifty per cent isn't. Gradually you'll get to seventy-five per cent and then finally a hundred per cent, and you won't even think about spirit."

Harriet said, "Yes, I just don't want to think about them at all now."

I said, "It's a slow process because you've got to reprogram your mind, and that's very difficult as you've found out."

Harriet said, "Yes, definitely. Now that they're fading out, I've got new things to focus on, like my thoughts and dealing with the fact it's coming from me now and how to process them."

I said, "It'll take you a while to get used to that. Have you started reading?"

Harriet said, "I've got a book, but I haven't started it yet."

I said, "It's a pleasant way of passing the time. It takes your mind out of everyday life, and you get into the story and a good way to relax, and it also focuses your mind and distracts you."

Harriet said, "It's so annoying, I've got someone saying to read a book, but I don't know who. I don't want to listen to spirit, but I want to read a book."

I said, "Well then, it's your decision if I say don't read a book and you want to, you 'll read it anyway won't you because you're making up your own mind?"

Harriet said, "Yes, I'd be making up my own mind, wouldn't I?"

I said, "Yes, so you had this thought about reading a book, and you're not sure whose thought it is, but you feel comfortable with it, then it's your thought."

Harriet said, "I don't want my guides to communicate and confuse things."
I said, "They'll help the same as they help most people, and that'll be in the background, and you won't know they're there."
Harriet said, "That's what I want. I'm getting paranoid now because I'm thinking I don't want to be hearing loved ones and guides coming through."
I said, "You're not going to. We've already set that up; all we need to do is clear you of what you've got at the moment. What I mean by that is clear you of your hang-ups and your fears and paranoia. Once we've cleared you of that, then you won't even know spirits are there. You don't hear from your loved ones or very much from your guides, do you?"
Harriet said, "No."
I said, "But they're there when you need them, and that's how it should be. There'll come a time when you don't need them because you'll be strong enough to deal with it yourself."
Harriet said, "I know better now I know spirit is going to mimic and pretend to be loved ones and guides. It created another paranoia if they were trying to get through to me. After this is done, and the spirits are all gone, will this happen again?"
I said, "No, it won't, but let's be clear about something, the spirits won't be able to get through because your defences will stop them."
Harriet said, "OK, when I said to you about getting my own thoughts together, and I know the difference between my thoughts and their thoughts., now they're

starting to play on my thoughts, and I'm more open about what I think. I'm training myself to say whatever I want in my own space. Now I ignore their comments because, before anything that I do, I'll get a comment on it. I'm training myself to say and do what I want. If I want to swear, then I'll swear. I can pretty much say what I want now, and it's been working great. But because it's working, they pick at my flaws and criticise everything, but I'm learning to ignore them, and it goes quiet. One of the spirits was talking about Matilda, and I dismissed it. There's no way she can come back, is there?"

I said, "No, everyone who was removed can't come back because you've put them in the custody of their guides, and they won't let them. If you get somebody who sounds similar to someone else, it's because they're mimicking them. They try and undermine your belief and make you think that you can't get rid of them. The idea is that you'll give up because you think it's not working. Now that attack you had the other day where everything came at once, it was to try and get you back on drugs. Because when you were on the medication, you were easier to manipulate. You weren't so resistant. Now that your mind's clear, you know what you want and can resist easier. That make sense?"

Harriet said, "Yes, it does because ever since I came off it, my mind is sharper about everything, and I've been putting logic into place more and thinking smarter. I'm not so laid back about it, and I'm latching on quicker to what they're doing. It's like my brain is changing, and it's such a dramatic change now I'm off the tablets I

noticed that straight away, so wow, so much difference, can't believe it."
I said, "If I'm a negative spirit and you're on drugs, and I'm in your face, you don't take much notice to start with because you're slow on the uptake. While I'm in your face, I'm doing other things with other negative spirits to confuse and harass you. Suddenly, you've got all of that to deal with at once. Whereas if your brain is clear, you can put a stop to it much quicker and stop the others from getting in. Automatically now, you don't even know about it, but you're rejecting attacks."
Harriet said, "Yes, as soon as I feel anything slightly spiritual, I'm putting a barrier up, which stops it straight away."
I said, "It's dramatic, isn't it?"
Harriet said, "It is, it's scary, but it stops it. It's like I've had enough of spirit now."
I said, "That's what you're supposed to do, that's what we're aiming at. We're working at your education and building up your ability to do that till, in the end, nothing will touch you."
Harriet said, "So it was wise to come off the tablets, I was worried at first because I didn't think anything would help with my mood, but it seems to be fine. I just thought I would be more of a target if I were off the tablets, but it's perfectly fine."
I said, "In fact, the reverse is the case, isn't it? You're more of a target when you're on them."
Harriet said, "Yes, I was, so that was all to get me back on medication."
I said, "So you can see how some of those people that

you've seen in the mental institution are having problems because they're on drugs. Of course, some may have an underlying problem and have brain damage or abnormalities in the brain. People can have damaged brains for all sorts of reasons, and some medications can help. Take someone with Parkinson's disease or Alzheimer's, their brain isn't working properly, and medication helps by supplying some of the chemicals needed. But with you and others like you, your medication doesn't help because it's not a brain problem, and that's the difference. It's not the brain; it's the mind. The mind is not physical, so chemicals don't affect it, but they can damage the brain. In recent research, it's been found that antipsychotics and antidepressants can damage the brain, and these are the drugs they use to treat people who hear voices."

Harriet said, "I know I'll get there in the end. It's the constant tricks they're doing are a little irritating, but I can recognise it quickly."

I said, "When they play games, you put a barrier up, don't you?"

Harriet said, "I do."

I said, "You're not getting as much interference when you're driving now."

Harriet said, "No, I think I've got that sorted now. One more thing, the spirits I send away definitely don't come back. But I'm worried about the ones I'm inviting in. I don't know how to stop that, and I'm a bit paranoid about it."

I said, "The ones that are coming in are the ones you're inviting in. What you're doing is when you've got the peace, instead of accepting it you're looking to see who's going to disturb it. When you look, you find. You said earlier you're beginning to accept the peace a bit easier and the more you can accept it, the less you'll be inviting. Don't worry if you make a mistake and invite somebody in. You just remove them. Practice makes perfect."

Harriet said, "That's what I keep saying to myself. Each one I remove is another chance to practise using the candle or the barrier or whatever it needs."

I said, "Don't forget to put your protection up in the mornings and evening. You still forget that, don't you?"

Harriet said, "I do it during the day."

I said, "Make a habit of doing it morning and evening, believe it, and forget until you're due to renew it."

Harriet said, "That's it. I've got no other questions I'm good to go."

I said, "OK, we'll talk next week unless you have major problem. You can deal with most things now."

Harriet said, "OK, see you next week."

I said, "Hi how're you doing?"

Harriet said, "After we talked, everything was OK, and it cleared up a lot of things. I started the day as normal, keeping busy doing my hair as well as watching TV, but the chatter was loud. I was focusing so hard on watching TV and my hair, so I was doing two things but still couldn't shake it off. I tried to block it by doing the driver's technique with the TV, but that didn't seem to be working, so I did the candle on top of watching TV, and I was still getting it so loud, and I was trying so hard to block it out. I called my guides, and they helped, and then it came back again, which I understand, so I thought OK I don't want to keep calling them, so I thought I'll have to try on my own. I watched TV for about an hour and tried the driving technique on the pictures, but I was getting so distracted by the background noise, and I couldn't shake it so, I started to bring up the candle, but I was blocking out the TV. I was doing two things at once that I was blocking out my own distraction; it was so confusing. I didn't know if I was doing it right, and I started to panic. I thought I better tell you if it didn't get any better during the day, then I'll know what to do for the rest of the week."

I said, "You were neutralising your distraction. Have you still got the chatter now?"

Harriet said, "It's pretty quiet now, I still notice the quiet moments, but when I'm distracted by spirit, it's so obvious. I know they purposely do it, and it's like a new irritation now. They're in the background, but they're loud in the background."

I said, "When I sit here with you, and I tell you to close your eyes and ask your guides to remove them, they remove them, don't they?"

Harriet said, "Yes."

I said, "Is that what you do when you're on your own?"

Harriet said, "Yes."

I said, "OK, so when you ask the guides to remove them, you know they've gone, simple as that. So, do it now."

Harriet said, "OK."

I said, "When you've done that, dismiss them. That quieter now?"

Harriet said, "Yes, it's good, and I know they're gone. When I invite the new spirits in it happens straight away, I feel like I don't want to ask them again."
I said, "You've got new ones there already?"
Harriet said, "Yes."
I said, "You've got new spirits because you expected it, you believe they've gone, but you expect new ones to take over, you're defeating yourself. You must learn to accept they're gone and dismiss the very thought of spirit; it's like a swinging door, as some leave others arrive. Your protection is useless if you can't believe it. I know it's difficult, but you've got to believe in yourself and your guides. We'll do it again, and this time, you know, they will be removed, and no others can get in because your protection will block. OK, now dismiss them. Are you going to work today?"
Harriet said, "No my hair takes hours to do so I'm just doing that today and watching TV. It's been raining all day so I thought I'd keep busy with my hair and sorting out my diet."
I said, "The voices have gone now, haven't they?"
Harriet said, "Yes."
I said, "There you are, you see what you didn't do the first time is dismiss them from your mind. Because your mind was on a different subject, it cuts them right out of your thoughts, and they've got nothing to work with."
Harriet said, "I believed they were gone, but I kept imagining the protection first and asking my guides to remove them."
I said, "You don't need to, do that just once in the

morning. If you try to do it too many times, then you'll open up, and you might as well throw the doors to your mind wide open. Just remember, simple is best, protection, and then dismiss all thought of spirit. If you get voices, use the candle and know it's working. If you feel uncomfortable, then ask your guides and then dismiss all thoughts of spirit. The sooner you learn to do that, the easier it will be."

Harriet wrote, "I just wanted to make something clear. I just want to know, when It comes to the spirits, when does the candle method come into play? Right now, my mind seems to be racing extremely fast. I know it's due to Cymbalta. I just need to learn how to switch off and relax, but I'm finding that hard. It's so fast-paced right now, from the adjustment of not being on meds, it's a little hard to think clearly. I know this will take some time to get used to, and from this point, it will just get better. It's just that I don't know when sometimes it's best to use the candle to block them out. For example, when I was doing my hair, I was watching TV. But, for some reason, couldn't fully concentrate. I was trying my best to ignore the voices, but it was still really distracting. Like loud background chatter. I was doing two things and still couldn't focus entirely. I'm not looking for them either, in fact, the complete opposite! So, it was weird. Of course, I asked my guides to help, and they did great! But I felt like during the time I was busy doing my hair and watching TV I was worried that calling them might become too often. So, before I really had to call them, I focused on the candle while watching

TV. But it felt wrong. I'm now seeming to be blocking out my own distraction with another distraction (the candle method) and got confused."
I said, "You're defeating the object by trying to do two things at once. The candle is to focus on and nothing else, so the only thing you have in mind is the candle."

Harriet said, "I have a few questions. I have been finding it hard to figure things out on my own and kind of need some advice. You might have to bear with me on a few things. I'm really sorry if I'm repeating myself, but I have to know a few things, to kind of sort things out, and hearing it from you would help."
I said, "What's been happening?"
Harriet said, "I had this dream last night, which was quite different. I was stressed yesterday, and I had a long talk with mum about a few things. Mainly how to deal with all that was happening – just life, mainly and new things that were happening. I wasn't focusing on having a bad dream, the opposite, more on having a good sleep. So, I went to bed, as usual, having had quite a positive day, even with its hang-ups. Then I got the dream. I haven't had this kind of dream for a long time! So, I thought I might mention it because a lot happened. OK, I was lying in bed, I was clearly in my room, but it felt like I was in 'half awake-half asleep state', and then I got a sudden attack. It felt like I was suffocating, so real, and the fear emotion seems to be rampant. I didn't feel I had complete control of the situation, but I remembered saying 'Go away' and the standard phrase of me saying 'Spirit guides, can you please help me

remove the spirits, and place them in the custody of their spirit guides'. Like I would typically do, when awake. The attack stopped, and I woke up. I got up out of bed, to kind of remove myself from the situation, and I felt the fear emotion, so I asked my guides to remove them, tried to go back to sleep and eventually slept. What do you make of this? I feel like I'm finally making my subconscious aware that I don't want this happening, even if I don't have full control of these dream states, like the other half of me is fighting back now?"

I said, "It appears your instincts are working, and you automatically defended yourself."

Harriet wrote, "Now that I'm off Cymbalta weird things have been happening! My senses are heightened. Which is driving me crazy right now. I feel like my hearing is super sensitive, and can't stand loud noises, so when I get an idiot spirit shouting at me, I really notice now, to the point it's quite distracting, and it makes sense why I couldn't focus. Remember when I said I couldn't focus on the TV? To the point, I was using a distraction with the candle because it was that bad. Before I could do it better, but now I feel like there's way too much background chatter like I'm picking up random people talking a lot more. I'm trying so hard to focus and be distracted, driving, reading, working, watching TV, music, anything, but it seems it's still very distracting, like I can't switch off. Like a crowd of people are in the same room as me talking, or always following me around, while I'm trying to get on with life, that won't shut up. I know that the Cymbalta was masking this from the start, which is why I was afraid to come off it. Because I knew it was dulling my emotions, I didn't realise it was dulling my senses too. I feel like everything is hitting me tenfold now. I realise how much the negative spirits are affecting me, I couldn't see that while on Cymbalta, but now it's obvious. It was masking everything they were doing and a lot more. Knowing this is great, but it raises questions on how to deal with this now, my senses are more alert. I'm struggling with these emotions and feelings that aren't mine, as well as my own feelings. You said something about me being an empath? Is that why this is so hard right now?"

I wrote, "Keep it simple if you focus on the candle, do it to the exclusion of everything else. Don't worry about asking your guides; that's why they're there. As for the dreams, you survived and understood what was happening. The Cymbalta was numbing you down, but now you're in a heightened state, try and stay calm and deal with things without fear or panic. I am going to clear you of everything now, so you get a breathing space. Put up your protection and believe in it. If you get pains, dismiss them, you know they aren't yours. Things will settle, you're doing a great job, trust in what you do and that you're doing it right."

Harriet wrote, "Thank you, I know you have your own things on right now. So, thank you for clearing me today that helped. I wasn't in the best of moods to talk, so I thought it would be best to not talk to you while I was in a foul mood and decided to talk later instead, once I calmed down. Then something interesting happened. I was in the right mood, realising more and more how much the spirits had control over me. I honestly wasn't dealing with that fact very well. I was under the covers trying to recollect my thoughts and think logically. I was pretty distraught. When suddenly I was assaulted by a spirit. It's hard to explain, like it was heavily implied in my head that someone was attacking me physically. I was so angry and annoyed by this because I just genuinely wanted to be alone and just have a good cry, without some negative spirit coming along and taking advantage of the situation. But as soon as I realised it was happening, I placed a barrier, like a bubble around me, imagining spikes on the bubble to push them back with, because I was that angry. I felt I needed to imagine that to get the point across, that I didn't want them there. And it stopped. I knew it was a straight-out attack, and I stopped it with the bubble protection. I calmed down afterward because I knew I needed to relax more. I feel highly stressed right now, and admittedly finding it hard just to relax, calm down and de-stress. But I know this will come with time, it's just exhausting fighting, I feel like I have to fight every day to stay on top of it. It's, of course, worth doing, just tiring.

"There is one thing I wanted to talk about for a long time. My ultimate fear, in a sense; I feel that I need to discuss this. I know this is a foolish question, and I don't know why I'm asking, but I need to get it in my thick head that this is true, Spirits, dead people and dead people alone behind this whole case with me, ever since Australia until now, who have been behind this. Let me explain.

"OK, you see, I need to know for a fact that all this time it's been dead people. I know that sounds stupid, me saying this now, but was told countless lies, was misled, doubts had spread, I spoke to numerous mediums, to people, and I got confused and lost along this path. But if you say this is the case, I will believe a thousand per cent. I just need an expert in this field, someone who knows what they're talking about because I'm blind and can't see what is generally happening/happened around me. I do not doubt you, sorry. If that feels like the case, I'm not, I followed you this far. I believe in you. I just need you to clarify for me one more time about this. It's still hard to believe that these things happen in real life. I just still feel a bit shocked that this is all real, spirit guides exist, and so on. So, I need to know that spirits, dead people (mainly the negative ones) are the cause? They cause fear, hate, anxiety, emotions, voices, thoughts, change appearance, mimic me, create images, visions, create sounds/smells. They go through my memory, drag it all up. I get physical touches, and they move things with energy. I'm guessing I know they can probably do more. Still, I'm sticking to what I think is happening to me or has happened, I should say. I know I'm protected, so I know there's more, just wanted to mention it, me having had this negative spirit case, does not mean it's linked to a bigger higher purpose, other than me learning to block spirit out. They're making a huge deal out of the fact that I'm scared of this having a higher purpose, and putting pressure on me to think that I need to suffer for a higher purpose. They're making me feel like I had to suffer to go through this just to help people, I know it's right to some degree, but they're making such a huge deal out of it! To the point, I feel pressured and scared because it's my destiny rubbish. I'm sick and tired of hearing everything happens for a reason, and I can't avoid it and feel like higher beings are watching me suffer for some experiment. I have no choice but to do it because I choose this, and I can't get over the fact that it's somewhat right. It's hard to stomach because deep down, I know I was meant to do this, and the fear of thinking, people are counting on my success is stressful. I just wish you can, just tell me there's nothing to worry about the whole destiny part and just go with the flow kind of thing. I hate that it feels like things are planned for us, and we're just following it until we die. Like we have little choice of what we do, because higher beings know, planned it, and are watching already. I hate the idea that my life is planned, and I feel like it's just another way of control, and I'm not living for myself. I've been controlled by the bad guys, and I thought I was looked after by the good guys. It feels like suffocating, and I don't want any spirit having control over me ever again. I wish I were just ignorant to the whole spirit stuff so that I could live peacefully without this paranoia. I pray I'm thinking way too hard about this. But it's playing on my mind a lot.

"So, to clarify, me having had these negative spirits does not mean it's linked to a higher purpose, other than I'm just getting rid of spirits, and I'm just learning to block them out. It has nothing to do with my race or my liver, all scare tactics. I'm doing this for a better life. And doing this for myself, not for anyone else. I don't need to sacrifice myself, making me feel like I need to hurt myself for a higher cause. I don't need to do or listen to what they have to say. Because it's all negative, they're negative, even if they act nice. No archangels, no Jesus, no god, no ascended masters, no fantasy being, no guides, telling me I need to die for humankind. Due to my liver, for example. It doesn't involve my liver and dying in the act of racism. My spirit guides would never tell me when my time is up or how I'm going to die. It's not a test; I'm not going to be judged by anyone, I'm merely getting rid of spirits, they caused all this, and made all this up. Just for mainly control and fear. From start to finish, it was them. Simple as that. So, it's pretty safe to say they're narcissistic, random people. Evil nasty pieces of work that continuously lied to me this whole time?

"I know, I know, this might seem stupid, but you have no idea how long these spirits had been telling me disgusting nasty painful lies. It's extremely hurtful and scary to all hell. The fear was just insane. I just need to know that this is all lies. Evil lies so I can move on from this. I feel like I'm making myself sick from stress, not getting confirmation that they're full of shit and calling them out on their bullshit. I just need to know. Talking has helped me vent and de-stress a bit, so thanks to you. I know I can go on. It looks obvious; they're just lying to me, but I need you to say too, please. You know more than me and can see more. Exactly what's happening, I feel blind and have no idea what's happening around me, so it's hard to just go on my feelings and beliefs alone. Please bear with me on this. I still don't fully grasp this whole spirit thing, even though I believe. Now I'm thinking more logically I have more questions lol I believe you. Can you confirm again? So, I can stay focused on my goal. And put this to rest, once and for all. Just been in pain with this for too long now. It's time to talk."

I wrote, "It's right what you say, spirits are dead people playing with your head. There are no demons, aliens, ascended masters, etc. but there are guides fortunately who are guiding us. Nothing is preordained; we have free will, and our life is not planned; we're free to choose. It may not seem like it sometimes, but if you think about it, everything that's happening is due to your reaction. They show you faces, and you react with fear, they attack you or abuse you, and you react with fear. Once your emotions are triggered, it's hard to think logically.

Harriet wrote, "Just realising how much control they had. I'm in a little shock right now, to be honest but managing a bit better each day. A flood load of questions filling my mind right now, knowing all of this. Just so messed up but I'm calm, I'm not panicking or scared or anything, but keeping my cool as much as I can."

The following week.

I said, "You've had an interesting week?"

Harriet said, "Yes, it's been a long week. I've noticed I can think more clearly, and I'm thinking more logically. I had so many questions, and I just wanted to clarify a few things so I can let go."

I said, "Are things more peaceful or not?"

Harriet said, "Yes and no. How to explain. There's one thing I did notice, when I was meditating with the candle over the past few days, I noticed I could quieten my mind to the point that I can think more clearly. My own thoughts are coming in, and it's me, and there's nothing else, everything is blocked out, and it's just me. It's so quiet it's a little bit scary at times. I've noticed I can do that, there are things I notice more now than I did before when I was on Cymbalta. I can just think clearly."

I said, "You've noticed a big difference since coming off the pills?"

Harriet said, "I have, and I noticed how much they were attacking me too. It's like dealing with both at the same time."

I said, "Yes, but they're attacking you like that anyway. If you retreat behind the pills, then there's nothing to stop them. Whereas if you're aware of what's going on, you're more able to block it."

Harriet said, "So even if I was on Cymbalta and it dulled my senses, and I couldn't feel them attacking me, they were still attacking me?"

I said, "Yes."

Harriet said, "That's so horrible, so nothing's changed. It's the same thing they've been doing. I just notice it more now because I'm off Cymbalta."

I said, "Yes, because you're more alert, and because you're more alert, you can do something about it. Whereas before you just let it slide, didn't you?"
Harriet said, "Yes, I even thought it was normal some of the things that were happening, now I realise it's not normal, and I can do something about it instead of suffering. I've got so many questions. You know when you said to me, I was empathic, was I empathic from birth?"
I said, "I would imagine so."
Harriet said, "When I said they were attacking me before, they weren't attacking me before Australia, were they?"
I said, "You didn't notice anything before, did you?"
Harriet said, "No."
I said, "Then they weren't attacking you. Look at it logically. Up until Australia, your life was normal, your own thoughts, your own actions and decisions. Once that started in Australia, everything changed, didn't it?"
Harriet said, "Yes, but you said about a trigger?"
I said, "A trigger, yes. Usually, when someone has a traumatic experience in their life, like a death in the family or a relationship break-up, it makes them more sensitive. They would then be aware of things that would normally go unnoticed. Once they become aware of the spirit world, it's difficult for them to turn off to it. If you've lost someone through either death or break-up, it can be lonely, and some people try to make friends with the spirits and don't realise what they're getting involved in. Once you get sucked in, they will torment you, as you know."

Harriet said, "So a trigger could be anything."
I said, "Yes, in answer to that question you had about aliens and ascended masters, just remember you're dealing with people who have passed over, nothing else. The proof of that is we've spoken to some of them and removed them."
Harriet said, "Sometimes, I try my hardest to remember what you say and think back on our conversation."
I said, "It's all recorded so you can listen to it again if you want. How are you getting on with the candle?"
Harriet said, "Good, I think."
I said, "Do you know why you're using the candle."
Harriet said, "I'm using it to block out the interference."
I said, "How?"
Harriet said, "By placing it in front of..."
I said, "It doesn't have to be a candle; it could be a pencil, a matchstick or a glass of water; it can be anything simple to visualise. You focus on that to the exclusion of everything else until you forget your surroundings or anybody around you. By doing that, you're controlling your mind, because you're focused on the candle. And nobody, be it physical or spiritual, can interrupt your thoughts. That's the object of the candle, to get to a stage where you block everything out just with a thought."
Harriet said, "I thought, it's easy to do the candle method on images and visions and stuff. I thought, how can I use it with feelings, energy, pain, emotions, and voices."
I said, "To block them as well, you mean?"
Harriet said, "Yes."

I said, "Well, in the first place, you have to get to that exclusion zone where nothing else matters but the candle. When you get to that stage, you won't get voices. You won't get pain or emotions simply because nothing can get into your mind because you've filled it with your thoughts of the candle. Your mind is locked down, and you're in control. If you're meditating on the candle and you're getting pain, then focus more on the candle after you've told the pain to go away. If you start getting mood changes, the best way to deal with that is to take a few deep breaths and count to ten, then focus harder on the candle. It's no easy task, but with practice, you can achieve it. Now, what's happening with the protection you're putting up?"
Harriet said, "Yes, that's really good."
I said, "What is the protection doing?"
Harriet said, "Just blocking out the emotions and stuff as well. I know I feel protected when it happens, and I feel like it's not as intense."
I said, "The protection will protect you, and you don't need the candle anymore. The candle can disrupt what you're doing at any given time because you've got to focus on the candle. If you can rely on and believe in the protection, that will work in the background and you won't have to worry about anything else."
Harriet said, "When I was at work, it was swamped, and I was trying so hard to concentrate on what I was doing. Still, I noticed the extra pressure attacks I was getting from spirit, like energy touches and knocking my knee and anything to get my attention. So, as you said before about putting up or imagining the protection around

me, I do that and dismiss it and get on with what I'm doing."

I said, "Does it go away?"

Harriet said, "I believe it does because I don't focus on it as much as I used to, so I believe it does help."

I said, "The operative word there is dismissing it, isn't it?"

Harriet said, "Yes. Also, coming off Cymbalta, I realise I'm not as relaxed as I was. I want this to stop, and I'm doing everything I can to dismiss them now, if that means putting the protection up and doing this and that. It's working so quickly, I thought it would take longer to make it a habit."

I said, "Don't look at the timeframe, look at them now, see the progress if it's working, fine, don't fix it if it's not broken. You have to be aware spirit will try to attack you more aggressively, so be aware. Spirit is teaching you to defeat themselves by attacking you. As they attack you, you get stronger. The stronger you get the less spirit will affect you."

Harriet said, "The more they throw at me, the more I'm defending myself; it's giving me a chance to practise. I just push back when they push me, and I'm trying to change my habit, so it comes naturally."

I said, "That's the idea of the protection. If you do that in the morning and know that you're protected, if anything impinges on your mind, dismiss it because you know you're protected."

Harriet said, "I believe I'm a hundred per cent protected now through learning all this."

I said, "The idea is that you dismiss it because it's not

part of your life. You concentrate on the physical rather than the spiritual. The less you focus on the spiritual, the harder it'll be for them to affect you. That's why you're putting the protection up, and you're just dealing with any excess. Try to dismiss it and get on with what you're doing rather than embracing it, because then you have to deal with it. You're making the spirit thing too big a part of your life by taking notice of it. The idea is to make it an insignificant part of your day by dismissing it. Use whatever you need to use to remove the interference. Have you removed anyone this week?"

Harriet said, "A few people yes, and they've gone. I was thinking about the new people that come in, how're they getting access to my memory so easily. I feel like I'm an open book, and it's disturbing me. I don't know how it works; it's like, people are attacking me, but there're also people watching. So, they know what's happening, and I was wondering how they're getting access to everything."

I said, "When you clear things, you expect others to take their place, and they're fulfilling your expectations, and you're opening the door to your mind because you're expecting them. You've got to get to the stage where you don't expect them. The way to do that is to get away from the thought of spirit being around you at all. When you remove someone, you dismiss them, and you dismiss the whole spiritual situation and get on with what you're doing. Your focus has got to be on your physical life, not spirit."

Harriet said, "It's hard to try and picture that because I

know spirits are around us all the time. How can I not think about them?"

I said, "Look at it like this; they're around your mum all the time as well, but she doesn't notice them, does she?"

Harriet said, "No, she doesn't."

I said, "Because she is not sensitised like you. For you to get back to normal, you've got to control your sensitivity. To do that, you need to be able to focus on what you're doing and ignore other things. What we're trying to do is get you to focus on your physical life only, that's why we use the candle because it's a mental picture of a physical object. You don't need spirit in your life at the moment, if ever. When you clear yourself or block them, you then carry on as if nothing has happened. Just like a fly that lands on your arm, you absently brush it off because it tickles. It doesn't register in your mind. It's a reflex, and the same thing has to happen with spirit. The more attention you give them, the more credibility you give them."

Harriet said, "I don't know how specific I need to be. I think I'm taking this too literally at the moment. For instance, things happened in the past that might have linked to spiritual stuff like a tune or movie, and I think should I watch it because it'll remind me of that occasion, or should I say it's just a movie and get on with it."

I said, "It's just a movie; it's entertainment; that's all, like reading a book. It's just a book, a story, nothing more. Leave the past where it belongs, in the past."

Harriet said, "Because my senses are heightened, I have

spirit on my mind all the time."
I said, "You're obsessing about it, and because you are, it's at the forefront of your thoughts all the time. I'm more sensitive than you, yet I don't even think about spirit unless I'm working. Accept that it's going to take a little time, but it's getting better, and you're getting more control. You're moving forward and getting less interference. Imagine if you moved into a house where there was a lot of traffic noise. You'd hear it all the time until one day it stops. It's slipped into the background and doesn't interfere with your thoughts anymore. It's still there if you concentrate, but if you don't, it's gone. It's the same with spirit; it's always going to be there. You don't have to be aware of them. Has your mum noticed any difference in you?"
Harriet said, "She says my personality is much better, back to my normal self."
I said, "You had some questions?"
Harriet said, "I'm feeling pain a lot more and certain body parts a lot more. Now it makes sense the pain is greater."
I said, "Are you telling the pain to go away?"
Harriet said, "Yes, and it's going. I'm also putting protection up as well."
I said, "No, just tell it to go away. You don't need to put the protection up; you've already done that in the morning."
Harriet said, "I see, so I don't need to worry about it during the day. Using the candle method for voices, pain, emotions and feelings, you said just focus on meditation because that should be enough. Should I

focus on anything else?"
I said, "If you focus on the candle when you're not doing anything to the exclusion of everything else, it will be enough because it'll block everything else out. The only thing you've got in your mind is what you're doing. Once you've done that, you then get on with what you're doing. You have to keep control of your mind, that's the objective."
Harriet said, "So, I don't have to implement the candle all the time, because I've been trying to implement it everywhere."
I said, "The candle is a focal point. It could be anything; we made it a candle because it was easier to visualise, and it's simple. The idea of the focal point is that your mind is on the candle and nothing else. That means you're controlling your mind and blocking everything out."
Harriet said, "I see, so the whole idea is to focus on a specific object, it doesn't have to be a candle, only when meditating, but when I'm out and about it could be anything else as long as I'm training my mind focusing on the candle."
I said, "No, you're training your mind to focus on what you direct it to. The idea is that, while your mind is occupied with what you're focusing on, nothing else can get in."
Harriet said, "Oh, I see, so the meditation on the candle is to help me focus on anything else other than spirit."
I said, "It's teaching you to focus on what you want to focus on."
Harriet said, "Oh, I see, that's cleared up so much."

I said, "That's why I say it's so important to practise and hold it there. The longer you hold it there, the longer you're in control. When you let it go, and you come out of your meditation, you should be relaxed, at peace, and things should be quiet. You've dismissed everything, and you move forward."

Harriet said, "Do my guides control what I get visually and verbally?"

I said, "No, they don't."

Harriet said, "Oh, they don't, so anything that happens, I can pick up on."

I said, "If your guides were controlling it, they'd stop the voices, the dreams, the moods, the pains."

Harriet said, "I thought they were controlling it, so there were certain things I can't hear."

I said, "No, they're there to help you, but you've got to help yourself when you help yourself, suppose you're able to protect yourself ninety per cent of the time, they'll do the other ten per cent. Guides don't control you or what you hear, see or feel; YOU do. Guides don't arrange for this or that to happen. They put the possibilities in your pathway; if they happen, they happen. If something detrimental happens like this, they'll use it as a learning experience, but it wasn't arranged for them and you."

Harriet said, "The spirits are close, but they're not close like inside me?"

I said, "Their thoughts are in your mind; they don't have a body, they're energy. The mind is the spirit and spirit communicate with other spirits naturally through the mind, but they don't have to be standing where you are.

They're not inside your body; they're projecting thoughts to you."

Harriet said, "They're putting thoughts in my mind to make me think they're there?"

I said, "If they were in your body, you'd be possessed, and they'd be controlling your body, and they're not. Spirit is just playing with your mind."

Harriet said, "So would that be the same with pain and discomfort, they're just putting that in my mind?"

I said, "Well, if you haven't banged your arm, for instance, why should it hurt? It's because they're either giving you the pain they're suffering, or bringing back the memory of a pain you've had in the past. So, there're two ways of doing it, one is by standing close and you being sensitive, will pick it up, or they push it on you. Or they use your memory to remind you of a pain you've had before. In either case, it's not real, so remove it."

Harriet said, "You said about the spirits that come near me. Is that like if I am walking and I feel a spirit there, I pick it up, or are you talking about humans?"

I said, "The spirits that are coming near you are attacking you, that's their focus to interfere with you. They're not attacking anyone else; otherwise, your mum would be getting attacked. When you go out, the same spirits go with you when you block them and don't accept any more coming in or remove them, you won't get that. Think about it like this, look at the difference between now and a month ago – it's a lot more peaceful. You're progressing, but you have to go at a pace you can cope with. You've also got to go at a pace where you can recognise what's happening and re-educate your mind and stop expecting them. That's your biggest problem; you can remove them all day long, but if you expect someone to take their place, they will."

Harriet said, "It does help to talk once a week and to get confirmation."

I said, "You've just got to believe in yourself."

Harriet said, "Yes, I can see the finishing line now. I'm now more confident this is going to stop. The more I remove and see it working, the more confident I get. I just get impatient."

I said, "Getting impatient is not helping you, and what you must remember is when you put protection up in the mornings that protection takes over from the candle, that's the eventual goal. It's not going to happen now because you're not ready. If you put the protection up and believe in it, you won't need the candle unless you think about spirit. If you can keep spirit out of your mind, you'll have won. When you can be at peace for two to three hours, you will be accepting the peace rather than expecting another attack."

Harriet said, "I'll get there, I know it'll take time, but as long as I keep doing what I'm doing, I'll get there."

I said, "You'll get there; it'll take as long as it takes. It's all to do with your ability to accept and reprogram."

Harriet said, "I feel like I have to retrain my brain again."

I said, "That's what you're doing, but it's your mind you're retraining, not your brain because your mind controls your brain."

Harriet said, "Coming to terms with it's hard, knowing

how much I've been manipulated and controlled."
I said, "Don't worry about that; it is what it is, we'll deal with it. They haven't controlled you as much as some people."
Harriet said, "They can produce hot and cold feelings, can't they?"
I said, "Yes, but everything they do, you can counteract because you're spirit too, you just have to work through your body, so it takes a bit more effort. If a mood or discomfort distracts you from dealing with the current problem, you have to deal with that first. You're as able as they are, but because you're in a body, you don't have the understanding and knowledge that you would have as the spirit. That's why education's so important to help you to understand that you're not ignorant of what's going on; you just don't know about it."
Harriet said, "So when I get sensations like that, just dismiss it, say it's not mine, go away and leave me alone and get on with whatever I'm doing. Believe that the protection's happening in the morning and at night, and I don't need to keep putting up barriers during the day."
I said, "But continue to meditate on the candle twice a day so you can keep control."
Harriet said, "I was thinking, of course, others naturally adapt to my mind settling down a bit after a while; it's racing a lot at the moment."
I said, "As your mind settles, your logic comes forward, and you're able to discern what is and isn't an attack, and you're able to deal with it a lot quicker. It's when you doubt that you struggle, you've been clearing yourself most of the time. I've only cleared you when it

got too much."

Harriet said, "It's hard right now, but it's getting easier, do they influence everything I do like turning my head and making me look at something? It's so subtle sometimes I don't know what's me and what isn't me."

I said, "If you want to do something, do it, don't be afraid you're influenced, just do what you want. Gradually you'll recognise when you're influenced, just work through it."

Harriet said, "You mean to be aware, but don't be aware, it's difficult, but I know what you mean. My meditations better now that my mind is focusing a lot more. I can focus on the candle and other things a lot more, and it helps me quieten my mind easier. I've got more control. I'm thinking a lot more, and it's more like my thoughts now in the meditation, and I don't hear anything else. I'm learning to control my mind better."

I said, "You'll notice we haven't removed any spirits today, that's because at the moment we're working to stop you inviting others to take their place. We're working on your acceptance that they've gone rather than expectance."

Harriet said, "So if I can think it, they can think it too, I just have to be one step in front instead of playing catch-up. I've noticed they're quite intelligent because they're starting to do other things now to make me doubt myself a bit more."

I said, "You're recognising they're doing other things now so you can counteract them, so you're still in control. Don't be frightened if you miss something, as soon as you recognise it deal with it. You aren't going to

get it right first time, every time. What matters is you deal with it?"
Harriet said, "Now that I'm off Cymbalta, the attacks are getting stronger."
I said, "The attacks are the same; you're just more aware."
Harriet said, "It's so hard to accept they would want to do that to people."
I said, "Don't overthink it."

I said, "Hi, how was your week?"
Harriet said, "I've had a good week, a particularly good week."
I said, "Tell me about it."
Harriet said, "I was out walking, ignoring the voices, and listening to my music, distracting myself, doing the safe driving technique while walking. I got a sudden loud voice shouting in my face, just shouting, shouting, really obvious. I thought, where did that come from? I was ignoring the normal stuff, but there was something stronger that came in, it scared me for a bit, and I thought what's going on. I tried to ignore it by doing the steps like looking at certain things and just getting my mind focused on something else. What this spirit was doing was trying to change my mindset to think of something else. To explain, if I was looking at a bird, he put another image in front of it. He was trying to make me think his way and not my way. That scared me because whatever I was looking at, he was purposely saying things and changing what I was seeing by putting an image in front of it. I thought, oh my god, what to do,

then I thought I couldn't ignore it, so I said to my guides, can you please remove this person and any others that are causing me problems, and it went. I thought, oh my god, just like that, it was so easy, and the other voices were trying to mimic it afterward, but it wasn't to the extent that person was. So, I knew he was gone, and I believed it more when the guides were taking people away even though I did believe it before. But now I thought, oh my god they're doing it, so I thought that was really good. I don't know how true that is, but hopefully, it's true."

I said, "That's right; trust in your guides. When you asked your guides to remove the spirit, you didn't ask them to remove everyone, did you?"

Harriet said, "I don't remember."

I said, "Well, he got removed, and then you had other voices mimicking him, so you didn't remove everybody. Also, if what you say is what you said, you didn't ask your guides to put him in the custody of his guides."

Harriet said, "You mean the specific person?"

I said, "Yes."

Harriet said, "I think I did."

I said, "You need to say, please remove all those who are causing problems and place them in the custody of their guides. Your guides can remove one or twenty just as easily."

Harriet said, "Say all of them, regardless. I thought it was going to be a heavy load to get rid of all of them."

I said, "No, it's not a problem. You're choosing who you want to get rid of, and your guides can only remove those you ask them to. Whereas if you say all of them,

you'll have some peace."
Harriet said, "OK."
I said, "Are you doing the protection in the morning and at night?"
Harriet said, "Yes, definitely."
I said, "Are you sleeping better?"
Harriet said, "I am, it's been pretty good; I believe it as well, so that's good. During the day, I don't imagine the bubble or anything, and if the spirits are imitating, I know just to dismiss it."
I said, "Does it go away when you dismiss it?"
Harriet said, "It does, it does, I ignore it straight away I don't even pay attention to it. I just ignore it."
I said, "That means you're getting more control over your mind."
Harriet said, "It seems it. I noticed that a lot this week when I was doing a lot. I didn't want to make it a habit of keep calling my guides unless I absolutely had to, like if I had that guy. It was too strong."
I said, "There is nothing to fear, so don't get scared if it comes on a bit heavy sometimes, just deal with it."
Harriet said, "Yes, OK. Meditating is going well now that my mind is quietening down, it's still a bit hyper, but it's quietening down a lot. When focusing on the candle, I notice I'm thinking a lot, and I've cut that down a lot to the point now I'm focusing on the candle in silence. I can hear them more because I've cut down my thoughts, but I'm ignoring it, and I'm still focusing on the candle, which is distracting me enough to ignore it."
I said, "Now you're finally getting the idea of why we're focusing on the candle, it's taken a long time for you to

realise the purpose of the candle. You're getting there."
Harriet said, "I get annoyed because I know it's working, and I know I keep hearing the spirits, and they're just trying to distract me. I know they're distracting me, but I keep going back and dismissing them. Am I dismissing too much? I still doubt myself, it's just annoying. I know it'll probably take time. It's been good, though. Just focusing on it now quietly in my thoughts, just focus on the candle. If I get anything that comes, they do stupid things and anything to get my mind off the candle, I just ignore it dismiss it, know it's blocked and that's it, it's done."
I said, "During the day, do you think about spirit, or do you think about what you're doing?"
Harriet said, "You know, no, I acknowledge they're there, but I don't focus on them if that makes sense, as much as I used to last week. I know it's a fact they're still there. The funny thing is because coronavirus happened. I'm more stressed out about that than about them, so it's pushing them way out of my mind. I don't notice them anymore because I'm so focused on watching the news, focusing on cleaning and so much stuff that I don't give spirit a second thought."
I said, "Now you understand the purpose of keeping yourself occupied, don't you?"
Harriet said, "Yes, I can see the importance of it now, but I was a bit worried about the coronavirus because if I can't go outside, how am I supposed to keep occupied."
I said, "Then you occupy yourself inside when they say you can't go outside, they mean you can't mix with

people, they didn't say you can't go for a walk."
Harriet said, "That's true, but they're saying about a lockdown."
I said, "You'll have to keep busy inside, then if you can't go out, then you'll have to walk on your treadmill, won't you?"
Harriet said, "Also, with being empathic, I don't know whether I realise this more and more or if it's just a case that I'm off the antidepressants. Or I'm more used to them numbing my senses. It could be both. I noticed when they mess with the emotions, they seem to override my emotions by putting their emotions over mine. I know it's happening, and I'm still in withdrawal, but I still have my own level of stress too, due to the coronavirus, and I'm watching the news, of course, they're going to heighten my fear, and it's like they've been doing that. But I've been noticing it and ignoring it, I still my emotions, and it's hard."
I said, "That's normal, though, isn't it when you hear about disasters on the news and situations like this. That's your thoughts."
Harriet said, "Yes, I was just trying to differentiate between the two. Because I'm ignoring and blocking them out and dismissing, and not getting sucked into their games."
I said, "Yes, so instead of running around chasing your tail, you're acting smartly by waiting until you have to deal with it, that's the smart way to do it. If they have you off balance, they can start giving you panic attacks. Whereas if you're relaxed about it, when you're ready, you say enough is enough, off you go. That way, you

don't react to every little thing."

Harriet said, "Now that I'm aware of what they've been doing, I'm trying so hard not to outsmart them specifically like being snarky or spiteful, which I have to admit I was a little bit. I've got to the point where I started thinking there's no point. Now I understand what they're trying to do, it's easier to ignore, but I was getting quite spiteful."

I said, "That's perfectly understandable. You wanted to get your own back. You have to remember spirit has got 24 hours to play their games. You don't; you have to sleep."

Harriet said, "Yeah, and I have no time, so I have to ignore everything. It doesn't matter."

I said, "By ignoring everything you're putting it in the background rather than making it the main object of your day. So, you're now thinking of other things instead of spirit, which is what we want."

Harriet said, "Is everything connected, feelings, emotions, energy, memory, images, sensations, voices, taste and smells? Once I block that all out by ignoring them, so I don't get anything, it won't be just the voices at the end of the day, will it all stop at once?"

I said, "Yes."

Harriet said, "So once I train my mind to block them all out, the voices won't just stop? It'll be everything that'll stop?"

I said, "Yes. Then you'll be normal you see, and by normal, I mean people do get influenced occasionally by spirit, even if they don't know it. In your case, you'll know it, but you'll just ignore the negative spirit. We need to go back to your question about empathy. I've given it some thought, you're not an empath you're just oversensitive due to coming off the pills. Don't worry about always picking up on things; you won't, once you settle down. You see, you only pick up on what's attacking you; you're not aware of interference around others, which means you're sensitive, not empathic."

Harriet said, "I know I shouldn't focus on spirit, but it's bothering me a bit at the moment. Having been highly sensitive, how does that affect me when I feel energy or they're pulling my leg or a limb, or they knock something over or move something? Is it because I'm highly sensitive, or is it because they know I'm highly sensitive so they can do that stuff more and people just don't notice it, and it'll just go away? I don't know how to explain, it's like I was trying to think of what was physical and what they could do in my mind. I know they can do a lot in my mind, like give me impressions, but I was thinking when it comes to the energy, the pushes and pulling my finger and lifting my hand, is that part of the mind or physical? I don't know, and I was getting a bit worried."

I said, "What do you think?"

Harriet said, "I think it's physical."

I said, "So if it's physical, you need to have somebody standing there doing it, don't you?"

Harriet said, "Yes."

I said, "But you haven't, have you?"

Harriet said hesitantly, "No."

I said, "So it's mental, isn't it?"

Harriet said, "Even feeling the energy, the strong energy

pushing you, it's all mental, in your mind?"
I said, "No, the touches can be a memory, but it's more likely they're touching you. It's not a problem, it's been happening for a long time, that'll disappear also. When you get rid of them, there'll be no one there to touch you, will there? You feel the energy because you're sensitive; when you become calmer in yourself and less sensitive, you won't feel the energy so you won't feel the touches. But it's not all in the mind; if it were, things wouldn't move by themselves, would they?"
Harriet said, "That's why I wanted to know for sure that was the case; So that means they're standing near me when they touch?"
I said, "When they're touching you or when they move something, they don't have to be there to touch, spirit can be on the other side of the room. They can still move something because they use their mind with energy; I don't know how that works. But they don't have to be there."
Harriet said, "Memories, my memory, is getting a lot better, I'm noticing what's mine and what isn't, my own memories are fine. There were certain memories I had of the past that they're using against me, which I block by putting the image of the candle over it. Remember I told you I did that when they put certain things onto me, like if I've watched a horror movie which frightened me? They use it against me like in the past, and I put a candle over it to block it out. I'm worried, will it affect me if I keep doing that with my own memories?"
I said, "No, it's not going to affect you in any other way except you're blocking it out. Why do you bring the

memory up, why do you think about it? The reason you think about it is, it's being brought to the front of your mind so they can use it. It's easier to make you fear something you feared in the past; you know it's in the past, so put it back. Focus on the future and move forward."

Harriet said, "Even if I use the candle method to block out certain things, like images and such, that's OK, did you say?"

I said, "There's nothing wrong with using the candle for that; it's helping you control your mind, isn't it? What you'll do in time is instead of using the candle, you'll put your own image on top of theirs, which will block it out anyway using your strength of mind or control and you'll notice how much more control you have now."

Harriet said, "A lot more in just one week."

I said, "It's not in just one week, it's over some time, but you've now understood what we're doing and how we're doing it and why, so it's now making sense to you."

Harriet said, "It does, it makes so much sense. If something comes in my head like a voice or anything, I open my eyes and immediately focus on what I'm looking at, and it cuts it off straight away."

I said, "That's what we've been working toward; you're starting to block things automatically; that's what we want."

Harriet said, "It's been so stressful, I know I've come a long way, but I just realised it this week, the difference is amazing."

I said, "I've been waiting for you to understand what

we're doing and how it works. Now you can move forward with confidence. Although I told you right at the beginning, the reason for the candle is to block everything out. You didn't understand what I meant by focusing on the candle to the exclusion of everything else. If you'd understood that sooner you would have been further forward."

Harriet said, "I'm just glad I've got to this stage. Just realising the difference is mental. OK, what I'm concerned about is going to sleep, I'm fine, but I thought even with the protection I feel a little vulnerable because when I'm drifting off, they seem to attack me even more because they know I'm vulnerable at that time. They talk to me a lot more, and I try not to talk back. I try to focus on the candle, but then I have to open my eyes and focus again to go to sleep, but I can't keep doing that if I'm trying to sleep. It's confusing to try to focus when I'm trying to go to sleep. I just feel like they're exploiting my vulnerability."

I said, "You've always known that the weakest points in your day are when you're waking up or going to sleep. So, we're going to try a little experiment, OK?"

Harriet said, "OK."

I said, "Close your eyes, imagine in your head that you can see a black velvet cushion. Now focus on that and concentrate until you can see it."

Harriet said, "Just the black velvet cushion."

I said, "Just the black velvet cushion and nothing else. Can you do that?"

Harriet said, "I think so, yes."

I said, "The idea is if you focus on nothing which is a

black velvet cushion, your mind has nothing to latch on to and nothing to stimulate it. So, you'll go to sleep, because it turns your mind off."

Harriet said, "Oh my god I realise this, I remember you spoke about this, ages ago, but when I was going to sleep because I couldn't open my eyes, focus on the candle and go to sleep as well. I took it a bit literally with the candle. I thought I have to think of the candle all the time. I get it now, when I was going to sleep, I noticed focusing on the darkness and nothing else helped. It was just like yes, that's a focus in itself even if there's nothing there it's still focusing."

I said, "Because you're focusing on that, there's nothing to trigger any thoughts or memories in your mind, and your mind slows down, and you go to sleep."

Harriet said, "I remember one night I was struggling. I thought if I just quiet down and just focus on nothing like the darkness, and it helped."

I said, "Focusing on nothing is hard; you've still got to have something in your mind to focus on; you can't focus on nothing. The reason we're using a black velvet cushion is that some people are afraid of the dark."

Harriet said, "I've got about four more questions. Senses overload, I know this will settle down after a while; I wondered, long term, what will that do for me with heightened senses? Will it be like that forever?"

I said, "Once you get used to it and it becomes familiar, like everything, it'll fade into the background. So, no, you won't have to worry about your senses after this is over. Everyone has senses; it just depends on what sense is highlighted at any given time. The more you focus on your daily life, the further you push spirit into the background."

Harriet said, "OK, thank you. You know I said I was quite sensitive right now. I was dealing with being specific in my phrasing. Sometimes I feel like when I go to sleep or have a headband on, I feel like someone's touching it."

I said, "Do you feel a pressure on your forehead?"

Harriet said, "Yeah, like someone's moving it or something. I've no idea what they're doing, so I just say go away and leave me alone."

I said, "Does it go away?"

Harriet said, "It does, yes. It's just because there are so many things happening. I get pain, discomfort, and I feel the energy, I think. With the pain, do I say 'This is not my pain go away and leave me alone'? With the discomfort I don't know if it's the same thing."

I said, "Yes, it's the same thing."

Harriet said, "And energy like moving clothing and stuff like that. Do I say this is not my sensation?"

I said, "Just ignore it, if it bothers you, ask your guides to remove the spirits that're disturbing you, and put them in the custody of their guides."

Harriet said, "But I'm feeling so much stuff now I'm off Cymbalta it's ridiculous I couldn't believe this was happening when I was on Cymbalta and not realising what was happening to me. Now I feel everything they do."

I said, "You're, hypersensitive right now, things will calm down Cymbalta was doing something, it was numbing your senses. Because it was numbing your senses, you weren't alert enough to deal with the situation. It didn't solve the problem. It just masked it; there was always going to come a time when you would have to deal with your hyposensitivity."

Harriet said, "Even with the pain and other interference, it'll all calm down?"

I said, "As your sensitivity calms, you won't get the pains, etc., because you'll automatically remove the spirits. Getting spiritual pains and interference is a normal part of life; it's just that you know about it and recognise it where other people don't. As I've said, if you get sudden pain, it probably isn't yours, so tell it to go away and believe it, and it will."

Harriet said, "Why is that the case when you say go away, they go, is it because they listen or is it that something happens?"

I said, "It's because you push the spirit away; that's doing it."

Harriet said, "Oh, you physically do it yourself."

I said, "No, you don't physically do it yourself; you log into your mind. It's not your pain, and if it's not your pain, why should you feel it?"

Harriet said, "Oh, OK, so you do it, but in the mind."

I said, "When spirit comes close, and they have pain, sometimes sensitive people will feel it. Other times the spirit will be projecting the pain on the person. By saying 'That's not mine, take it away", the spirit realises what they're doing by mistake or what they're doing on purpose you know about, and you're not accepting it. It's the nonacceptance that rejects it. That's why when you say take it away, you believe it and then dismiss it."

Harriet said, "Even if they're purposely doing it, that

would still work because you're dismissing it?"
I said, "That's right."
Harriet said, "Wow, it shows how powerful the mind really is."
I said, "If you were trying to do this through your brain, it wouldn't work because you would be working with five senses instead of six."
Harriet said, "So with the pain, unless it's a mega pain, I'll just say go away and leave me alone, the same with energy and stuff like that."
I said, "If the pain is sudden, go away and leave me alone, if you have a pain that gradually gets worse you may need to see a doctor but try go away and leave me alone first. If it doesn't go away, then maybe there is something wrong. If you find you have a pain, but there's no reason why you have it, then it's not yours."
Harriet said, "Sometimes it's a bit hard to determine whether it's yours, especially when you're ill. It's so hard sometimes."
I said, "You're not ill, are you?"
Harriet said, "A little, but I know they can create memories and make it worse."
I said, "Don't fear them making it worse; you'll recognise it and deal with it. You're building up your protection with the bubble twice a day, and it's like armour, and you won't feel half of what you feel now because it won't get through your protection."
Harriet said, "I see, so I am building up protection."
I said, "Let me try to explain. You understand now about the candle and the purpose of it, and the reasons behind it, it's the same with the protection. At the

moment you believe it works, but you're not sure. When you're absolutely convinced that it's working, you won't get any interference, it'll take over protecting you, and it'll protect you all day without any worries."

Harriet said, "Will that just happen in time?"

I said, "Of course, but you've got to build up to it the same as you have with the candle. We're replacing the candle with the protection; then, you don't have to think about the candle. You won't have to think about the protection so you can get on with your life without even considering spirit. But it's a gradual process because you've got to learn and get used to it and experience it. As you experience it, you'll become more convinced in your own ability."

Harriet said, "Oh, like the fact that I believe my guides take them away, but I believed it for a fact when they took that loud voice away."

I said, "Yes, because you were convinced, weren't you? You couldn't deny it."

Harriet said, "No, I couldn't; it was gone."

I said, "That's the thing you see, it's all very well believing something, but until you actually do it and it happens, you're not convinced, you've always got that little doubt."

Harriet said, "It's like I want to believe in the protection, I try and believe it as much as I can, but I don't focus in on it."

I said, "Wanting to believe is not the same as believing."

Harriet said, "Yeah, I know, I do believe it; it's just disheartening when I get another one."

I said, "Who are you convincing, me, or you?"

Harriet said, "Me, myself."
I said, "Are you trying to convince me that you believe it?"
Harriet said, "I believe it; it's just when it gets difficult. I start to doubt a little."
I said, "Don't."
Harriet said, "I know my guides are trying so hard, I know I'm doing it with their help, but it's just constant."
I said, "When you say you're doing it on your own, you mean you're controlling it. You're not doing it on your own, in the sense that if you ask your guides to remove somebody, they're removing them on your behalf. What you're doing is saying when you'd like some help, you're discerning enough to decide you'll have a go yourself first; if you run into a problem, then you ask for help. Rather than sitting there, expecting your guides to do it for you, so you're in control working toward protecting yourself. But don't think your super-girl and you can do everything, you can't."
Harriet said, "I know, but if I can train my brain so I can deal with this."
I said, "It's your mind, not your brain."
Harriet said, "Yes, of course. I know my guides have their stuff to do to help me, and I'm going to have to do most of it, that's why I'm focusing so hard to train myself to do a lot of it, instead of relying on them to do everything."
I said, "That's good, but when you say they've got their own stuff to do, the stuff they do is on your behalf; that's their job. Your guides have to let you do it yourself; it's only by making mistakes that you learn.

The pathway that you've taken has been difficult, and there's been a lot for you to understand. I have to say there are a few people I know in a similar position as you who I wouldn't be able to help. The reason for that is they don't have your determination, which has all got to come from you."

Harriet said, "The attacks I'm getting now are not as obvious as they were before, I don't know how to take it, instead of being loud and vocal they're being quiet and trying to command me by whispering in my ear."

I said, "They're playing a different game, you deal with them exactly as you did before, do what you've been doing, and don't put up with anything."

Harriet said, "I thought when it's quiet, and they do that and purposely be quiet, they're trying to pretend they're blocked out. If I say something and they pretend to block themselves, so I'll think I'm doing it. I'm getting to know their tricks now, but when I'm meditating, and they're quiet on purpose, should I take advantage of it?"

I said, "Yes, why not, there's no point rattling a stick round in a bee's nest if the bees are being quiet and leaving you alone."

Harriet said, "I was so worried that they were pretending to be quiet; I wondered what they were going to do next."

I said, "Are they pretending to be quiet, or are they having trouble getting through?"

Harriet said, "That's another thing I didn't realise, that they might be having trouble getting in."

I said, "Yes, because you've got protection up, haven't

you? So, stop worrying about it. Those times when you think it's quiet or they're hiding from you, they're the times, that's when the protection is working, and they can't get through very well. It's going to get better and better until they don't get through; you won't even be aware of them."
Harriet said, "I was worried if I'm actually blocking them out now, or they were just quiet, I was scared about what to think."
I said, "You are blocking them out, only deal with the annoying ones. With the best will in the world, you're not going to keep them out all the time at the moment, and now and again they'll attack you. When you get attacked, deal with it. Worrying is like looking, stop it."
Harriet said, "Thank you. See you next week."
I said, "OK."

We were unable to speak this week due to Harriet looking after her parents, who both have the coronavirus. It'll be a testing time for her as she can't go out, and keeping her mind occupied may be a struggle. Harriet will be vulnerable to spirit interference more as she's already anxious about her parents. On the other hand, it may be that she's so focused on them that she'll put spirit entirely out of her mind. We shall see.

I said, “How’re your parents?”
Harriet said, “It was quite scary at first, but they’re both recovering now. We’ve all been in isolation for nearly two weeks now.”
I said, “How’re you getting on?”
Harriet said, “Me, OK, it’s been hard. The spirits have been active because I’ve been stressed out what with looking after my parents and worrying about my sister. Because of what’s happening, I’ve tried to ignore spirit and not to overthink things and scare myself.”
I said, “I would think it’s making it a bit difficult for you since you can’t get out to keep yourself occupied at the moment?”
Harriet said, “No, although I’ve been busy cleaning and sanitising the house. Spiritually it’s been hard, but I knew they would take advantage.”
I said, “Maybe, but you’ve coped. Have you been removing spirit?”
Harriet said, “I have been quite a bit to be honest, which helped enormously. But I know I have to ignore them as much as I can. I can’t keep removing them; I need to start blocking them, so they don’t even come into my mind. I’m trying to get a balance, and if it gets too intense, then I remove them. Otherwise, I try to keep myself focused on what I’m doing around the house like cleaning and cooking and washing. I’ve been meditating, but it’s been hard, but I’ve been trying to do it once a day. I tried twice one day. It’s been so stressful this week, everyone’s been ill, I couldn’t

concentrate. But I know I need to push myself to keep doing it."

I said, "OK, at least you're trying, but you've still got to try and focus away from spirit and on your physical life. At the moment, the spirits are still in the forefront of your mind, aren't they?"

Harriet said, "It's difficult to put them out of my mind when they're talking."

I said, "Yes, I bet it is, but when you put your protection up in the mornings, do the voices stop, and how do you feel about the protection working?"

Harriet said, "I'm still unsure to be honest, although the voices do stop but not for long. I know it's going to take a while, but I can't wait until I get to the point where it starts to make a difference. I think when things calm down with this virus, I'll settle better."

I said, "You were starting to get out and get on with things, but it's set you back a bit not going out. But it's a good opportunity to learn to keep yourself busy at home."

Harriet said, "In a sense, they haven't been in the foreground as much. It's hard to explain because I've got new things to stress about, what with the illness and things I'm focusing on in real life. It's what I wanted anyway, so it's a weird mix, and because I'm focused on daily life, they're taking advantage. I haven't been as diligent, what with all the other stuff. It's like because I'm a bit fearful of the virus and the stuff that's happening now, and they're drawing in on it."

I said, "Yes, they've got a hook into your fear of things that are happening around you. Don't doubt yourself;

you'll get through it, you've got through the last two weeks, and I can only imagine what you've had going through your mind. I'm talking about your thoughts, not spirit, and having them on top would make things harder, so well done. You've got through it because you've been using the mechanisms we've put in place?"
Harriet said, "I have as much as I can, I had to there's no other choice as I'm stuck indoors, it's either do or die really."
I said, "What's bothering you at the moment?"
Harriet had a few tears and said, "I don't normally cry, and I don't know why I'm crying now, maybe it's a release of emotions. It's worrying that I'm at risk as well, and people are dying left, right and centre, and I'm thinking should I write a letter to mum in case I don't wake up. It's horrible stuff like that."
I said, "With this virus, you'll get a warning with the cough and the temperature so it wouldn't be sudden. You'll have plenty of time if you do catch it, you're not going to go to sleep and not wake up."
Harriet said, "Yes, I suppose so. My sister is ill too, and we have to keep our distance. It's hard as I don't have a mum to help me at the moment, she's still getting over the virus."
I said, "Try not to worry about the virus. If you catch it then you catch it. The more you worry, the more stress and then you'll start getting anxious and paranoid, and then your buttons are going to get pushed. Just take deep breaths and try not to react. You've done well so far."
Harriet said, "It's just so hard because I know I can deal

with life's stresses, but it doesn't help when you've got spirit saying you're going to die, and telling me to do this or that or you're not going to wake up."

I said, "Look on the positive side, your mum and dad are recovering and you're OK. You can't do anything to change things, so accept it and work through it."

Harriet said, "The problem is I'm the highest risk in the house with asthma and cancer, so I'm a bit worried. I came through the swine flu, so we'll just have to see. Now that mum's taking care of everyone, I can isolate myself, and I may be lucky and not get it. There're people worse off, so I count my blessings. I set up a routine of things to do in the morning, like to get me out of bed and moving around. The first thing I do is my protection then prepare myself for what I planned to do. The spirits pretend to be my thoughts and say, you've got to do this, and don't forget to do that. Making me remember things I forgot like I might forget to do something, and they jog my memory."

I said, "Why would they jog your memory when you remember something? It doesn't come as a voice. It comes as a thought, doesn't it?"

Harriet said, "I'm not too sure."

I said, "Well, if you think about it, you'll find it was silent, no voice. You recognised your thoughts recently, and you could tell when it wasn't your thought. Well, your guides are jogging your memory."

Harriet said, "That's true."

I said, "Because you've had so much to deal with, you're not thinking you're reacting. If you get a thought come in, decide is that what I want to do? If it is then do it, if

it's not, then don't."
Harriet said, "Even if it's not my decision?"
I said, "You make all the decisions; it's your mind, you're in control. If you make a wrong decision, it's your fault, but you decide. Sometimes you'll get it wrong, we all do, that's life. The important thing is you're controlling your thoughts."
Harriet said, "I don't have much to ask this week apart from the virus because I wasn't thinking much about spirit. I could hear what they were saying, but I just ignore it as much as I can. It's hard to ignore it completely, but when I'm going to sleep, it's like I want a moment to myself to have some logical thoughts about everyday life and what's going on in the world. I quieten my mind to think and get constant chatter. The thing is I know to ignore it and think about it rationally and be logical."
I said, "Just remove them and have a little bit of peace where you can think your own thoughts. You're still getting the peace a little, aren't you?"
Harriet said, "Yes."
I said, "We'll make use of it to examine your thoughts, and you'll see the difference between their thoughts and yours. How often have you used the candle recently?"
Harriet said, "I meditate every day, and I've used the candle to distract me, but I try and occupy my mind with my own thoughts first. If it gets too difficult, then I use the candle."
I said, "Yes, so you're focusing, but you're doing it without the candle, you're using your thoughts to

distract you, are you?"
Harriet said, "Yes."
I said, "That's good because it means you haven't got to concentrate on the candle before you can clear things. It means you can change your thoughts just by changing your mind about what you focus on."
Harriet said, "That's what I've been doing, just changing what's in my mind, and it goes."
I said, "You're controlling your mind now, that's what we've been trying to do. With the protection, you just have to accept it's working; you've had evidence that it does, believe it. You'll notice if you have a problem, it's not as harsh as it has been in the past."
Harriet said, "No."
I said, "That's because you don't get upset, excited, or depressed because you're getting interference, you just remove them."
Harriet said, "That's another thing, because I knew to mentally get prepared for what they're going to say and I prepared myself to stay kind of content. When they hit me with the emotions, I just remove it as soon as it happens, I'm kind of on guard all the time but not aware that I'm on guard. It's a bit weird. I thought I would be crying and more emotional because I thought they would be putting everything on me. It feels like they are, but it's not all getting through."
I said, "That's right, that's because your protection's working, but it's not working as well as we want."
Harriet said, "It's like they're desperately trying, but it's as though it's not happening, they don't seem to be as strong."

I said, “That’s because you’re controlling it; you’re not thinking about it all the time. You just deal with it when it happens.”

Harriet said, “Yes, it’s if it turns up, I’ve got so much on my mind that isn’t spirit. I don’t even think about it.”

I said, “So keeping your mind occupied is working, isn’t it?”

Harriet said, “It is.”

I said, “So you’ve got control of your emotions. When you start getting interference you remove it, you’re getting the peace with no voices. Take advantage of the peace and stop worrying about somebody else coming in.”

Harriet said, “I feel like there’s less and less, but I know it’s going to be like this for a while now, and they’ll be there for a bit longer.”

I said, “No, you don’t know it’s going to be like this for a while, because next week it could all be over. What I’m saying to you is you’re expecting it to last a long time. You’re not expecting it to be over next week or the week after, are you?”

Harriet said, “Not really.”

I said, “No, so you’re expecting it to last a while, so we come back to expectations, don’t we? When you clear somebody, you expect someone else to come in, don’t you, or you were? Now you’ve changed that expectation to it’s not going to end in the next two weeks it’s going to take longer, it doesn’t necessarily have to. You’ll start to get your mindset right when it’s quiet all day, and you don’t dwell on spirit.”

Harriet said, “Yes, you’re right if I do get someone who

is loud or abrupt, I just dismiss it and think right what am I going to do now, and it just gets rid of the interference straight away."

I said, "All we have got to do now is get you to a stage where it's automatic, it doesn't hit your consciousness; it's dealt with subconsciously. Like the fly on your arm, you don't even think about it. You just brush it off."

Harriet said, "I was thinking, with the pain, I dismiss it a lot more now, but I do get twinges of pain that come on suddenly, and I know it's them. I do immediately say go away; that's not my pain. Is that still OK?"

I said, "Of course, that's the advantage of going through all this, if you can call it an advantage. You've learned to tell the difference; most people think it's their pain."

Harriet said, "I think the pain is less intense. I've had no pain in my arm; in fact, I'd forgotten about it."

I said, "Sometimes it can take a week or two to overcome the expectation regarding particular pains. Take me. I was getting headaches, which I don't normally have, so I dismissed it for a couple of days, but it persisted, so I took paracetamol, and it went. The point I'm making is once I'd taken the pill, my mind accepted it had gone, and it did. It's the same when dealing with the voices, it's just pain, instead of words, it's coming from the same place. All you need do is stay positive, deny it, dismiss it. The problem is you have to decide when it's your pain and when it's not, that can be hard sometimes. But the rule of thumb is, if it's sudden, it's not yours, if it's not sudden then it could be. If you tell it to go away and it persists, then take something and forget it. Remember, we all get pain now and again for no apparent reason, so don't think you're under attack all the time. Now, you're not getting those voices in the background anymore, are you?"

Harriet said, "I only get the loud voices now, no more chitter-chatter."

I said, "That's because the waypoint is working. The spirits looking for help are getting helped by your guides instead of bothering you. Your mind has accepted your guides can deal with that without you. All we have to do now is get your subconscious to accept the protection is working, and you won't need to remove anymore because they can't get passed your protection. So, you can see some improvement there, can't you?"

Harriet said, "Yes, I had forgotten about the chitter-chatter, is that what it's going to be like with the voices, one day they'll stop?"

I said, "Yes, you won't even think of them. But like in the past, we'll have little setbacks to overcome before it's over. Each time you have a setback, you come forward stronger, and you deal with it. Once you overcome something, you won't get it anymore, take your arm, for instance, and the chitter-chatter. The same for your moods and emotions, you've got them under control now. It's not a miracle; it's the education and understanding that's got you where you are now, and the hard work you've put in, putting it into practice. That's why it can't be a quick fix because you have to learn how to do it. Which is what you're doing."

Harriet said, "I've been more content this week although I've been worried about the coronavirus. But

I don't get the emotions as much anymore because I'm blocking them out. It's more like when I'm thinking about horrible stuff, of course, they're going to say do this or that. I should know better, but once I cried, I know they're human, and they know how to push my buttons. They've never tried to be friendly and help me out, it's always some kind of control. I always see it as control, even if they do point out things I've forgotten, I know it's them. The last thing I want when I'm stressed out is voices telling me what to do, and I know it's all fake to try and control me again. Sometimes I get angry, and then I have to chill out and keep blocking them out regardless of what they say. It's hard sometimes when they act like they're trying to help and they don't, I don't believe them anymore. I know they're trying to get their hooks back in, if that makes sense."

I said, "Well, of course, they are."

Harriet said, "I'm not falling for it anymore. I just tell them to go. I know it's not over yet, so I'll keep practising removing them, and do what needs doing. Other than that, it's been stressful just dealing with my stuff, not dealing with them for a change. But I still worry about everything that's happening."

I said, "You're a worrier anyway, aren't you? Just think about this for a minute, when you worry about something, does it make it go away?"

Harriet said, "Make it go away? No, I see what you mean."

I said, "If you don't worry, it still gets resolved, doesn't it?"

Harriet said, "Yes it does."

I said, "So why worry? People spend most of their life worrying about what doesn't happen. You were worried at one time about spirit coming in every time you cleared yourself. So of course, you worrying about it made it happen; if you don't worry about it, it doesn't happen so much, that's because you're dismissing them and not keeping them at the forefront of your mind. That's the proof you need that worrying is not helping.

Harriet said, "Yeah, worrying and panicking about everything."

I said, "Panicking is definitely a bad thing."

Harriet said, "Yes, I know, and that's the thing about me, I need to be so careful about my emotions. I know if I do start panicking it's going to be harder to recover because of what's happening still with me with the spirits. I know that it'll go, but I also have to be realistic in thinking I have to be careful that I don't get too sad and depressed. They're going to play on it, so I can't let that happen. I have to keep my emotions level the whole time."

I said, "That's one of the things you've got to learn, to stay level and don't react, that way there's nothing for spirit to work with. It'll affect your everyday life because when someone says something nasty, you'll just let it go. When there's no reaction, people won't bother to try and hurt you with words."

Harriet said, "Yeah, it's funny you know when I said I don't cry that much, and I thought once I came off the antidepressants, I'd be all over the place. But it's like you just said, I'm not emotionless, but just level or I control it a lot better. I noticed that so much more this week after being hit with all this news. I was accepting it but not stressing about it. I thought that was bad because hearing the bad news, it was building up inside, and I'm not reacting to it. That's why I said it was weird I wasn't crying so much as I thought I would be. I guess as long as it's not making me ill, it's a good thing."

I said, "Well, it's not, is it? How would it make you ill?"

Harriet said, "You know when people say you bottle up your emotions or you don't show your emotions, and if you get bad news, you don't react to it, they say it's not healthy.?"

I said, "You just take it in your stride rather than get upset about it."

Harriet said, "Yeah, that's it, take it in your stride but not suppressing everything that happens."

I said, "All you're doing is accepting something has happened, and you can't change the past, so there's no point getting upset or excited about it because it's already happened. When you accept it, you don't react? You also accept you can remove spirit, so you're not reacting as much. Because you're not reacting, spirit is losing interest. You'll notice it's not so intense now."

Harriet said, "So I don't need antidepressants, I can manage it on my own."

I said, "So how are you going to occupy yourself today?"

Harriet said, "Not too sure, I've got a few things to write up. I was going to play some games with my sister, but I don't think she's well enough. I'm not a hundred per cent myself; I feel a bit weak at the moment."

I said, "You could read a book; if you don't have any

check out Kindle. There are quite a few free books on Amazon. It's important that you read a novel, so you'll see that they're not interfering with your mind while you're reading, because you were worried about that, weren't you?"

Harriet said, "Yes, I know, it would be another thing out of the way."

I said, "That's why you need to read, it's another part of your life that we need to put back together. You used to like reading books, didn't you?"

Harriet said, "Yes, all the time, there're quite a few things I haven't been doing because of this. I haven't been listening to music or playing my PlayStation, which I used to play a lot to de-stress, but now I get worried if I play a game."

I said, "You're associating your PlayStation with de-stressing. You're not associating it with just playing a game; you're looking at it as a tool to stop you from getting stressed. You need to change your thought pattern and look at it as something to do to pass the time. You're playing the game because you want to, not because you're stressed. It's how you think about things."

Harriet said, "Yes, you're right. I need to change the reason why I do things."

I said, "You've got your PlayStation, books and music, while you're stuck at home you might as well bring them back into your life, they're as good as anything to keep you occupied. Thinking about it, you could read *Working in the Realms of Spirit*; that's the one that explains the hierarchy and how the negative spirits

control lost spirits and the structure."
Harriet said, "OK, I'll have a read of it. Another thing, you remember I told you I went for a walk, and I had this person come in really intrusive, and he was attacking me strongly and shouting very loud at me?"
I said, "Yes."
Harriet said, "He was trying to change my mindset and rubbish what you've been teaching me. First, I tried to ignore it and it wasn't going at all, so I asked my guides to remove him, and he was gone instantly. Ever since then, I thought if anyone came in, I could easily remove them, and I realised I'm not scared anymore."
I said, "It proves to you that you can deal with any of them with the help of your guides, and you can control them."
Harriet said, "Yes, definitely, because I have to admit it was scary knowing I had this kind of power, and I couldn't do anything about it. That's why I had so much trouble in the past with this because I didn't know what they could do, and how I could stop it because it's spiritual. I couldn't attack it. I couldn't do anything."
I said, "The trouble was you didn't know what you could do, did you?"
Harriet said, "No."
I said, "Now you do."
Harriet said, "But I think the guides did that, so I didn't do anything."
I said, "Well, the guides removed them only because you asked them to, sometimes you need help, your part of a team, you're not on your own. You must accept your part of a team, and when you try and fail, you ask

the rest of the team to help you, the same way as you help them. Once they've gone, you still have to do your part by dismissing them. If you don't do that, there's no point in removing them."
Harriet said, "So if I don't dismiss them afterward, it means I'll invite more in?"
I said, "It means you're open to someone else coming in. When you dismiss the negative spirits and don't think of spirit anymore, they haven't got a channel into you because you've blocked them. If you don't dismiss them and you're thinking about spirit, you're looking for them. Just dismiss it, slam the door and move on to something else, which is what you've been doing. It's what you did with that loud spirit, isn't it?"
Harriet said, "Yes I did, and it worked, it just gets so disheartening. I do dismiss them and I try so hard to not focus on them, and I hear a voice, and I think here we go again, and I just ignore it as much as I can."
I said, "You're reacting, aren't you, because you say 'Oh, here we go again'. Whereas if you take it as a matter of course and don't react to it, then it's not going to upset you. Remember the fly if it lands, brush it off, you don't expect it, but if you get something, you'll deal with it and get on with your day."
Harriet said, "OK, I'll remember that. Thank you, talk next week?
I said, "Yes, OK, don't forget; don't react."

The next time we spoke, Harriet said, "My parents have recovered more or less from the coronavirus. I had it for about a week, and my sister is recovering. It's been pretty hectic what with one thing and another. I was fragile and couldn't eat, I had no energy, and I had to stay in bed as I couldn't even get dressed. We have to stay isolated until everyone recovers and see how it goes. It's been hard trying to look after everyone and deal with my own stuff with the spirits."

I said, "How has the spiritual side been?"

Harriet said, "Hard. I told myself I know they're going to take advantage of my situation, so stick to what I've learned, and I can keep everything under control and keep myself distracted, even if I'm in bed. Like you said, just keep doing something. I've been playing my Playstation, which helped, and I've looked at the Kindle books, and I'm going to get a Kindle. The Playstation worked a lot, keeping my mind occupied."

I said, "Apart from your illness, it's been easier this week, has it?"

Harriet said, "Yes."

I said, "One thing you said, you expected it to get hard."

Harriet said, "I know expecting it's not good; that's why I had the conversation once with myself because I knew if I kept bringing it up, I'd be thinking of spirit too much. It's hard. I know it's there, but I mustn't think about it."

I said, "You just deal with it if it happens. You've got all the methods in place now; all you need to do is apply whichever method appropriately."

Harriet said, "I know I shouldn't say it, but I thought it would be harder, but it was OK. I suppose the same when I was ill, I didn't focus on anything but how I felt due to the virus."

I said, "So when you were ill, and you weren't focusing

on the voices, were you hearing them?"
Harriet said, "Sometimes."
I said, "When you were playing the Playstation, were you hearing them?"
Harriet said, "Yes, sometimes, I believe it's mainly my thoughts when I'm playing the Playstation, to be honest."
I said, "OK, so you're not getting interference when you're playing the Playstation. When are you getting interference?"
Harriet said, "When I needed a rest, I was focusing so hard just to try and do something, even if it meant I wasn't resting, which was wrong because my body was screaming to rest. I was worried as well because I knew as soon as I rest, I'm going to have that quiet time, and that's when I felt on edge."
I said, "You got worried because you thought the spirits would interfere and what you worried about happened, didn't it?"
Harriet said, "I needed to rest and quieten my mind and switch off from everything, including the daily stress of life. I knew if they were to interfere, the best time for them would be when I was quiet. So even when I'm resting, I'm focusing on getting control of my thoughts and keep opening my eyes to refocus just to cut the chitter-chatter. I know that whatever happens, I'll just deal with it, but I've been so stressed, it's hard not to think about it. So, I've been trying to maintain that balance and not focus on spirit and just focusing when I have to."
I said, "While you've been a little stressed with life, you

haven't had so much of a problem?"
Harriet said, "I don't think so, no."
I said, "If you're working all day and you're thinking about your work and what you're doing and when you finish work, you'll be thinking about what you're going to do with your time off. So, you won't have much if any time for spirit, will you?"
Harriet said, "No, I want to work, but it's a difficult time at the moment with the lockdown. The chances of getting a job are zero with so many people laid off. It's frustrating at the moment because I just want to work and get this under control. I know I have already, but it's the next step."
I said, "You have it under control now; it's just a case of keeping yourself occupied until you can go and do something else. It's good that the Playstation is helping you with that. If you get yourself a book, you can relax and read, that'll give your body a chance to heal, and it keeps your mind busy."
Harriet said, "Yes, that's true. I'm a little concerned when I want a lie-in and just want to lay there and think I can't do that. I can, and I do, but I feel like I have to distract myself all the time and keep my mind busy. It gets a bit stressful because I think I can't lie there. I have to get up and do something. That's why I was talking about resting because I felt I had to do something to distract myself."
I said, "OK, so isn't thinking distracting; when you think with the candle that distracts you from spirit, doesn't it? If you think about what you want to think about, those are your thoughts, and they'll also distract you.

So, you're controlling your mind with your thoughts."
Harriet said, "That's a good point. I had a few moments when I had no choice but to rest, and I had my own thoughts, and that blocked them out."
I said, "That's what we're working towards, you not even thinking about them because you're busy thinking about something else."
Harriet said, "You know when I put that stuffed cat behind me to stop spirit from touching my back. Well, I haven't been using it lately. I've been ignoring it and just turning over whenever it's necessary, and it's been working, and it doesn't play on my mind anymore. I didn't think there's anyone in the bed anymore because I had the cat behind me. Now I don't need it because I know nothing can get to me."
I said, "You see what you've just done there? You know, and because you know, you no longer need the cat. When you get to that stage with your protection that you know it's working, you won't even think about it not working. And so, you'll have succeeded, won't you?"
Harriet said, "Yes. I don't even think about interference like that anymore. But it helped to start with."
I said, "It's done the job hasn't it?"
Harriet said, "I also started to feel lonely."
I said, "That lonely is not you; spirit is making you feel lonely so that you'll look for company."
Harriet said, "OK, but I've been looking for mum and my sister for company. That's where I got confused, and I thought it was me being alone."
I said, "Being alone and being lonely are two different

things; being alone is being on your own but happy to be on your own. Being lonely is wanting other people there all the time, and the problem with being lonely is that, if you think right back to when you first got this interference, it was company for you, wasn't it? They're trying to entice you into the same situation again. If you need to be alone, that's fine, but don't ever be lonely, you've always got your guides with you anyway."

Harriet said, "I'm alone, but I know they've been trying all sorts, but I've just been blocking it out. I've had so much to think about that I've been blocking them out automatically. When I first started to feel lonely, I wondered where the feeling was coming from. I thought, was it them? I didn't want to think it was, so I was thinking it was me because I didn't want to think of them as bringing up emotions all the time, I wanted to think it was just me and sorting it out by being with mum and my sister."

I said, "Yes, because you didn't want to think they could do that to you."

Harriet said, "It's more like I knew they could do it. I just didn't want to focus on it instead of assuming it's them, may be thinking it's me that's alone and that I wanted to be with mum and Charlotte. As soon as I started thinking I'm lonely, I thought maybe I should get Charlotte in the room instead."

I said, "That's the right way to do it, make a decision, don't think lonely, think alone – there's a big difference. If you're alone, you can think of things you want to do, but if you're lonely, you want someone to entertain you. Never think of yourself as lonely, there's nothing wrong with being alone; it gives you time to think."

Harriet said, "I like it, it feels that way because being alone is peaceful, and I can think what I want to think without interference, it feels great. But when they put thoughts of being lonely, and you need company and all that stuff, I just think maybe I should go and speak to mum or Charlotte or have them come and sit and chat for a while, and it just goes."

I said, "You see, you're directing your mind rather than spirit."

Harriet said, "Yes, and it works so well because when I'm feeling a little depressed, or someone's attacking me, I don't concentrate on the attacking method itself. I think of ways to deal with it, and if that means speaking to mum for a bit, it dismisses it straight away because I'm not thinking about it at all. It's like they're attacking me, but it's not affecting me."

I said, "You're transferring the way you deal with things before you would sit there and bring up the candle to block it. Now you get up and go and talk to your mum or sister and that's a natural block. You're controlling your thoughts and actions naturally. That's how life is, and it's only those who won't talk to people who get isolated and start to have a problem. It's healthy to talk to people and keep your mind engaged in different things. There're times when you want to do things on your own and times when you want to do things with people. Providing you can do those things without interference. You're living a normal life. If on occasions you get a voice that's annoying you, just remove it, don't think about it, just do it. Just swat the fly. It's good

that you're transferring things. How many times did you use the candle this week?"
Harriet said, "Hardly at all, only when meditating. I just use distractions all the time now."
I said, "You don't need to use the candle so much now?"
Harriet said, "No, I don't use it at all; the only time I use it is when I'm meditating, that's it."
I said, "When you put up your protection in the morning and at night, you then forget about it, don't you?"
Harriet said, "Yes I do, and it's working. I just put it up and it's done. Then I think about what I'm going to do for the rest of the day, and it's gone into automatic and just carry on. If I get visions of the protection, I just dismiss it because I know they're trying to bring it to the forefront of my mind as they do with certain images, visions and words to trigger a reaction. I just dismiss it and move on."
I said, "So, you deal with it."
Harriet said, "Yes, it's good, but it feels tiring at the same time."
I said, "That's because you're still working on both sides of life, aren't you? When you're working on one side of life (the physical), it will become normal. It's just that you're doing the transition at the moment, from being aware of spirit to not being aware."
Harriet said, "Yes, it feels like I'm trying to find a balance between it."
I said, "Yes, you'll get a balance, you don't need to worry about the candle as much now, it's done its job in helping you to regain control of your mind. But it's a useful tool to have as a backup. Now you're using

distraction just like anyone else, like if you want to do something you do it. If you change your mind, that's your choice. If you want to be alone, then you can be alone with your thoughts because they're your thoughts, and you recognise what's not your thoughts. When the thoughts aren't yours, you remove them or block them, and how do you block them?"

Harriet said, "By thinking of something else, I distract myself with visual or mental images."

I said, "Yes, so you don't think of the candle, do you? You do it the natural way as everybody else does."

Harriet said, "Oh, I see it's getting used to it, but it's working because my mind's doing it automatically at some points."

I said, "So, as a percentage, how much peace do you get during the day, how much time do you get where spirit isn't present?"

Harriet said, "I'd say on average, about sixty per cent."

I said, "That's good. Before you were hoping to get to fifty per cent weren't you, and now you estimate sixty per cent. Only forty per cent to go, that forty per cent includes you thinking of spirit in the morning and at night when you put protection up. Then you forget about it, and if something comes to mind, you dismiss it. How many times do spirit come to mind in a day apart from the protection?"

Harriet said, "I'd say about three times in the morning, and it doesn't last long, because I either block it or remove it. In the afternoon, it's a bit more noticeable, but I can still remove or block it."

I said, "So, what's happening is in the morning you're

fresh and more alert, and you deal with it immediately, but as the day wears on, you're not so alert, and it takes a little more effort.

Harriet said, "That's right."

I said, "I think your per cent is about right."

Harriet said, "You're right, when I get tired or stressed out, then if it happens, I have to calm down and focus, and then it goes. When I'm tired, it hits me harder."

I said, "Yes, so what's happening is when you're tired and drained, you react, whereas in the mornings you don't react, you just deal with it. You see the difference?"

Harriet said, "A little, but sometimes I feel like in the morning I react, I try not to."

I said, "You will sometimes, every day is not going to be the same."

Harriet said, "You're right; it's not always like that. But as soon as I wake up though it's like wham, I'm not thinking about anything. I'm just lying there thinking of the day, and it just happens. I get annoyed sometimes, I'm not even thinking about spirit, and it hits me."

I said, "That's your weakest point in the day when you've just woken up, getting yourself organised and getting your thoughts together. That's when they come in, and you just put your protection up and get rid of them. Once you've done that, you can forget about them."

Harriet said, "Right, straight away, no messing around, do it immediately. I have to admit I don't always do it straight away. I have to remind myself to do it, then it goes."

I said, “Do it straight away, every time.”
Harriet said, “Yes, OK, if I’m going to sleep, do I do it straight away then?”
I said, “Yes. The more you dismiss spirit, the less they will come in. You’re starting to dismiss them automatically, and you’re also building the strength of your protection.”
Harriet said, “Yes, I noticed that when I was meditating on the candle. I’ve got into the habit of using my voice to get back into focus. It’s good and it works. When it comes to the quiet moments, say if I want to go to sleep, I don’t want to be waking my mind up again just to refocus, like I might say to myself focus on the candle. I’m training my mind to focus on the image without saying anything, and it’s working.”
I said, “So why don’t you focus on going to sleep?”
Harriet laughed.
I said, “Have you tried the velvet cushion?”
Harriet said, “Yes, I do, and that works too; I focus on the black velvet, and it calms my mind down, which is good, and next thing I know, it’s morning. I don’t have many questions this week.”
I said, “That’s good, that means things are going in the right direction, and you’ve got things under control.”
Harriet said, “When I do the meditation, I still open my eyes to refocus, which helps. But I feel like I’m opening up too much sometimes. I’m not meditating properly, because I’m not closing my eyes to focus and imagine it more. Even though I’m still focusing on the object and it still blocks it out, it feels like it’s not full meditation because I’m opening my eyes.”

I said, "It doesn't matter; what matters is that you're controlling the situation. It doesn't matter how you do it. We want you to be able to get your mind under control when you need to. If you focus on worrying about not doing the meditation properly, that's a distraction in itself."

Harriet said, "I see that because it still worked, it's refocusing my mind and dismissing everything anyway. Even when I'm not meditating, it still works, and I'm focusing on things around me, and it helps. I don't know why I asked that, I already knew."

I said, "You asked because you wanted clarification. Now you've got that."

Harriet said, "Going back to the visual imagery instead of vocal. It's the kind of thing that I wanted to do, but I don't know. When I said to you about focusing on, I'll give you an example. I try not to get angry or frustrated, but sometimes I do, and I know to snap back out of it and focus on something else. I know there's no point getting angry anymore, so I'm way better at doing it now. But when I get someone shouting out of the blue, it makes me jump. Which is weird, before I was so used to it."

I said, "So now the voices are unusual rather than normal, like you weren't expecting it. Before you knew where it came from, you expected and accepted it. Now you get a voice, and you think where's that come from?"

Harriet said, "Yes, it's like, what?"

I said, "What do you do when you hear that voice suddenly?"

Harriet said, “It, kind of shocks me at first, but then I just ignore it or think of something else or look at something and take note of the detail, and then it goes. But if sometimes it does persist, like it’s still quite loud, more than normal, I ask my guides to remove it after I’ve tried if I can’t shake it off, and it goes. It’s a bit weird, it’s scaring me now because I wasn’t expecting it.”
I said, “There’s nothing to be scared of, nothing at all. It’s just like if you walk around a corner and someone shouts at you from about two feet away, it’d make you jump, wouldn’t it? It’s the same sort of thing, only you can’t see them, and you just learn not to react to it.”
Harriet said, “It’s good, though that I dealt with it as soon as it happened and dismissed it. Another question, I thought this morning, if I have so much protection and I’m blocking them out and having the guides remove them, and they know this, why is it still happening?”
I said, “Because you’re still letting them in. You’ve got to get to a stage where you know that no one else is coming in. It’ll happen, just be patient.”
Harriet said, “Will that happen automatically and things will be normal?”
I said, “It’ll get less and less. There’ll always be someone who’ll put a lot of energy in to try and disturb you, and they’ll get through the protection, but gradually that’ll stop.”
Harriet said, “I’ve no doubt spirit is always going to be around.”
I said, “You’re not going to be listening to them, are you? It seems to me your life now apart from the stress

of the coronavirus is a lot calmer."

Harriet said, "Yes, it is, which is funny because what with all that's going on, it does feel calm. I know it's working and I know how to deal with it now. To be honest, I'm not expecting it so much."

I said, "That's why it surprises you when it happens, that's a good sign. I think you're more surprised that someone gets in, and if spirit gets in, you don't think about it. You just deal with them straight away."

Harriet said, "The weird thing is I don't even want to think about my guides because it brings up their association with the negative spirits."

I said, "You don't want to be thinking about any spirits; just think about life. The less you think about your guides, the less you'll think about spirit. You've got to put your guides in the background. Where they can get on with what they do, and you don't have to be aware of them. From what you're telling me you don't get as many coming in as you were."

Harriet said, "No, I don't."

I said, "Now you've got less thought about spirit and more about your daily life, you're at sixty per cent now and moving forward toward a hundred per cent."

Harriet said, "Regardless of what the spirits do, I just ignore them, block them or dismiss them. But now that it's working so well with the blocking, they're doing a lot of other things to try to get through, more subtle things. It's like they're trying to make me doubt my guides."

I said, "The idea is to try and get you focusing on spirit, be it your guides or themselves, they want to try and keep you off balance. You must remove them without thinking of what they're doing; you're just not interested. Even if you try to remove your guides, they won't mind (you can't), but you just clear your mind of all spirit."

Harriet said, "That's funny, I thought, why do I think about my guides? I don't want to be thinking about them. It's like the spirits are making me think about them, but I was getting conflicted too because we're a team, and they're supposed to be helping me. I'm supposed to think of them to help me, and I didn't know what to think with them. That's why I got angry and frustrated with it because I knew I had to think of my guides to help me, but then in a way, I don't want to think about them."

I said, "You've got to accept that your guides are doing their job, and you're doing your job. When it comes to teamwork, if they persist, then you ask your guides to remove them, and they do their job. That's it; there's nothing more to it than that, then dismiss them all from your mind. As you get less interference, you won't think of your guides so much."

Harriet said, "With pain and sensations, I feel it but not as much as I felt it before. It's like I feel the emotions, but it feels numbed down."

I said, "It's not numbed down; it's not getting through so strongly, that's your protection working. Gradually you'll get to the stage where you don't feel anything; it's your trust and knowing that the protection is working. Let's go back to the cat; don't use that now, you don't need it because you know it works. You've got

to be at the same stage with everything else as well; you know it's not going to happen."
Harriet said, "I do know, I just need more confidence, but I feel like it's going to end soon."
I said, "I reckon another month or less, and it will end."
Harriet said, "You know when you said about the protection, I believe it's working; it's blocking out everything, isn't it?"
I said, "It will do."
Harriet said, "I say that because even when I get the voices when it happens, it doesn't seem to be getting through as much as it used to."
I said, "You're at the stage of believing in your protection but not knowing it; when you know it, then it will be stronger. OK, is there anything else?"
Harriet said, "No, that's it, but I thought you don't have to talk to me every week now, I've got things under control. If I need you, I'll drop you a line."
I said, "That's good that you feel that way, but we'll talk next week and see where we go from there. OK, see you then."

I said, "Hi, how are you today?"
Harriet said, "It's been an interesting week. I had a day when I didn't call my guides at all. I just dealt with them. I was really proud of myself. I didn't let it go to my head, but I thought it would be something to note, my first day in control. The next day was a bit harder, I know I shouldn't, but I had it in the back of my mind they might pop up a bit more, and they did."
I said, "Be careful what you think."

Harriet said, "I did everything just to act normal, not overreact, and it did work. I didn't think everything was going to pop up or anything I just got on with it. Then yesterday all hell broke out. I didn't know what happened. I wasn't expecting it, I don't think. I was just getting on with things, and it came quite quickly. Suddenly there was a lot of loud talking and I was asking my guides to help, after trying to ignore it, and went back to what I was doing, listening to music and reading, playing games and talking to mum, and still it persisted. In the end, I had no choice but to ask my guides to remove them, but then about an hour or so afterward, it came back. I thought what's going on? I was confused. Also, I'm finding when going to bed, I know to shut off and not think or just focus on the velvet pillow. It was still hard because I know they were playing on my nerves."

I said, "Why were you thinking about getting rid of them?"

Harriet said, "Because they were really loud, and there was a second one there."

I said, "Don't think about them; just remove them, don't think about it, just deal with it. Spirit is trying to get back in, and by doing that, they're testing you to see if you're going to do anything. All the while, you don't do anything; they'll push to get more in your face. You've got to not care; it's irrelevant, remove them and dismiss them."

Harriet said, "The problem was I didn't want to keep relying on my guides; I wanted to do it on my own."

I said, "That's what they're there for, your part of a

team, and you work together. The more time you spend removing spirit or not removing them or asking your guides, the longer they're there, and the more they impact on your thoughts. As soon as you're aware of them, remove them. If you can't, then ask your guides to. You don't want to give them any of your time."

Harriet said, "I've been trying so hard to distract myself and get rid of them because I thought that's what I should be doing, so I didn't have to keep calling my guides. I thought I had to do it on my own."

I said, "No, you haven't got to do it by yourself; that's why I'm here, and your guides are here, we're here to help you. If you get any kind of interference at all, you just dismiss it. You don't want to take any notice, the more you think about it, the more you build up the fear and expectation of others coming in. So, the day you didn't have to call your guides, did you get any voices?"

Harriet said, "I did, but I ignored it, and it went."

I said, "OK, and the next day it got louder?"

Harriet said, "Yes, it did."

I said, "The reason it got louder is that you were ignoring it, and they wanted to see how far they could go before you removed them. So, you should accept no interference at all; you must remove spirit immediately in whichever way you feel is best."

Harriet said, "I'm worried I can only ask my guides so many times, then they'll stop helping."

I said, "Your guides have waited five years for you to start rejecting the interference. They're not going to give up now you're getting somewhere. They're there on call, every time you ask them to remove somebody they do, don't they? It's not a problem for your guides; it may be a big deal for you, but for them, it's an everyday occurrence. That gives you the space and time to readjust; you mustn't dwell on spirit at all. We don't want you thinking of spirit in any way. You said something about when you were going to sleep?"

Harriet said, "Yes when you said about them pushing me, especially when I said I didn't ask my guides that day, I felt they were pushing me. So, when I go to bed, I know I'm more vulnerable than normal because I'm half awake, half asleep. It's a bit hard to concentrate on my thoughts and ignore everything. Because it was louder, it made it harder to ignore."

I said, "So remove them."

Harriet said, "I wasn't thinking so much about spirit until yesterday when it was horrible, and I thought this is wrong; I shouldn't be thinking about them this much. But they were so prominent I couldn't ignore them."

I said, "That's because they wanted you to be thinking about them all the time. It makes it easier for spirit to interfere. That's why I'm saying to you it's so important you don't think about spirit; you just remove them without a thought. As far as vulnerability is concerned, when you're going to sleep and waking up, you shouldn't be as vulnerable as you were because you've got your protection. You can rely on that protection because, like the candle, it will stop the interference. So, you've got to get the thought out of your mind that you're going to be vulnerable when you're going to sleep or waking up. You see, you're expecting it, aren't you?"

Harriet said, "Yeah, I haven't even been resting because I think someone's going to pop in and start talking rubbish."
I said, "If you need to rest, then rest, if someone pops in remove them, you have to have zero-tolerance. You were starting to get to the stage where you dealt with it automatically. The spirits persisted and pushed a bit, and they've become louder, so they're more on your mind. You have to go back to how you were, don't think about it, don't consider it; just do it."
Harriet said, "I know why that happened, because I got the idea in my head that I could do this on my own; I stopped asking my guides. I was determined to do it on my own without any help, and it was so hard, and it showed."
I said, "You have to remember there are so many different ways they can attack you, and you've got to think what they're doing so you can get rid of them. Whereas it doesn't matter what they're doing, you just get rid of them anyway. You don't need to know how or what they're doing; all you care about is they're gone. If they're not there, then you've removed them."
Harriet said, "Yes, they do attack me in loads of ways. It's more the voice now, everything else seems to be stopped, because of the protection, I guess. Even the voices, I still feel the protection is making a difference; it seems more subdued."
I said, "You're watering down your protection by thinking about them, they're not important. If you can do that over the next few weeks and accept your protection is working and not think about them, your

protection will kick in automatically. You won't even need to be aware of it happening. That's the objective, the more you think about your life and the less you think about spirit, the less you attract them and the harder it is for them to get in. You need to trust your protection is working; you only need to put it up in the morning and at night and be aware you can distract yourself any time you need to."

Harriet said, "You know you said to read if I want, I notice I don't imagine as much as I used to, or if I did, I'd drop it because something would pop in. Now I'm letting my imagination run longer like imagining characters in books doing things. The weird thing is, when someone does pop in, I'm reading, and they put their emotions to it which are not mine. I ignore it and the protection works because before it was obvious, but now it's a lot less. But the imagination bit is hard because some other thought comes in and changes it completely, and I have to either fight it or ignore it. I'm finding it hard to decide whether it's safe to imagine or should I ignore it or fight the images and think what I want to think, I'm getting a little confused, I don't know how to sort it out."

I said, "Don't worry about it; just enjoy your book, and when you finished, put it away. If you get influenced in your imagination, then OK, they're taking it further than you wanted. It doesn't matter; it's just a book. Worrying about it gives them a weakness to exploit. Everything you worry about can be enhanced, so don't worry. You may have noticed as things have got better, you've had one thing on your mind, and that's where you get the problems. When you've dealt with that, you have something else on your mind, which they then attack. They'll always try to exploit your weaknesses, so don't give them any."

Harriet said, "It used to be so obvious, once I learned how they were attacking me, but it's not so clear now. With everything that's happening regarding the coronavirus, on top of everything else, I've found more to worry about, although I've also had plenty of distraction. It's like a double-edged sword. I don't want to keep saying I was expecting it, but it's hard not to."

I said, "If you say to yourself if something pops in, then you think it might, so subconsciously, you're expecting it. If you don't think about it, it's less likely, as your mind is on other things. I know it's hard; this is where it gets subtle, and if you're continually looking, you will find. Your focus should be on what you're doing, and nothing else. You may get interference, you may not; deal with it accordingly."

Harriet said, "With the pains I get it's been a bit hard to know what's mine because I've been ill, but it has reduced or been removed when I've asked. I'm a little confused, do I tell it to go away or try to ride it out?"

I said, "Why would you accept pain that's not yours?"

Harriet said, "Because I didn't want to think about them."

I said, "You don't think about it; you just take it away and then dismiss the thought. In asking for the pain to be taken away, it's the same as asking your guides to remove the spirits. If you specify the one that's causing me pain, that's all they'll remove. But if you ask for

them to remove all the spirits that are interfering with me, then they'll remove all of them."
Harriet said, "I noticed the difference between asking for one or all of them to be removed."
I said, "Good because you're the centrepiece in this; the only way things get done is by your actions, either by you removing them or by asking your guides. Which is what you've been doing. When you've done it correctly, then you've been cleared. Your guides are always there; you only have to ask because they know what's happening to you and are ready to give a helping hand if you ask. They know when everything is OK and when there's a problem. They're alert and ready to guide you through it."
Harriet said, "So, as soon as I'm aware of someone I remove them, it doesn't matter who?"
I said, "Yes, we don't want you thinking is this a guide or negative spirit, or what they're doing, we don't want you thinking about spirit at all. Just get rid of them."
Harriet said, "So just to be clear, I get rid of anyone at all?"
I said, "Yes, anyone, even that little voice you hear sometimes. The longer you allow it to go on, the bigger wedge it makes in your protection; the longer you leave it, the more comes in, and the harder it is to get back to the peace because you have multiple attacks going on at the same time. That's why as soon as you're aware of spirit, swat them."
Harriet said, "When I'm asleep, I don't need to worry about the protection because my mind's shut off, even when I get dreams, I don't have to ask my guides."

I said, "Your mind's always alert, but your brain is resting, and it's when you're not in a deep sleep that you get dreams that make an impression on your brain, and then you react. If you need to ask for help to remove spirit, then do so and remember it's only a dream. Turn over, and go back to sleep. Because you're asleep doesn't make you more vulnerable, your protection's still there, that's why you renew it before you go to sleep. Your protection is at full strength when you renew it, but during the day it gets attacked. If spirit gets through your protection, it weakens your resolve because you then have doubts that it's working. Usually, they get through because you've mistakenly let them by thinking about spirit. If you become aware of any spirits, you just remove them and again place your trust in your protection."

Harriet said, "By doing so, I would be asking my guides every time?"

I said, "No, if you change your thought pattern at the first hint of spirit, you'll block them; that's what I do, that's what everybody does. If you have thoughts you don't want, then just think of something else. If that doesn't achieve the objective, then ask your guides."

Harriet said, "I'm learning to do that more now, and most of the time, it blocks them."

I said, "The idea is that you've got to control your mind; that's the whole object of this exercise. So, the thoughts in your mind are yours, and if other thoughts that aren't yours get in your mind, you can remove them. It's hard for you, I know, having had these other thoughts for so long, but you will succeed. Because you have been,

you've had good days and not so good days."
Harriet said, "Yes, I have, and I know it's possible. It's just tiring sometimes."
I said, "So don't waste your energy on them."
Harriet said, "OK, see you next week."

I said, "Hi, how're things?"
Harriet said, "I had a nasty dream during the week, which caught me by surprise, but I dealt with it and went back to sleep."
I said, "Have you had any other problems this week?"
Harriet said, "Nothing like that, but I still hear voices when going to sleep and waking up. But I'm getting better. I will go to bed when I'm exhausted which helps, so I go to sleep quicker. I know I don't have to do that, but it did help a little. I started to think more of the candle, which helped me focus, and my mind wasn't wandering."
I said, "Are you getting the voices during the day?"
Harriet said, "During the day, I hardly notice anything, and if I do, I dismiss them. But when I go to bed and in the mornings, that's when it's the most obvious."
I said, "So, during the day, you've got other things to think about and do so you're not getting interference, but during the night, you have a problem."
Harriet said, "It's frustrating because I do the candle and they fight back, I don't expect them to, I just keep refocusing on the candle. I feel I'm constantly fighting something, and I think it's wrong, but I'm trying so hard to focus on the candle. I eventually drift off; it's just that initial fighting all the time, I don't know if I should be

fighting them or not because that means I'm paying attention to what they're doing. I try to think of something else and come back to the candle and trying to find different ways of sorting it out and seeing if it eased off. What I mean by fighting is they keep changing the image all the time, so I'm constantly trying to rethink the image in a different position and keep fighting that way. I don't feel I'm trusting what I bring up because they do it so often it gets hard to believe I'm doing it, focusing on it properly."

I said, "You're winning, aren't you? You're getting to sleep and you're overcoming the interference. We need to see why you're getting it at night but not during the day now. I think that's because you have a fear of going to sleep."

Harriet said, "I'm not going to lie, I am a little bit afraid, more because of my health than spirit, but I think they're going to interfere with it and I'm worried about getting enough rest."

I said, "Don't worry about that; you'll get enough rest, maybe not every night, but overall. Your sleep patterns are no different than anybody else's; some nights are better than others; that's normal. The difference is you're looking to see who's attacking you, most people just put it down to a bad night. Instead you should concentrate on going to sleep. You can deal with everything that comes up now; it's coming up less and less, so that means you're succeeding. I know it's difficult with the lockdown because you can't go out and occupy yourself in that way. You're managing quite well during the day, but you're going to get a backward step now, and again it's how you cope with those that's important. Don't waste time on it; just talk to your guides and remove them, dismiss them and move on. Don't tolerate them at all; just remove them."

Harriet said, "I know you said there was no limit to how many times I call my guides, but I keep getting this idea that I can't keep calling them all the time."

I said, "You're getting a thought in your head that you shouldn't keep calling them. Where do you think that's coming from? You just do what you want to do; you know your guides are there to help you and that as a team you're stronger, use your advantages."

Harriet said, "You know when you said about me allowing them to come in, is that what happens? Even when the guides take them away, I'm intentionally finding someone, or they just come in."

I said, "Now it's a bit of both, they attack and find a chink in your protection and get through, and you're looking to make sure they don't find a chink and, of course, the idea there might be a break in protection makes one. Go back to what we said before, the less you think about spirit, the less they're going to be able to attack you because if there's no thought to begin with, there's no way to get at you. Your mind is on other things occupied with life. You don't think about spirit all day now, do you?"

Harriet said, "No, not at all, unless it pops up, then I think oh OK, and just get rid of it."

I said, "Does it disturb your day?"

Harriet said, "No, as soon as I remove them and dismiss them when I've said that I focus on mum or Charlotte or TV or whatever, and it goes. I try to refocus naturally, not because of the interference, like I'm making a choice."

I said, "You've got that more or less sorted out now, it's just the going to sleep part to deal with. That's no different from during the day, what worries you is once you go to sleep, you're not consciously aware of what's happening."

Harriet said, "When I go to sleep, I feel fine because I don't have to think, but when I'm just dropping off, they talk and I feel like I talk back. I realise what I've done, and then I go back to trying to sleep. It's like starting all over again."

I said, "It's a natural response when someone speaks to you, you automatically reply, don't you?"

Harriet said, "That's when my concentration's low and more open, and they know that."

I said, "You know that too, so focus on the candle and don't talk to them. Don't tolerate anything; just remove and dismiss the spirits even at night. It's the same as during the day, except you're not physically doing anything. You need to control your mind; that's what the candle is for."

Harriet said, "I know, but it's hard when you're trying to fight them all the time."

I said, "That's why you remove them and then focus on protection and then fill your mind with the candle and sleep."

Harriet said, "OK, I should know that."

I said, "It doesn't hurt to have a reminder."

Harriet said, "No, but it's frustrating when a spirit jumps

in right after I've removed someone, it's like OK, dismiss it when it pops up, I don't get angry anymore if it doesn't go then I call my guides and ask them again. Even if they've just removed them, someone can pop in straight afterward."

I said, "Yes, they can, you know that because you've experienced it in the past. What this is all about is you learning to control things. I can't, and I've never said I could get rid of all the voices, but I said we could reduce them and control them. Which is what you're doing, but you've taken it a step further. You've got rid of the voices during the day pretty much, haven't you?"

Harriet said, "Yes."

I said, "So that means we've got a good chance of doing the same at night, but there's always going to be a day, six months, a year down the line when you'll get interference. If you do, you know how to deal with it, and so you do and just carry on with what you're doing. It may well be that's going to be a part of your life, I can't say, it all depends on you. What we're trying to do is give you your life back, and from what you tell me, you've got most of it back now."

Harriet said, "Yes, even reading is so much better, anything pops up, dismiss it, either continue reading and get back into the story, or if it lingers, I call my guides, and it's gone and go back to the book and carry on. I don't expect anything to pop up; in fact, I'm assuming it's going to be quiet. I don't even think about it, not being quiet. I'm slowly accepting it's normal to be like this, that this is generally normal, you know, not hearing voices."

I said, "We need to look at the times when you get fearful, the times when you feel weak and incapable."
Harriet said, "OK, I know exactly when – going to sleep. I'm a little fearful that I'm going to come under attack."
I said, "Has it occurred to you that you could take a book to read?"
Harriet said, "I did that on my phone. I've got some books on that which I'm reading."
I said, "Yes, and did that help?"
Harriet said, "Yes, it really did."
I said, "How many people do you know of that take a book to read before they go to sleep?"
Harriet said, "Loads of people."
I said, "It's normal, most people can't go straight to sleep, so they have a read which takes away all the worries and stresses of the day and helps quieten the mind. When you feel tired, you put the book down and go to sleep. The only thing on your mind is what you've been reading. If you dream, it's more likely to be about something in the book. If you wake up from a dream, you just turn over and go back to sleep; it's only a dream."
Harriet said, "With dreams, I try to ignore all of them, regardless of whether it comes from me or not. That's because I sometimes think they are going to manipulate me."
I said, "Just accept it as a dream, don't think or worry about somebody manipulating it, half the time you'll manipulate it yourself."
Harriet said, "I considered that it could be spirit, but it could also be me or me altogether."

I said, "Just don't consider spirit, but if it persists, then deal with it because someone's propagating it. Generally speaking, a dream is just a dream; many people analyse dreams, but what's the truth? The truth is the mind puts the day's events in order so you can access events easier at a later time, it's just your mind clearing up for the day. If you look at it like that, it's much easier to accept that when you have a dream, you've focused on something, so treat a dream like a dream."

Harriet said, "Going back to the weakest parts of the day, what you said about reading a book that helps. I find when I'm just lying there, my mind wanders, but with the book, my mind's focused."

I said, "That's the idea, to take your mind off the day and yet still keep it occupied, you don't have to think, you just read. When you say that's the weakest part of the day, it's because you haven't got a routine. As I mentioned last week, initially going to sleep and waking up were the most vulnerable parts of your day, but they're not anymore. The reason they're not is that you control them better."

Harriet said, "Yes, and because I know where my weakest parts are, I'm more prepared."

I said, "By being more vigilant you're focusing, you don't want to treat that part of the day any different than the rest of the day. With your protection, you don't need to be always looking; just take it naturally, go to bed, read if you want, and then go to sleep."

Harriet said, "OK, so really, I know what could happen, but I don't expect it. Sometimes I watch TV and then go to sleep, just so long as my mind is occupied."

I said, "That's fine as long as you turn it off before you go to sleep."

Harriet said, "I was trying to figure out what I was so afraid about going to sleep, what's worrying me the most. I thought I knew the reason, but I don't want to admit it. It's because I'm scared of hearing silence. I'm scared of it being quiet, and something pops up, and I'll hear it a lot more."

I said, "That's what we're trying to get you to understand and accept, the quiet. We said a few weeks ago that you'd have a problem with silence because you're not used to it. If you can accept it, that's the way things should be."

Harriet said, "As I said, I'm slowly getting used to being silent, but at the same time, I'm still scared of it. I'm trying to ease myself into accepting it's normal."

I said, "The problem is it's quiet, and you're trying to decide why it's so quiet instead of accepting it. You're on edge all the time, thinking something is going to happen. You've got to not look at it like that at all. I know it's difficult after what you've been used to, but try and accept it. You'll find the more silence you get, the easier it'll be."

Harriet said, "That'll only happen if I keep up what I'm doing with the focusing and remove the spirits then dismiss them straight away."

I said, "Yes, quiet is good because you can focus on what you want without interference. Trust in your protection, and you'll be fine. Do you get chatter in the background?"

Harriet said, "No, I just get the odd voice. Having said that, I feel like the voice isn't as loud."
I said, "Yes, it will be quieter because it's got to come through your protection. Each time you reinstate your protection, it gets stronger, and the voices will get quieter until they stop. Overall, I'd say you're almost there. Your days are more or less clear and your nights are getting there."
Harriet said, "Believing in the protection has helped a lot, I don't think about it so much now. Soon as I do it, I forget about it, and that's evidence that it's working."
I said, "What about your moods? Do you get angry or anxious so easily?"
Harriet said, "No, not at all, and if it does happen, it's very slight, like it might last for a few seconds, and I realise what it is, and it's gone."
I said, "That's normal, everybody gets emotions and mood changes, it's how you deal with them. Sometimes you stoke them up and let them take over and consume you, more often than not you just dismiss it by changing your thoughts."
Harriet said, "Sometimes I can tell the difference when it happens. If I disagreed with my mum, I know it's me if I get angry, I can tell that it's me. I'm starting to know who I am and my faults now."
I said, "When you get angry, and you know it's you, what do you do?"
Harriet said, "I just take a few deep breaths and calm myself down because I know it's not worth getting angry, and it dissipates. Sometimes something stirs my emotions, and as soon as I recognise it, I dismiss it, and

it goes. It's so much better now I'm off the antidepressants to manage my emotions, I feel happier and better. I feel like I'm genuinely laughing because I'm laughing. I thought it's been a while since I've felt like this, happy. I realised the medication was stopping me from releasing my emotions properly. That was bad, not knowing that I couldn't do that properly, laughing felt different, new even."

I said, "What we're expecting in the coming week is getting control of your sleep and getting no interference."

Harriet said, "Well, I know what can happen, and I can deal with it. I'm not going to give any attention to spirit; I don't feel I need to anymore."

I said, "That's good because you don't want to be relying on me all your life when you don't need me, then you're there. It doesn't mean we won't catch up now and again. We'll talk again next week, OK."

I said, "Hi, how're you today?"

Harriet said, "I'm okay. I know I keep bringing this up, I've been trying not to think of spirit and of course that makes me think of them more. They say things like Oh, your guides aren't here, and my mind automatically thinks of my guides I'm trying to stop that. Then they say a word any word, and that goes round and round my head."

I said, "It's a trigger, they say guides, and you immediately think of them."

Harriet said, "Yes, exactly, it's annoying. I try not to think of them, but once they're in, I just remove them."

I said, "You might have to remove them a few times to start with, but once you set the thought up, it'll gradually become instinctive."

Harriet said, "Since I've come off my medication, I feel I've got more sensitive."

I said, "It's because you're more alert you're looking to see what's around, and that's what's making you more sensitive. I know it's hard, but you have to try and put spirit out of your mind completely. Until you can do that, you're always going to get some interference. You know how and when to remove them. You just have to do it subconsciously. The more you understand, the less you'll get sucked in, you need to stop looking for them. Take your protection, what're you thinking about when you renew it?"

Harriet said, "I wonder if they're going to interrupt me and get in."

I said, "There's the invitation right there you have doubt, there's no point putting up protection if you're going to think that, it's self-defeating. You should be thinking only about renewing your protection, then dismiss spirit from your mind, don't think, I hope this is going to work. Know it will and trust in your guides and yourself."

Harriet said, "It's so hard not to expect after all this time I'm so used to hearing voices it's a difficult habit to break. I want to break it, but it's frustrating when I remove them, and then another voice pops up."

I asked Harriet's mum if she had noticed any changes in her. She said, "Harriet is happier and more confident and not asking so many questions of clarification of things. She's more or less getting there she's beginning to understand what she has to do. Sometimes Harriet finds it a bit difficult and likes to question things and find out. She takes things literally and analyses too much. That's what gets her in trouble; I talk to her about it and tell her to forget it, and if she has a quiet moment, just think of something she wants to do. I tell Harriet to live in the now and plan for the now and celebrate the quiet time to do something fun and to think fun things. Not to let anything come into her thought (because they're not interfering now, they might come back). I try to get her off that track, to focus on now and everyday life and stuff like that. It's not easy for her. It's been such a long time, and it's become a way of life. She's finding it hard to get out of that routine and forget about it and just get on with her life.

Harriet was very anxious when she got palpitations. I told her what to do, but she had to hear it from you. You said the same as I told her, so it was good that you reaffirmed what she had to do, deep breathing, and tell them to take it away. I have to reaffirm her every-day when I come home from work. We have chat's every-day. I try to get her to forget about the spirits and just do what she wants to do. Harriet is slowly but surely getting there in that respect, I must say. We go for walks and things and spend a lot of time together. It's nice to be able to help her move on with her life. It's an ongoing project, you might say, but we're getting there. I tell her every night, well done, you're doing well, you're making good progress, I'm so proud of you. All those positive things to reinforce her and I am proud of her she's come this far she's almost there, and I just want her to enjoy the fruits of having a normal life. So, it's important that she stays grounded and focus on what she wants to do in life."

Harriet said, "I think it's important that you know I want that too before I wasn't sure about it, but now, I want to get out of this habit and start living my life."

I said, "So, you've got no more question's, have you?"

Harriet said, "No, I don't."

I said, "This is a good thing because we've been talking for half an hour, normally it takes an hour to sort out your problems, which means you're getting fewer problems. You're more capable, and you've moved forward a lot in your understanding and education."

Harriet said, "Yes, I've noticed during the week when I don't speak to you. I realise I answer my own questions. It's like I know what you would say, and I think there's no point bringing it up because it's all the same thing, so just ignore it, it doesn't matter what they do or say, anything they do just dismiss it. It always comes back to ignore it, remove it, dismiss it. I'm finding it easier to read a book now I don't worry about my thoughts being interfered with anymore."

I said, "That's good now you can enjoy books again. Is there anything else?"

Harriet said, "No, that's it; see you next week."

MAY 2020

I said, "Hi, how are you this week?"

Harriet said, "Good, very good."

I said, “So you’ve managed all week without too much interference?”
Harriet said, “Yes, honestly, the past three days spirit wasn’t even an issue. I focussed on doing a diet with my mum and doing things in general. I haven’t been focussing on anything or even lingering on thinking about spirit.”
I said, “That was the plan, wasn’t it?”
Harriet said, “It’s been excellent, there were a few times I called my guides to remove them, but mostly I ignored them and concentrated on what I was doing, and they went. Whereas before I was thinking did I do it right, now I know I am.”
I said, “Are you still putting protection up in the morning and at night?”
Harriet said, “Yes, I do it, religiously.”
I said, “Do you think you need to renew it?”
Harriet said, “I not sure what you mean.”
I said, “You think about it when you put the protection up, and you believe it works.”
Harriet said, “Yes.”
I said, “So you don’t need to put it up anymore, you know it’s there.”
Harriet said, “I see, so that was just to reassure me that it’s there and working.”
I said, “Now, you don’t have to do that every day; you don’t have to put protection up at all. You know it’s there and protecting you. by not focussing on your protection, you won’t think about spirit at all, will you?”
Harriet said, “That’s true I won’t need to bring spirit to mind, I can just forget about them is that what you

mean?"
I said, "Yes."
Harriet said, "My sleeping has got a lot better. I've noticed it's more my thoughts than anything else now. I just calm myself down and go back to sleep. During the day, I get a little uptight dealing with life, but that's good because there're no spirits involved. "
I said, "How many times do you think you asked your guides to remove spirit during the week?"
Harriet said, "In the first few days about five, but it got less until I didn't call them at all. When I heard anything, I just change my thoughts, and it goes. I talked to my sister about things, and she said she didn't realise what I've been going through. By telling her about it, I felt I was letting go and felt lighter afterward. If that makes sense."
I said, "Well, you seem to have things under your control. You can deal with everything that comes along; I'd say your there now."
Harriet said, "What do you mean?"
I said, "I mean it's over; you've got your mind back; it's all under your control now. You may have to remove someone on the odd occasion, but all in all, you have control, haven't you?"
Harriet said through her tears, "Yes, that's amazing, thank you so much."
I said, "I will continue to check in with you each week, but basically, you've won. You remember I said it would take a while, well it's taken us ten months."
Harriet said, "Wow, thank god it's over, I don't know how many doctors I've spoken to, to try and explain

what was going on and they've not listened to what I've been saying. I'm glad I was honest about it, but at the same time, I was annoyed. They seem to have certain guidelines, and if you do this, then you're put into that category, and if that, then some other category.

I said, "If you think about it, you had it for five years when we started, and you're in control of your mind again."

Harriet said, "Can I call my mum so you can tell her?"

I said, "Yes, of course."

Harriet went to get her mum.

I said, "Hi, I think we're at the end of the road."

Harriet's mum said, "Are we, that's fantastic. Oh my god, thank you."

I said, "Harriet has it all under control now."

She said, "So what's the long-term plan for Harriet?"

I said, "We'll check-in for ten minutes weekly, and gradually we'll reduce the frequency until Harriet feels comfortable."

She said, "I don't know what to say I'm so excited it's such a relief, I keep telling her she's nearly there just keep focussing and believe in yourself. I tell her these things every day, don't question, don't sway just focus on what you need to achieve and go for it and stay grounded. I pleased I'm pleased. I'm so pleased. Thanks for everything."

Harriet said, "Thank you, Mike, see you soon."

I said, "We'll talk next week."

Harriet called two weeks later to say she was sorry because she forgot our appointment the previous

week. When I asked how she was getting on she said in the past t wo weeks I've had three moments when spirit interfered briefly before she removed them, other than that nothing. She said she also forgot to meditate and was feeling very positive.
Because Harriet forgot our appointment and hasn't been meditating is a good sign that she no longer needs to. As she say's "I feel comfortable in my own body and am moving on with my life, so thank you for your help I will keep in touch.

This is a case study of one of my clients and as you can see there are difficulties when trying to overcome the medication and influences of discarnate spirit. By gradually reducing her medication Harriet was able to control her mind better. Is it any wonder people suffer so much when the condition is misdiagnosed and the medication only numbs the brain and has no effect on the cause? Unfortunately, not all people who have been diagnosed with a mental health problem can be helped. There have been failures where the patient was unable to find the strength and determination required to persevere against the evil manipulation they endured. We can see that as Harriet understood what was happening and why, she was able to counteract the attacks successfully. She had her good days and bad days but gradually with reassurance and constant reminders she was able to overcome the attacks. It was fortunate that I as a medium was able to guide Harriet to a successful conclusion but it couldn't have been done without her courage and fortitude. It's unfortunate that the medical profession is unable to accept the possibility of interference from outside the body. Because of the lack of understanding by mental health professionals many people suffer the side effects of unnecessary drugs all their lives.

It's been a long and sometimes traumatic journey for Harriet but with her determination she got there. The case study reveals difficulties Harriet experienced to overcome spirit interference. Make no mistake, it's a difficult task to understand the way the spirit realms interact with the physical plane, and why they pick on certain individuals to play their evil games. Now Harriet can take her place in society and live a peaceful life.

Printed in Great Britain
by Amazon

23502835R00215